FR. JOHN MURPHY
OF BOOLAVOGUE

1753-1798

BY

Nicholas Furlong

Published in Ireland by
Geography Publications,
Kennington Road,
Templeogue, Dublin 6W

ISBN 0 906602 18 1

Cover Design by Caroline Moloney
Typesetting by Phototype-Set, Drumcondra, Dublin 9
Printed by Colour Books, Baldoyle Industrial Estate, Dublin 13

DON DOCHTÚIR "PAX" Ó SIONÓID,
(1901-1957)
INA CHUIMHNE AGUS LE BUÍOCHAS

Boolavogue

At Boolavogue as the sun was setting
O'er the bright May meadows of Shelmalier,
A rebel hand set the heather blazing,
And brought the neighbours from far and near.
Then, Fr. Murphy from old Kilcormack,
Spurred up the rocks with a warning cry;
"Arm! Arm!" he cried, "for I've come to lead you,
For Ireland's freedom we'll fight or die!"

He led us on 'gainst the coming soldiers,
And the cowardly yeomen we put to flight,
'Twas at the Harrow the boys of Wexford
Showed Bookey's regiment how men could fight.
Look out for hirelings, King George of England
Search every kingdom where breathes a slave,
For Father Murphy of County Wexford,
Sweeps o'er the land like a mighty wave.

We took Camolin and Enniscorthy,
And Wexford storming drove out our foes,
'Twas at Slieve Coillte our pikes were reeking,
With the crimson stream of the beaten Yeos.
At Tubberneering and Ballyellis,
full many a Hessian lay in his gore.
Ah! Father Murphy had aid come over,
The Green Flag floated from shore to shore!

At Vinegar Hill, o'er the pleasant Slaney,
Our heroes vainly stood back to back,
And the Yeos at Tullow took Father Murphy,
And burnt his body upon the rack.
God grant you glory brave Father Murphy,
And open Heaven to all your men;
The cause that called you may call tomorrow,
In another fight for the Green again.

Air: Traditional *Words:* P. J McCall

Geography Publications wish to record their thanks to the following major sponsors who contributed towards the production of this book.

WEXFORD COUNTY COUNCIL

COMÓRADH '98, CONTAE LOCH GARMAN

MICHAEL MURPHY, GOLDEN PAGES

GREENCORE, P.L.C.

PEOPLE NEWSPAPERS LTD., WEXFORD

Acknowledgements

Throughout the years since 9 January, 1974, when I started research on the life and times of Fr. John Murphy, I have been helped by many people to whom I owe a great debt of gratitude. They include Professor Patrick J. Corish, Maynooth; Anna Drury and the staff of Wexford County Library; Dr. Denis Kennedy, Dublin Archdiocesan Archivist, Fr. Bartholemew Egan and Fr. Patrick O'Sullivan of the Franciscan House of Studies, Killiney; Fr. Laurence Murphy, Guardian, Franciscan Friary, Wexford; Bishop Donal J. Herlihy, Custodian of the Ferns Diocesan Archives; the staffs of the National Library, and Trinity College Library; Frank Corr, Archivist, Irish State Paper Office; Fr. Declan, Archivist, Passionist Fathers, Mount Argus, Dublin; the Curator and staff of the County Museum, Enniscorthy; Francisco Gonzalez Garcia, Rector of the University of Seville; John Bigger, Secretary of the Irish Embassy, Madrid; His Excellency, Dr. Jose A. de Yturriaga, Spanish Ambassador to Ireland; Kevin Danaher, Daithi Ó hÓgáin and the staff of the Department of Irish Folklore, University College, Dublin; Commandant J.N. Bergin; Professor Patrick Gallagher, Spanish Department, University College, Dublin; Philip Deacon, Spanish Department, Trinity College, Dublin; Chief Superintendent Anthony J. McMahon and Detective Sergeant Niall Heron who constructed an identikit likeness of Fr. John Murphy from contemporary descriptions.

I am indebted to six trusted friends from different disciplines who at various stages read the manuscript carefully and contributed critical assessments. They were Mairéad Furlong; Kevin Danaher, University College, Dublin; Professor Charles McCarthy, Trinity College, Dublin; Fr. James B. Curtis, P.P., V.F., St. Martins, Piercestown, Dr. Kevin Whelan, University College, Dublin, and Eithne Scallan, Wexford.

For kindly help and for contributions, written and printed, I am particularly grateful to Bill Cronin, Editor, *Wexford Free Press;* Michael Roche and my colleagues on the staff of the *People* Group of Newspapers, Wexford; Dr. Tom Sherwood of St. Peter's College, Wexford, for the translation of Latin documents and advising me on matters of Canon Law; Fr. Henry Peel, O.P., Cork; Fr. Hugh Fenning, O.P., Tallaght; Fr. Patrick J. Brophy of Carlow (a collateral descendant of Fr. John Murphy); Brother Linus, Patrician Brothers, Galway; Dr. Edward Culleton, Piercestown, Curator, Irish National Heritage Park; Phil Tobin, Kilmacow, Screen; Maure Roche, Ballyhoobeg; Chris Halsall, Oxford; Gerard Donovan, New Ross; Brother P. B. Jacob, C.B.S. Callan; Fr. Fergal Grannel, O.F.M.; Tomas Lyng, N.T. Kilkenny; Margaret Hall, Boolavogue and her family; Philip Sullivan, Gurteen, Bunclody; King Milne, Ballymorgan; Ben Chapman, Tobergal; William Walsh, Ballyorley,

Boolavogue; Josie Cashin, Knockaree, Tinakilly, New Ross; Sean Scallan, St. Magdalens; Joan Nolan, Parklands, Wexford; Dr. Barty Curtis, Wexford; Dr. Aidan Ryan, Wexford; Margaret Reck, Mulgannon; Molly Conboy, Rathaspeck; Seán O'Grady, Colchester, Essex; Aidan O'Leary, Ealing, London; Breda Kelly, Strand Hotel, Rosslare; James Delaney, Athlone; Michael Foy, Editor, *Biatas*; Art Sinnott, Boolavogue; Seán Óg Ó Dubhghaill, Enniscorthy; Martina Kealy, Castleknock; Seamus Cullimore, T.D. Wexford; Andy Doyle and Comóradh 98; Noel M. Dillon and Wexford County Council.

In the protracted and exhausting work involved in uncovering the buried life and times of Fr. John Murphy the project would have been dropped were it not for unselfish support. Were it not for the understanding, the patience, the encouragement in dark days, and I would like to think, affection, from Mairéad Furlong and also from Dan Nolan of Tralee this work would certainly not have been completed. For final polish I salute a young warrior in a seventeen year campaign, my friend, Dr. Kevin Whelan of Clonegal, Newman Scholar, University College, Dublin.

Nicholas Furlong
Wexford, May 1991.

Nicholas Furlong was born in Wexford in 1929. He has contributed to many journals, national and provincial newspapers, television and radio. He is a permanent contributor to *The People*, Wexford and the author of four stage productions. *Insurrection '98*, commissioned by the Wexford Opera Festival in 1965, was an outstanding success. He has written five historic tour guides. In 1974 his biography *Dermot, King of Leinster and the Foreigners (1110-1171)*, was published by Anvil Books. In 1986 he was commissioned to write, *Foster Son to a King*, for school children by The Children's Press. He is a Council Member of the Wexford Opera Festival, responsible for the famed fetival tours, a member of the Wexford Historical Society, the Uí Cinnsealaigh Society and is a Life Fellow and Council Member of the Royal Society of Antiquaries of Ireland. He combined with camera technician John Hayes in the acclaimed two volumes of early phtographs *County Wexford in the Rare Oul' Times* Volume I (1985) and Volume II (1987).

Contents

Chapter 1

Early Years

John Murphy was born in the townland of Tincurry, parish of Ferns, county Wexford in 1753.[1] He was the youngest son of Thomas Murphy, a tenant farmer, and Johanna Whitty from nearby Tomgarrow. The Murphys had four sons, Moses, Philip, James and Patrick, and one daughter named Katherine. Their home was concealed in the rolling slopes overlooking a tranquil stretch of the river Slaney from which the fields and hills extended in waves to the Blackstairs Mountains on the horizon. They farmed about seventy acres and, in addition, Thomas Murphy was a bacon curer supplying the Dublin market in a normal Wexford trading pattern. The soils in the Tincurry area and in north Wexford generally are amongst the best multipurpose soils in the world, easily worked and with a particular facility for producing top quality malting barley.[2] So great was the output and so excellent the quality of barley produced and exported that one eighteenth-century writer defined the county as 'the granary of the kingdom'.

The Murphy name had been in that area as far back as records extended but the Gaelic regime was altered drastically by the Elizabethan plantations, followed by Cromwell's thorough purge of 'Irish Papists' in the 1650s.[3] The planting of English colonists on the farmlands of north Wexford had been so extensive that in the townland of Tincurry alone the Murphys were surrounded by ten farming families of English descent, all members of the Church of England, Protestant and Reformed.[4] The Murphys of Tincurry were in a precarious position, being tenants at whim. The actual owner with title, the landlord of Tincurry, was Robert Uniack Fitzgerald of Cockbeg, county Cork, who had accumulated considerable property in county Wexford as well as in Cork county and city.[5] He rented his property in Wexford to a middleman, Thomas Richards of Brookville, Wexford, who in turn sublet it for him to other farmers, amongst whom were the Murphys.

The Murphy children attended a hedge school in their parish.[6] Hedge schools evolved during the days of the severest application of the so-called 'Penal Laws' against Catholics enacted by King William of Orange

1

and Queen Anne. The last of these laws remained on the statute book until 1829, but the worst of their bite was eroded in the late eighteenth century.

The 'Penal Laws' were not designed to eliminate the Roman Catholic religion[7] but to consolidate power and wealth in the hands of reliable London loyalists who were by tradition Protestants. They aimed to keep the antagonistic Irish poor and politically harmless, without a prospect of power in their own land. Had the Irish elected to convert to the Established Protestant Church *en masse,* other means to frustrate them would have had to be designed. In time the hedge school gave way to cabin accommodation, but either shelter was tenaciously availed of. The hedge school teachers were supported by the parents who gave their children pennies to take with them for the school masters' upkeep each week. In addition to teachers based in the one parish there were also travelling teachers with special skill, and in county Wexford in the latter half of the eighteenth century there was the prospect of a reasonable training.

The name of the hedge school master who taught the Murphys was Martin Gunn. Of John Murphy's early life and adolescence very little out of the ordinary is known but he enjoyed one scholastic advantage. He had an aptitude for languages to the extent that he became the equal of Martin Gunn at Latin and Greek. This facility with languages is not unusual in people who are bilingual, as a great many in county Wexford were.[8] In the early part of the eighteenth century the spoken language of the rural population was Irish. The greater proportion spoke English by the end of the century but Irish was still the main language used everyday in the north and west of the county.

When John Murphy was nine years of age an unexpected development took place. The parish priest, a former hedge schoolmaster, died and an exceptional priest was appointed to succeed him.[9] The new parish priest was a member of a powerful church institution which had come under papal displeasure, the Society of Jesus. His name was Fr. Andrew Cassin, a Doctor of Divinity and a man who inevitably had a direct influence on John Murphy's life. The unprecedented appointment of a Jesuit to rural parish work took place in the period of the Society's defamation on mainland Europe. The bishop of Ferns, Dr. Nicholas Sweetman, of determined and independent vintage, befriended the Jesuits at the time of their oppression and Cassin, a gifted and experienced man with firm Wexford links, was one whom he sheltered. Cassin's talents were quickly employed. He was appointed Vicar General of the diocese of Ferns, but although the title rang of venerable prestige, his place of worship consisted merely of a mud-walled, thatched chapel situated outside the Ferns village limits at Newtown, and he took lodgings with a farmer at Effernogue.

Apart from languages, John Murphy was not noted for any other academic talent, but there is a living tradition of his prowess in field sports.[10] He excelled in athletics. He relished physical tests of strength and agility and became a superb horseman. In one particular sport he was long remembered. That was handball, a mass sport at the time because it made few demands on space or landlord property and was played against a wall with single or double competitors.

The nearest large village to the Murphys was Ferns, over three miles away, once a cathedral town and the medieval power centre of Gaelic Leinster. The nearest town was Enniscorthy, six miles distant, with about five thousand inhabitants. Its streets and buildings were grouped around a stone bridge across the river Slaney at the point where it ceases to be tidal. Enniscorthy was a busy town with turreted castle, market house and courthouse. Markets of cattle, sheep and pigs were held four times a year and the riverside wharfs were busy with barges and gabbards plying to and from the port of Wexford. Presiding above the hills of the town, the steep streets and thatched houses, was a lordly rock outcrop called Vinegar Hill. This town was on the rim of John Murphy's boyhood horizon.

In the Murphy household, as in most Irish rural households, there were two recurring annual irritants. The first was the rent due to a landlord for land which had been confiscated in the lifetime of Thomas Murphy's grandfather. The second was the payment of tithes to the minister of the Established Church, the church identified as that of the planter and English establishment loyalist. That there were periods of turbulence and bitter hatreds there can be no doubt, but despite the swings of fortune the Murphys were never evicted presumably because they must have been good rent-paying tenants. The eldest son, Moses, married Margaret Proctor the daughter of a nearby tenant farmer from Crane and she came to live in the homeplace at Tincurry. The only girl, Katherine, or Kate as she was known, married John Walsh of Effernogue in her home parish and went to live there. Little is known of Philip Murphy, but Patrick Murphy eventually became the ultimate political activist. He fought throughout the rebellion of '98 and was killed at the last great battle on Vinegar Hill.[11]

A kinsman of the Murphys, Anthony Ryan, wrote that the remaining brother, James Murphy, was sent to Seville to study for the priesthood but returned because of ill health, and in time 'married into a farm' near The Harrow. Students for the home mission were not sent abroad for training without first being ordained but it could be that James went to Spain on a ship bound from Wexford on the grain run, to investigate his

3

prospects. There were enough Wexford contacts in Cadiz and Seville to facilitate this. John Murphy himself took up the challenge and became an aspirant to the priesthood towards the end of the 1770s.

Seville Cathedral *(Patronato provincial de turismo de Seville)*

Chapter 2

Ordination

John Murphy spent his apprenticeship under the direction of his Jesuit parish priest, Dr. Andrew Cassin. Because of the severe restrictions of the times the practice was to ordain aspirants to the priesthood before they began their studies in theology and philosophy in the various colleges of mainland Europe. There were no Catholic seminaries in Ireland. This premature ordination involved considerable risk and was undertaken only after the candidate was vouched for and sponsored by his parish priest. At the time of John Murphy's studies, discipline in the diocese had been tightened considerably and only the best students were acceptable to an alert Bishop Sweetman.[1] The onus of certifying the worthiness of any candidate was placed upon his parish priest. Under Cassin, John Murphy was trained in the basics of the Church's liturgy, sacraments and services. Had it been required, he could have gone to specialised private teachers in the county as other candidates did for courses in Latin, mathematics and classical literature, but with Martin Gunn in the vicinity, as well as his own superbly qualified parish priest, this was hardly necessary. Throughout his pre-ordination training he lived at home and took part in the day-to-day affairs and pastimes of the parish. Finally, in the autumn of 1779, Andrew Cassin formally declared him worthy of ordination.

According to the usual procedure, John Murphy was then summoned to Wexford town by Bishop Sweetman for the ceremonies and stages leading to his final commitment.[2] Other candidates from the diocese also arrived in Wexford and they were all lodged in houses around the town. The day after their arrival they assembled in the bishop's fine slated house in High Street. There they were confronted by Nicholas Sweetman, one of the most flamboyant figures in the Irish Catholic Church. An unrepentant supporter of the exiled and Catholic Stuart Kings, Sweetman had been tossed into a Dublin Castle dungeon on the charge, laid by one of his own priests, that he had collected arms for 'The Pretender'. As an administrator he knew every square inch of his diocese and every priest and significant family in it. He was a member of one of the county's most powerful families who can only, in their cir-

5

cumstances, be described as an underground aristocracy. The Sweetmans were extensive tenant farmers at Newbawn in south Wexford but technically, like their old Irish compatriots, were tenants at whim. From their sturdy thatched abode they wielded remarkable commercial as well as ecclesiastical power. The loyalty and respect they commanded from their fellow countymen suffering penal deprivation was extraordinary while they themselves, using the talent which they could legally exploit, had merchant and shipping bases extending from Placentia in Newfoundland to Cadiz in Spain. Nicholas Sweetman, brilliant and energetic churchman, who was compelled to walk a tightrope of suspect legality and taut discretion all his life, was more than a bishop. He was the undeclared figurehead, inspiration and stabiliser of a native stock still recovering from the humiliations of the previous one hundred years.

On the first day of their meeting Bishop Sweetman conferred the minor orders and the sub-diaconate on the candidates. A few days later they were ordained deacons. Finally, with the rest of his colleagues, John Murphy was ordained priest. All the rubrics, the solemn laying on of hands, the liturgy and that most moving of the Church's ceremonies, ordination, took place in seclusion behind closed doors in Bishop Sweetman's chambers.

The Murphy family celebration did not follow immediately after Fr. John's ordination. By the custom of the day, that took place several weeks later when he had celebrated his first Mass in the home place in Tincurry. The caution and reverence involved in the Eucharistic ceremony at that time was such that he had to return to Wexford to confer with Bishop Sweetman and receive permission to say Mass. It was at this visit that the bishop had to declare his choice of European college for Fr. John's future training. He selected the Dominican College of St. Thomas, Seville, in the south of Spain. It had an outstanding reputation of which Sweetman had direct confirmation, for it was the *alma mater* of a scholar friend, Dr. James Caulfield, parish priest of New Ross.[3]

There was but one further problem and that was getting Fr. John to Seville, for France and England were once more at war and the English Navy blocked all French ports. Transporting fugitives or free men to or from mainland Europe was now a centuries-old art form in Wexford port, so it is beyond doubt that he took the sea route on the grain run disembarking at Cadiz and proceeding up river to Seville.[4]

The twenty-seven-year-old priest reached Seville in July 1780.[5] The contrast between the green lanes of Tincurry and the scorching sun of southern Spain was great, but the sight which was bound to overwhelm anyone of John Murphy's background was the spectacle of the Holy Roman Catholic and Apostolic Church triumphant.[6] The city presented him with a visual splendour that was totally out of his ken. It was entirely surrounded by an intact fortified wall on which there were 176 high towers. A colossal stone aquaduct built by the Romans dominated the adjacent landscape. Here the Moslem world and Christian Spain met and the hand of the Moor greeted his eyes unaccustomed to such architectural splendour. There was a profusion of glowing Catholic churches redolent of age and dignity, magnificently endowed with sacred art of comprehensive range and richness, but the single creation which inspired most awe was the cathedral, one of the wonders of Christendom, a monument that appeared of cosmic proportions. Its decorations, Madonnas, saints and tabernacles almost bewildered the senses. One single altar, constructed of a mass of solid silver, was enhanced by the riches left by supplicants as well as the grateful. In an interior of blazing candles the tabernacle for the Sacred Host was more than twelve feet high and was supported by forty-eight columns. These riches themselves were trifling when compared with the gold and precious stones which had been deposited in the cathedral's caverns by zealous Catholics when the wealth of the Americas flowed into Seville. The priceless glories of the cathedral rendered numb the memory of Ireland where deprivation and stealthy worship were the constant companions of Catholicism.

John Murphy arrived at his lodgings in Seville on 13 July, 1780.[7] It was a residential house for 'worthy priests, poor and infirm', an indication of the meagre resources which sustained his education. He was fortunate in his new superior, the Dominican Don Francisco Aquilar y Ribon, a dominant figure in Church and Seville university life for almost half a century; an enthusiastic reformer, he is still noted as one of the most accomplished *alumni* of Seville's university.[8]

The Wexford priest started his five years' studies in theology and philosophy and gave them the single-minded attention which he was later to devote to every project he undertook. He took his lectures through Latin amongst an international gathering of students from several continents, all convening in the college of St. Thomas Aquinas. From the beginning the authorities looked upon him as a sober student, an obedient man, and one seen to give good example. He was earnest and diligent and throughout his years in Seville he attended lectures without interruption. He had little financial scope to behave extravagantly in his new and exhilarating environment; his only means of self-support was from Mass offerings. Strict orthodoxy prevailed in the Spanish Dominican's teaching of theology and philosophy. Passive obedience was the theological fashion at the time of John Murphy's residence, and, like all clerical students in France or Spain, he was indoctrinated in the 'Divine Right of Kings'. One aim was clear. The Dominicans in Seville did not intend to train and export radicals. The service of 'the Sacred Mission' in whatever diverse climate was the target of their zeal.

A vibrant Irish colony had been established in Cadiz and Seville, by the time of John Murphy's years there.[9] Bishop Sweetman's brother, Patrick, was well placed in business in Cadiz. Many of the Irish exiles were merchants who had brought Irish people over to work with them.

They had introduced at least one favourite delicacy to Seville, for Irish salted butter had become a daily item on the city's breakfast tables. The great phenomenon to John Murphy must, nevertheless, have been the fact that ordinary water was sold just like tobacco, clothes, food or wine; it was sold in such quantities in the busy sun-baked city that the vendors lived for the rest of the year on what they earned during the summer heat.

Fr. John remained in Spain for the entire duration of his course of studies. At the end of his five years there he was given a diploma. While it did not proclaim outstanding academic qualifications it certified that he did his best, gave no trouble, studied and did what he was told. On 5 March 1785, the parchment which formally ended his college life was issued:

IN THE NAME OF GOD, AMEN

We, the undersigned Rector, Regent and Professors of Sacred Theology and Arts in the venerable major college and in the pontifical, imperial and royal public schools of general studies of St. Thomas Aquinas, of the Order of Preachers in the city of Seville, do hereby make it known to each and every reader of this document, that the Reverend John Murphy from the diocese of Ferns did earnestly and diligently and without noticeable interruption, attend the philosophy lectures of Melchior Cano for a period of three full years in our public schools.

In recognition of this, we, as the juridical authorities of this major college present him with this document under the lesser seal of the college. Given on the 5th day of March, 1785 A.D.

There was another document of fundamental importance, which would be of particular interest to his bishop in Wexford. It was the certificate declaring his fitness and worthiness from his superior in Seville, which was finally given to him a fortnight afterwards.

I, the Reverend Franciscus de Aquilar Ribon, priest and doctor of theology of Seville, member of the royal university and prebendary of the metropolitan and patriarchal church of that city, and present administrator of this residential house for worthy priests, poor and infirm, do hereby certify that the Reverend John Murphy, a priest of the diocese of Ferns in Ireland, who came here for the purpose of his studies and who had been here from the 13th day of July, 1780 to the present day, did reside and accept maintenance in this house, piously attending the spiritual exercises and showing good example and obedience. From here he attended, with permission, the philosophical and theological studies at the major college of St. Thomas Aquinas of the Order of Preachers.

In virtue of this, we adjudge the said Reverend John Murphy to be fit and worthy to return to his own country so that he may assume his sacred mission and his spiritual duties.

In witness to this, I hereby put my signature to this document, dated March 29th, 1785.

In the early summer of 1785, Fr. John set out for home. He was thirty-two years of age. Back in Tincurry, nephews and nieces he had not seen previously told him of the changes that had taken place. The old ecclesiastical warrior, Bishop Sweetman, was alive, active and in control at eighty-nine years of age but he had a new coadjutor bishop in Dr. Caulfield, parish priest of New Ross.[10] The countryside was stirring with industry. Tillage had increased dramatically and the grain export trade out of Wexford port had expanded.

John Murphy was not given long to rest at home. He was posted immediately to the vacant curacy of Kilcormuck in the neighbouring parish of Monageer. The place was better known as Boolavogue, where the thatched chapel was situated.[11] The parish of Monageer was well treated by its liberal landlord, Lord Mountnorris, who permitted Catholics to have two thatched chapels. The other thatched chapel, used by the parish priest, was in the village of Monageer. Such facilities were not enjoyed everywhere. There were parishes in Wexford where no Catholic chapel was permitted by the landlord, where the most the parish priest had was a moveable altar or temporary shelter in an open field, subject to the weather conditions at all times.[12]

The new curate had the advantage of being near home and his married sister, Katherine Walsh, lived not far away at Effernogue, while his brother James resided a couple of miles distant at The Harrow. Consequently, the usual search for local knowledge, atmosphere, keep and lodgings was very much shortened. His immediate superior was Fr. Patrick Cogley, the parish priest of Monageer, who was only two years his senior. Fr. Cogley's qualifications were ideal for the mixed community in which he had to serve with discretion. Bishop Caulfield was to define him as 'a proper and discreet man of quiet disposition'.[13]

Bishop Sweetman had placed John Murphy into a social and farming situation with which he was familiar. Like Ferns, his new parish contained some of the richest soils in Ireland. As in Ferns, a high proportion of the lands in the Boolavogue region had been planted a couple of generations previously.[14] The counties of Wexford and Wicklow were the largest areas of England's loyalist plantation outside of Ulster. In Wexford the planted families of English Protestant descent were concentrated to the greatest extent on the best soils of the county, above the town of Enniscorthy. The proportion of the population which was loyalist and Protestant in Fr. Murphy's new parish was estimated at between fifteen and twenty per cent, but they held a greater proportion of land. Their spiritual welfare was cared for by the Protestant rector of Kilcormuck, Rev. Edward Tottenham, an elderly gentleman of a nationally known Wexford family, possessed of formidable loyalist credentials.[15] His father had been prominent as a member of parliament for Wexford and was at one period in his career appointed High Sheriff of the county by the Crown. The Tottenham family, however, had become reduced in property and status, a decline epitomised by Kilcormuck's rector.

Boolavogue's Catholic curate was given lodgings in the home of John Donohue, a tenant farmer at Tomnaboley, half a mile from the chapel of Boolavogue. Donohue provided the new priest with extra means of support. He let him keep two or three cows on the farm, and this meant that he would have a few pence of his own from the cows and their produce to give him a little independence. The relationship between the priest and the family with whom he lodged through his years in Boolavogue must of necessity have been intimate, but it was with another neighbour that his name and fortunes became persistently associated. That neighbour lived alongside the chapel at Boolavogue Cross. His name was Thomas Donovan.[16]

Tom Donovan, his wife and family were the caretakers of the thatched chapel because it was on their rented land that the chapel had been built. In Tom Donovan's case that relationship carried an additional edge.[17] A generation or so previously his family had been guilty of what was regarded as the unforgivable in rural Irish society. They had become Protestants. That was seen as joining forces and collaborating with the governing establishment, and attending the English language Church services for immediate social and commercial gain. Tom Donovan had, however, placed himself under establishment odium by leaving the Protestant Church and reverting to Catholicism. As with most converts, he became fanatically zealous in his adoption of the old religion. His first cousins, the family of John Donovan of Tobergal, who lived a short distance away, had remained Protestants, and by doing so they nourished a focal point for local bitterness, especially the loudly voiced criticism of Tom Donovan.

Fr. John celebrated Mass each morning in Boolavogue chapel and breakfasted afterwards in Tom Donovan's. Thus from the earliest days Tom Donovan and his family became a prime source of information, mirth and gossip for the new curate, having daily, as everyone knew, 'the ear of Fr. Murphy'.

John Murphy was a well-built man of medium size, well fleshed, with handsome, regular features. He was light in complexion, with a rather high forehead, but the most noted feature of his face was a pair of bright blue eyes.[18] From his first days in Boolavogue he made an impact on young and old, but especially on the youngsters because of his considerable skill as an athlete.[19] It was not long before they discovered that he was the most adept ball player and a 'born horseman'. Horse-riding was a priest's only method of travel in all weathers, and this meant he had to endure many rigours. Fr. John took advantage of the central position of Boolavogue and galloped the roads and hills around him, so that even distant areas became known to him intimately.

One year after Fr. John's posting to Boolavogue, the old order in the Catholic Church in county Wexford suffered abrupt if inevitable changes. His mentor and tutor, Dr. Andrew Cassin, S.J., died at sixty-eight years of age.[20] He was followed by Dr. Nicholas Sweetman, the bishop who ordained Fr. John. The bishop had turned his ninetieth year but his death meant more than the passing of an aged prelate and his replacement by the coadjutor bishop. With Sweetman's death, the complexion of the Catholic Church in Wexford, or, as it is termed, the diocese of Ferns, was altered. To his last breath, he maintained his unbending loyalty before God to the Catholic Stuart monarch in exile in Rome, thus unambiguously branding the rival, *de facto* monarch in London, the Protestant King George, an usurper and thief.[21] Sweetman's successor, his former coadjutor bishop, Dr. James Caulfield, reversed all that, in the conviction that the Catholic Church must reconcile itself to the political realities. To Caulfield's own clergy, therefore, as well as to the government, it was evident at once that a new situation in diocesan affairs, a sharp break with the past, had taken place, and Bishop James Caulfield took open steps to emphasise that this was so.

For a start, the new bishop made certain that there would be nothing furtive about Church conferences or meetings, especially as far as the Government was concerned. He embarked on a new series of regulations and regular meetings of the clergy.[22] In John Murphy's area the venue for such meetings was Enniscorthy's main hostelry, which was owned by a Protestant and loyalist, John Rudd. Dr. Caulfield took the precaution of having the notices and agenda of these conferences openly published by a Protestant printer. The time-table scheduled the meetings for 11 a.m. and the bishop was explicit in his instructions. The meetings would take place in Mr. Rudd's 'and nowhere else'. Bishop and priests would lunch together in Rudd's dining-room at 2 p.m. and the priests depart for their separate parishes at 5 p.m.

The meeting of Fr. John with the new bishop took place in conference with all the priests of the deanery of Enniscorthy. The bishop's words, his views and instructions were awaited with unusual interest, but, the clergy gathered at Rudd's must have speculated on whether they would not shortly be looking at his successor. Caulfield was like a wraith, a delicate, sharp-nosed gentleman with high white hair, whose physique bore but poor comparison with the bodies and complexions before him, country priests rendered ruddy and rough by years in the saddle.[23] He was full of grace and airs, a little wisp of a man whose demeanour communicated punctiliousness. He wore a high-collared black coat and a shining white neckerchief. It was evident that any slip from etiquette, sobriety or discretion would inspire in him the keenest displeasure.

Bishop Caulfield informed the gathering that he had appointed four places for conferences in the major towns of the diocese, to be held in the fairweather months from April to October only. The purpose, he pointed out, 'was for the information, instruction and direction of the clergy; particularly for the younger and less experienced clergy.' They were, he continued, 'for the consideration and discussion of cases of conscience such as occur in the course of moral theology.' He went on to define the political guidelines and, as expected, made clear his orders about their future conduct as Catholic priests. John Murphy absorbed the new regime's abrupt change of direction as itemised in the bishop's finely chiselled words:

> Agreeing or consenting to any measure which tends to turbulence, to disturbing the public peace and good order, to opposing the King's government and the legislature, or violating the established laws of the land is to be marked with detestation and reprobation, as contrary to the doctrine and example of Jesus Christ and His Apostles; and to all social good order. Loyalty and fidelity to the gracious good King George III; submission to His Majesty's government and to the constituted authorities; obedience and observance of the laws are to be a religious, conscientious, and indispensable duty to every Roman Catholic.

These then were the unambiguous guidelines which he and his fellow priests were enjoined to take back to their flocks for acceptance. The people were to reconcile themselves to their unalterable circumstances. The emphasis stressed by Dr. Caulfield confirmed, nevertheless, that his flock were of contrary opinion. An abrupt transference of loyalty to the Protestant King George of England, along with submission to his laws, regime and government, was a physic unpalatable to many.

Boolavogue chapel 1798. (*Drawing by Stephen Hannon from a plan by Kevin Whelan*).

12

Chapter 3

Revolution

On 14 July 1789, the world was changed. In Paris the 'untamed' teemed out of their lairs and threw the fabric of civilisation and society into desolation. The Bastille prison was stormed and captured by Parisians. France erupted, town by town, city by city. The hierarchy of power in which kings, lords and bishops ruled by divine right was demolished. The very basis of property and existing power was attacked with sustained ferocity. No one suspected of association with the old order of things was safe from violent assault and death. The meanest mortal in clerical garb became fair game for a lamp-post hanging.

The violence was not limited to a week or even a year. England watched, initially fascinated, as France tore herself apart; as month followed month and year followed year, outrage after outrage was visited upon the nation's once indestructible institutions, England's horror turned to fear. Fear saturated the mind and imagination of those involved in power, property or politics in England and mainland Europe. The King of France, Louis XVI, was kept alive in prison until January 1793, when he was guillotined. His Queen, Marie Antoinette, was executed in October of the same year. The heads of aristocracy, minor and major, and those of their families and serfs who chose to remain loyal sliced from the guillotine into baskets like slates in a gale. The Pope and the Roman Catholic Church looked on aghast as every cherished tradition, norm and citadel of faith was invaded with venom and destruction. The crowned heads of Europe seemed stunned in a stupor of inactivity, appalled by the words of a Revolutionary Assembly member. 'Let us tell Europe,' declared Deputy Brissot, 'that if the cabinets of foreign courts attempt to stir up a war of kings against France, we shall stir up a people's war against the kings!' He added that: 'A people who after twelve centuries of slavery have won liberty, require a war to consolidate it.' These were not idle words. The revolution bred an army which in ten years became the most powerful and feared machine of war in Europe.

Probably no event since the sack of Rome produced a cataclysmic effect upon European society equal to the French Revolution; the terror with which its progress was regarded, even in countries as fundamentally stable as England, was unsurpassed by any event in modern times. It is not surprising then, that if the politically influential classes in England shuddered, the political ascendancy in Ireland, ever fearful of the immense Catholic majority and ever conscious of their latent hostility, were terrified, particularly in a situation over which they came to have increasingly less control. 'We are afraid of the guillotine,' wrote one prominent Irish Government official'.[1]

Nevertheless, it took time to gather the tinder for conflagration in Ireland. Wexford's passion was ten years away and in quiet Boolavogue life followed a normal course. Nothing happened to bring Fr. John to prominence. The normal church business was carried on, the sacraments were administered, the sick and dying visited, the dead prayed over and the new arrivals baptised. As he worked amongst the people, his faults, virtues and characteristics were identified.[2] His amiable manner made him popular, but he was not an easy-going curate. He was described by some as 'terribly active'. He was also unbending in principle and rigidly committed to Bishop Caulfield's directives. As time went on, it was recognised that he was a valuable man in many roles. People went to him and came to rely on the advice he offered. Wherever there was trouble or bereavement he went to help and organise the work. He gave his considered opinion freely, but his inflexibility was such that he was 'terrible when opposed'. A phrase encountered in the folk memory says that 'He was a right sort of man … but he could be hot.' His education and travel gave him entry to many houses, including that of Lord Mountnorris of Camolin Park, where his conversation 'commanded admiration even from Cromwellian and Williamite'.[3]

Mountnorris's practice of entertaining Fr. John and his likes was regarded as foolhardy by the extremists amongst his class, but Mountnorris was a liberal, who courted Catholic support.[4] Fr. John also became a guest in the homes of two of the most influential old Catholic families who had maintained the substance of county gentry, the Hays of Ballinkeele and the FitzGeralds of Newpark.[5] These contacts, and his undoubted popularity among his own parishioners and family connections, gave him comprehensive information throughout his twelve years of residence in Boolavogue.

There was much to be seen and hotly argued as the 1790s advanced. The significance of the French Revolution, of which several of Wexford's greatest families, Protestant as well as Catholic, had been made acutely aware, did not percolate to the chapel gates for some time. Nevertheless, with a volition which appeared to have a momentum of its own, trends escalated to stimulate unrest. A general election to the Irish Parliament, in which Catholics as usual had no vote, took place in 1790.[6] The consolidated ruling faction in the land divided between the Protestant supremacists on the one hand and the liberal Protestants on the other who were anxious and willing to introduce reforms and redress Catholic grievances.

In Wexford the election was fought with corrosive bitterness. Catholics were no more than partisan spectators, but the result had a deep effect on spectators, voters and participants alike, for the extremists were victorious over the liberal party. Following the election one Wexford Catholic of aristocratic antecedents articulated the despair of many when he grieved at his 'civil degradation as a Catholic', a condition regarded with growing discontent.[7] This smouldering resentment resulted in the formation of a national body known as 'The Catholic Committee' to win civil liberties, a body which was greeted by the governing ascendancy with suspicion and hostility.[8] When the Catholic Committee's secretary arranged for county conventions and the election of delegates to a national convention in Dublin he was accused of 'issuing writs for a general election'. Ascendancy bodies all over the country raged in voice and printed proclamations, but the ruling authority's position was succinctly defined by John FitzGibbon: 'Catholic Emancipation would lead to the reform of parliament and a reformed parliament would break the connection with Great Britain, a connection which is essential to British safety and Irish social stability'.

In 1791, a young Protestant lawyer, Theobald Wolfe Tone, helped to found a new society named the Society of the United Irishmen.[9] His aim was to bring Irishmen of all persuasions, Catholic, Protestant and Dissenter, into a movement for far-reaching reform. The Dublin Society of the United Irishmen was joined by supporters of the liberal Protestant party in Wexford, the best known of whom were the popular landlord and barrister, Beauchamp Bagenal Harvey of Bargy Castle, his brother James Harvey, William Hatton of Clonard, Samuel Cooper, John Grogan of Healthfield, Anthony Perry of Inch, George Powel and Edward Sweetman of the Newbawn family.[10]

A branch of the new society was formed in Gorey towards the end of 1792 and Captain Sweetman, a former French army officer, announced its inauguration to the Dublin Society on 21 December. It adopted, he reported, 'the resolutions of the Society in Dublin and those of Belfast'. It was one of the first branches in the provinces and was joined by more enthusiasts from the Protestant liberal party. No list of founding members of the Gorey society survives but it is likely the earliest members in Wexford, supporting at first only parliamentary reform and Catholic emancipation, included Anthony Perry of Inch, George Sparks of

15

Blackwater, Captain Matthew Keugh of Wexford town, a former British army officer; Henry Hughes of Ballytrent, Robert Graham of Inch and John Boxwell of Sarshill, Kilmore, – all Protestants; Dr. John Henry Colclough of Ballyteigue Castle, Kilmore, a Catholic member of a junior branch of the great Tintern Abbey landlord family; John Hay, a former French army officer and his brother, Edward of Ballinkeele; Nicholas Murphy of Monaseed, Edward FitzGerald of Newpark, Edward Roche of Garrylough, Nicholas Sweetman of Newbawn, a nephew of Bishop Sweetman; Esmond Kyan of Mount Howard and James Edward Devereux of Carrigmannon; all Catholics.[11] The early members of the United Irishmen's society in county Wexford were all respected, widely connected men of substance. They were also possessed of one other vital political facility. They lived in well dispersed locations all over the county, from the slopes of the Wicklow Mountains to the entrance to the Irish Sea.

A new Catholic Relief Act was pushed through Parliament and Lords by Pitt's influence on 2 February, 1793. It added greatly to the political privileges of Catholics who were exempted from all penalties for non-attendance at the Established Church service on the Lord's Day, and cottages were exempted from the hearth tax. Catholics were deemed capable of holding civil and military offices or places of trust or profit under the Crown and those with a property qualification were allowed to vote. As a qualification for these privileges, every member of the Church of Rome was required to swear the formula of allegiance prescribed by Parliament in 1774, and to take another oath avowing his detestation of the principle that it is lawful to murder or injure any person under the pretence of his being a heretic; declaring his belief that no deed in itself unjust, immoral or wicked can be justified on the grounds that it is done for the good of the Church, or in obedience to any ecclesiastical authority; affirming that it is not an article of the Catholic faith that the Pope is infallible, and testifying that the individual adjured will not exercise any privilege, to which he may be entitled, for the purpose of disturbing or weakening the Protestant religion and Protestant government in the Kingdom.

To make certain that the *status quo* in government remained, the same Relief Act stipulated that Catholics could not become members of their own country's Parliament, could not become members of the bench, sheriffs, Privy Councillors or general officers in the armed forces. Resentment amongst politicised and informed Catholics no less than amongst liberal Protestants, especially in Wexford, continued to fester. Frustrated in their demands by a faction of ascendancy extremists, they bristled with anger. At the very same time, the governing ascendancy advanced into a daily state of fear. Aghast at the continued growth of

16

the French 'terror', they were disagreeably aware that their own titles to power and property rested on forceful seizure. The fear was given impetus when in that very year revolutionary France declared war on England and Holland.

The hierarchy of the Catholic Church welcomed the Catholic Relief Act as a significant step out of the catacombs, and acceptance of the Act's requirements and oath was urged upon all Roman Catholics. At the same time, Dublin's ascendancy Parliament decided to add a restraining act called 'The Convention Act'. This forbade the formation or gathering of all and any assemblies purporting to represent a large section of the Irish people. The Catholic Convention was dissolved.

To Theobald Wolfe Tone, a former secretary of the Catholic Committee, and his closest comrades, the new acts consolidated the grip on power by the ascendancy. The Society of the United Irishmen was now steered by him towards a new and radical course, a course supported by fellow members who were abandoning restraint. It turned towards revolution. The society's articles of association were changed into an oath of secrecy and fidelity. Its objectives of reform and emancipation were abandoned for nothing less than armed revolt, the rupture of the connection with England, and the establishment in Ireland of a republic on the principles exemplified by the revolutionary government of France. Wexford was to become one of the most thoroughly involved counties in the new direction of the organisation.

How far the many developments of 1793 affected digestion at Fr. John's breakfast table in Tom Donovan's of Boolavogue is hard to gauge. Tom's teenage son, Jerry, lame since birth, had become another contributor to the morning dialogues. One thing is certain, local drama did not escape dissection or diagnosis. Rev. Edward Tottenham, the aged Protestant rector of Kilcormuck, died in the spring and a new clergyman arrived to occupy his benefice.[12] The new rector, Rev. Thomas Handcock, was a stranger to Wexford. Handcock, son of a clergyman and the grandson of the archdeacon of the Ulster diocese of Kilmore, set about securing his income in the rural areas of Monageer-Boolavogue by employing the services of two tithe proctors to collect the tithes due to him in law. Both of the men he employed were Catholics, one of them named Murphy, and both were inevitably seen by their fellow Catholics as poachers turned gamekeepers. Handcock appeared to treat the Catholic clergy as if they did not exist, and where they did exist he regarded them as inflammatory demagogues.[13] He became as dominant a character in the locality as Fr. John himself, and an undoubted magnet for Tom Donovan's invective, but no account of contact between the two clergymen comes down to us, even though the Protestant rector was a competent recorder himself.

Handcock's arrival coincided with unprecedented violence. The Irish Parliament established a militia in 1793.[14] It was a locally recruited and locally commanded part-time defence force of the British Army, intended for the most part to contain local outbreaks until regular army units could be brought into action. A much hated parochial ballot was introduced to pick men for the militia. Their officers in Wexford were of the extremist ascendancy faction, but the rank and file were predominantly Catholic. In their first engagement in active service in Wexford, they compounded a disaster which was to have lasting effect from end to end of the county. In July 1793, a country crowd marched on Wexford town to demand the release of comrades arrested after a big tithe protest demonstration.[15] The crowd was met at the outskirts by regular British Army soldiers commanded by a veteran of the Spanish Wars, Major Vallottin. Vallottin went to parley with the crowds' leader, John Moore. Whatever transpired between them, both men attacked and mortally wounded each other. The military opened fire and a detachment of the 38th Wexford Regiment of Militia, under their captain, James Boyd, ambushed the fleeing hundreds at nearby Bettyville. In all, a total of eighty people were shot down and five captured men were tried and hanged, one of them an innocent bystander. After witnessing and surviving violence on a scale never before experienced by anyone, the compulsion to protect themselves by arms became widespread. The manufacture of pikes started to take place in secret and on a large scale.[16] Wexford was never the same again, and the United Irishmen were to reap that harvest of growing fear.

Conditions favouring the United Irishmen accumulated throughout 1794 and 1795.[17] On mainland Europe, the French armies overwhelmed all enemies in the field and took possession of Belgium and Holland. Fearful and informed of growing unrest in Ireland, England's Prime Minister, William Pitt, appointed a new Lord-Lieutenant of Ireland, Earl Fitzwilliam. Fitzwilliam came to Ireland determined to get rid of the leading ascendancy politicians. He openly supported the full franchise for Catholics but his extremist enemies in the Dublin Parliament insisted to King George III that to admit Catholics to Parliament would violate the monarch's coronation oath. Fitzwilliam's well-intentioned policies were repulsed and he was abruptly removed in March. His replacement was Lord Camden, a sterner political associate of William Pitt. The extremists in Parliament further fertilised antagonism when Grattan's Bill for a repeal of the so-called 'Popery Laws' was rejected by a massive majority. The question of full Catholic emancipation was dismissed from the Irish Parliament, to be raised again as opportunity arose for purposes of faction but nevermore with a serious prospect of acceptance.

18

Branches of the Society of the United Irishmen spread to most parts of Ireland in 1795, news of which reached William Pitt from a variety of spies. Pitt had the courses of every worthwhile individual with French revolutionary convictions plotted.[18] Wexford's senior member of the United Irishmen, Beauchamp Bagenal Harvey, had not merely his activities reported to Pitt by the spy, McNally, but his personality and characteristics as well. The imponderables were the masses of the people as well as the Catholic rank and file in the militia regiments. As time went on, the dependability of that militia rank and file became sharply suspect.

Wherever John Murphy's heart and instincts lay, his single-minded loyalty remained with Dr. James Caulfield and his conservative policy. He attended the monthly conferences with the bishop and the situation did nothing to cheer. The United Irishmen had made inroads into their people, an organisation which, the bishop noted, had the most sinister flavours: French, revolutionary, free masonic and Protestant. Warnings from the altar against membership of oathbound societies had only elicited ridicule. Caulfield persisted. The United Irishmen's oaths were noted by him 'as they ought to be', and emphasised as unlawful, perjurious and wicked. There was not the slightest degree of leniency allowed. 'I tell you,' Caulfield declared, 'that every action, every attempt to conspire or join with United Irishmen, or any agreement or consent to any measure which tends towards turbulence, to disturbing the public peace and good order, or opposing the King's Government and legislation must be marked with detestation and reprobation.' Such activities, the bishop insisted, 'are contrary to the doctrine of Jesus Christ and his Apostles and to all social and good order, loyalty and fidelity to our gracious good King George the Third.'

Submission to His Majesty's government was emphatically propounded as being the indispensable duty of every Roman Catholic. Fr. John Murphy was under direct orders from his bishop to make this clear to his parishioners.[19] Even as he did, there was an inexorable evolution of events both far off and close to home whose strange combination was to alter his life and the lives of everyone around him in the rural seclusion of Boolavogue. On 24 February 1796, the ambassador of the United Irishmen, Theobald Wolfe Tone, was before the French revolutionary leader, Carnot, in Paris, and the negotiations to induce a French intervention in Ireland commenced.[20]

The excitability of Fr. John's daily breakfast companion, Tom Donovan, was a family trait shared by his Protestant first cousin, John Donovan of Tobergal. John Donovan had a persecution complex that Tom Donovan did not have. He had married a local Catholic girl.[21] That alone created a brittle atmosphere so that very little mischief-making was required to boil the blood, and John Donovan happened to have blood easily brought to the boil. He was readily available for taunts, for he drank heavily and in public. The public house in The Harrow village was the venue for the men of the locality and in all respects John Donovan was indigenous. By no stretch of the imagination could he be classified as of Cromwellian or Williamite lineage. His attendance at the Protestant Church in Kilcormuck could not obscure the fact that like any bearer of his name he was of old Gaelic stock. As such he was as likely to be despised by the class he emulated as by the class to which his convert cousin Tom returned. The sophisticated art of taunting is well practiced. It is also well resisted in rural public houses, provided the subject of the taunts is not unduly vulnerable.

John Donovan was vulnerable and he was tormented. In 1796, however, a development took place which gave him the chance to elevate himself above the ranks of his begrudgers. The Government, fearful that the Catholic rank and file in the militia would prove unreliable, created a new force of part-time soldiers which they called the yeomen.[22] Commissions in the yeomanry were from the Crown and were paid for by the Government. It was a body whose function was declared as 'arming the property of the country'. The interpretation made by many was that the new force was a means whereby Protestant loyalists could be legally armed for action against Catholics, an interpretation which had a disquieting resonance in north Wexford. John Donovan decided that his best interests were served by the new force and so he enrolled in the cavalry unit based in the village of Camolin, alongside Lord Mountnorris's seat at Camolin Park.

Recruiting for the yeoman units exceeded the government's expectations. They anticipated about 20,000, but within six months there was an armed force of 37,000 yeomen, and later 50,000. Catholics joined the yeomen units as well, many in a deliberate United Irish policy of infiltration and exploitation of the opportunity to undergo military training.[23] This ruse was later frustrated by expulsions but at the time of the rising there were twenty-five yeoman units in county Wexford. Their numbers varied greatly from town to rural units, but a fair average was fifty men. By 1798, there were one thousand three hundred and seventy two yeomen in county Wexford.[24]

A new Government act called the 'Insurrection Act' introduced in 1796 allowed the Lord Lieutenant to rule through martial law in districts estimated to be so disturbed that they required harsh military government. It imposed the death penalty for administering an unlawful oath and transportation for life for taking such an oath. Magistrates were authorised to seize suspects and 'press' them into the British Navy. This drastic act already admitted that the situation in Ireland was deemed desperate by the government but initially its rigours were not felt in Wexford. The first area to feel the full fury of the 1796 Insurrection Act was the province of Ulster.

It is not known when exactly Tom Donovan of Boolavogue and his son, Jerry, became sworn members of the United Irishmen but despite the principles of their friend, Fr. John Murphy, and the mortal peril of subversion, the enticement to do so proved too strong.[25] Whether they took the United Irishmen's oath before or after their cousin John Donovan joined the yeoman cavalry is not known either, but there is no doubt that there were few prospects to thoroughly sicken Tom Donovan and his Catholic neighbours of The Harrow or Boolavogue than the sight of John Donovan of Tobergal in the scarlet coat, the white riding breeches and the black boots of the Camolin Yeoman Cavalry.

During the autumn of 1796, the preparations of the French for landing in Ireland were openly discussed.[26] The United Irishmen prepared to meet the event and to counteract the army of yeomen. Directions were issued by the United leaders to their men all around the country, requiring the formation and disposition of military units, along with the collection of weapons and ammunition. These directions were carried into effect as far as possible. The well informed historian, Plowden, estimated the number of armed men recruited in Ulster alone as 100,000, and the total number of United men in the whole of Ireland in 1796 as half a million. The comparison of populations in the three adjacent countries poised for war is remarkably different from that obtaining today but serves to stress the peril England faced and the resultant anguish of her loyal subjects in the grave situation. France with a population of twenty seven million was the most populous nation in Europe. By contrast, the population of Great Britain and Ireland together was not more than sixteen million, of whom five million were in Ireland.[27]

Chapter 4

The French Intervention

On 16 December 1796, the French expedition to Ireland left Brest, eluded the British fleet, and five days later anchored in Bantry Bay.[1] It consisted of thirty-five ships of the line and carried 12,000 troops under the command of General Lazare Hoche. Before embarking, Hoche had issued a proclamation 'To the French Army destined to assist the Irish Revolution'. He made it clear to his troops that they were going to people who were friends. 'You must treat them as such, and not as a conquered people.' The instructions of the French Directory were simple. With the help of the Irish revolutionary party, the British were to be expelled and an independent Irish Republic created. It was to be the first phase in the overthrow of England.

Despite a safe arrival the expedition's fortune was wretched. In eluding the British fleet outside Brest, Hoche's ship was swept off course and did not join the expedition at Bantry. One calm day, 21 December, was used in waiting for Hoche. The next day the heavens opened to unleash rain, snow and gales upon a mountainous sea. The gales became the great storm that signalled one of Europe's worst winters. By 27 December, the storm had developed hurricane force. Next day the last ship of the expedition left Bantry Bay for home ports. Notwithstanding British naval supremacy, Ireland was for one week at the mercy of revolutionary France whose path towards the conquest of England was stemmed by the elements alone.[2]

The report of the arrival of the French fleet created consternation in Dublin and London. The withdrawal of the expedition, however, stunned those who had prepared to join in. Miles Byrne later remembered the scene in the chapel yards of north Wexford: 'It is quite fresh in my memory and I shall never forget it, the mournful silence, the consternation of the poor people at the different chapels on Christmas Day and on the following Sunday after learning that the French had not landed and that the French fleet had returned to France'.[3] The frustration of the United Irishmen and the shock absorbed by the Government resulted in vigorous recruitment to both the United Irishmen and the yeomanry throughout 1797. The Government armed and equipped the yeomen in every part of the country for active service. The United Irishmen did not long bemoan the French withdrawal. They acted as if another landing was imminent and prepared an extensive plan for organising all Ireland.[4]

In a short space of time Wexford seethed with preparations for organised revolt. In their upper echelons in Wexford the 'Revolutionary Party', as the United Irishmen were being called, possessed experienced officers from the best European armies and at least one veteran of George Washington's army. Anthony Perry of Inch, a Protestant with Down and Dublin connections, was the county organiser, a task he tackled with urgency, especially in the parishes divided between colonist and native stock in north Wexford.[5] He sought new members everywhere, even foraging amongst Catholic priests. The parish priests held firm behind Bishop Caulfield, but a number of curates began to break ranks. The curate in Kilrush, Fr. Edward Sinnott, and the curate in Blackwater, Fr. Thomas Dixon, became United Irish activists and recruiting officers. Both were detected by the bishop, bitterly castigated and suspended.[6]

Boolavogue and its curate came sharply into focus in the spring of 1797. The good offices of Fr. John's opposite number in the Established Church, Thomas Handcock, were rewarded by the Government when he was appointed a magistrate. His appointment coincided with a spasm of new political activity in the parish. In the month of May, Boolavogue and Monageer became focal points of an intense United Irish recruiting drive.[7] The organisation headquarters in Dublin sent a man down to direct the local effort. He was Charles Nowlan, nephew of a pawnbroker, Timothy Nowlan of Greek Street in Dublin. Nowlan's dangerous mission involved a door-to-door canvas of 'safe' houses, that is, houses which could be relied on to keep his business a secret. It generated unprecedented excitement. His importance was confirmed by the man who directed him around the parish and introduced him, the schoolmaster, Hugh Maguire. The testing of the local temper by Nowlan and Maguire was so encouraging that they decided to embark upon an extension of their work. They elected to indulge in a time-honoured after-Mass political rubric – the distribution of their literature amongst the congregations. This they were allowed to do and whether Fr. John gave wholehearted approval or acquiesced quietly it is easy to visualise the tranquilising urgings of Tom Donovan, just in case the priest had any obstructive misgivings.

On the following Sunday Nowlan and Maguire openly distributed United Irish leaflets and pamphlets in the chapel yard of Boolavogue. The leaflets promoted the United Irish policies of organised revolt and

23

the grasping of Ireland's opportunity by her people. The words and ideas were consumed with relish but the bold enterprise reached the ears of Handcock within hours. Alert and alarmed, Handcock mounted horse and rode from house to house in the parish demanding of recipients that they hand the subversive documents over. He next went in pursuit of Nowlan to arrest him but the Dublin United man had disappeared. Handcock reported the outrage to Dublin Castle and there can be no doubt that the episode was swiftly brought to the attention of Caulfield, Fr. John's bishop.

The curate of Boolavogue was in trouble. He was not the only one, as the authorities, with clear evidence of support for disaffection, later rounded up fifteen of Fr. John's parishioners. Seven of them were placed on a capital charge of high treason, eight were charged with being sworn United Irishmen and all fifteen were marched down to Wexford jail to await trial. Boolavogue had emerged from obscurity. So had its priest. It is more than probable that it was in the aftermath of this development that John Murphy was first reproached and reprimanded by Dr. Caulfield.[8] The arm of the lawful authority did not, however, stop the United Irishmen's growth in Boolavogue, for the vacancy left by Charles Nowlan was filled by Thomas Howlett, the miller of Inch.[9] Boolavogue had now become politicised, and to keep the emotions at fever pitch there was a summer general election in the offing.

For Fr. John the swing of events might well be described as alarming. At the early meetings that year with Bishop Caulfield, the situation in Europe, which the Catholic Church recognised as deteriorating, was discussed. The commander of the French Revolutionary armies, Napoleon Bonaparte, had invaded the Papal States and forced a treaty on the aged Pontiff, Pius VI. Bishop Caulfield reiterated the peril of the developing situation as he judged it. Back the priests went to their parishes to maintain an orchestration of pleadings, warnings and blandishments against the French 'disease' gaining ground rapidly in their midst. Fr. John Redmond, parish priest of Camolin, another priest on visiting terms with the liberal landlord Mountnorris, went further than threats. He refused to hear the confessions of United men, and those he recognised as such he turned away.[10]

The daily dilemma in which the curate of Boolavogue found himself was further compounded by the return to Wexford of a turbulent old acquaintance. He was a fellow priest with whom he could at least debate the issues one way or another. His name was Fr. Mogue Kearns, a native of Kiltealy on the slopes of the Blackstairs Mountains.[11] Had Bishop Caulfield been aware of the companionship which developed between them, he would have been appalled, for Kearns was only too well known to him, 'being notorious for drinking and fighting'. That was not all. Kearns had earlier been sent on loan from the diocese of Ferns to the parish of Clonard in the far north of the diocese of Kildare and Leighlin. He was not long there when his superiors discovered he was industriously working as a political activist. His adopted parish priest and bishop saw him as an agitator and sacked him without compunction. As a student, Kearns had survived a hanging by a Paris lynch mob during the revolution.[12] Living dangerously was not new to him. His brother, Pádraig Ruadh Kearns, was the senior United Irishman in the mountainous district of Kiltealy in west Wexford.[13]

Fr. John and Fr. Kearns had family connections on both sides of the Blackstairs Mountains and they frequently met to ride together, to go hunting and after a day's sport to rest in the houses of relatives, especially Murphys of Rathgeeran on the Carlow side.[14] They became well known as companions and were regarded locally as 'great sportsmen'. Whatever about that familiar aspect of Irish life the outcome was that at sport or mealtime two men of like mind, Fr. Mogue Kearns and Thomas Donovan, had the ear of John Murphy.

Conditions promoting revolt grew rapidly in a seemingly unconnected sequence. The Irish Parliament was dissolved in July and a general election was called. The campaign, which went on throughout the high summer months, was fought with a political bitterness exceeding the personal enmities of the previous general election in 1790.[15] The contending factions were the same. The loyalist extremists advocated the full rigour of English and ascendancy supremacy and were violently opposed to any further concessions to Catholics. Opposing them were the liberal Protestants actively supporting Catholic emancipation and civil rights. The extremists in Wexford included the powerful names of Ogle, Ram, Stopford, Ely and Tottenham. The liberals included the names of Carew, Harvey, Grogan, Colclough and one other of specific relevance to Boolavogue and a wide hinterland of north Wexford, the landlord, Lord Mountnorris of Camolin Park.

The election was the focus of debate in mansion, farm house, chapel yard, crossroad and forge; while the overwhelming bulk of the population could do nothing to influence the result, they were partisan in their support. The Catholic community itself became polarised between young radicals bursting for change by force if necessary, and the conservative elder segment insisting on a low profile, watch-and-wait policy. In the end, when the votes of the electorate were counted, the liberals anxious for reform were beaten, but only by a narrow margin.

The frustration suffered in the election result was rendered far worse by the greatest economic catastrophe visited upon Wexford's entire grain industry in the century.[16] New malting legislation was introduced. In addition to an increase of duty and an increase on malt and malthouse licences, the decision was reached to end the carriage bounties on corn shipped to Dublin. This legislation had dire effects in seafaring Wexford where the shipping of malt alone had earned annually around one sixth of all the Dublin carriage bounties on grain and flour. Then came the legislation which affected a wide segment of society. A new act outlined the regulation of licensed maltings. The idea of the proposers was that the quality of malt delivered to the brewers in Dublin would be improved. The effect of the act was catastrophic. Over half the 242 maltings in county Wexford closed as they were judged too small to be licensed. Apart from the maltsters, millers and ship owners, the suffering extended to labourers who lived by farm work, malting or sailing. The tenant farmers in the tillage areas of the county, their main livelihood gone, were compelled to consider new enterprises and a husbandry of a different sort, namely cows, milk and cattle.

In the previous year, 1796, the price of barley per barrel to the grower was 26 shillings. It was a high price for barley and it had obvious results. Many speculating farmers and middlemen took land to rent for the 1797 crop at inflated rates. Competition for tillage land rented for one season was exceptional. In 1797, that market and stability were wrecked as a result of Government policies. The price of barley was slashed to nine shillings per barrel. In some parts of Wexford the price was even worse. The Colcloughs of Tintern, powerful landlord family though they were, were able to procure only 5/- a barrel. Labourers of all trades and no trade were rendered unemployed. Tenant farmers and middlemen who had paid top rents for land lettings were now in desperation. The collection of Church tithes and land rents was found to be an impossible task even with the threat of eviction. Inevitably there were many bankruptcies, especially amongst the maltsters of Wexford port.

Rev. Thomas Handcock noted the change in attitudes and reckoned the turning point on the road to revolt had come with the collapse of the price of corn. 'Incendiaries were sent down from Dublin to fan the disaffection. A visible change took place in the temper and manner of the lower classes'. 'There were secret meetings now,' he noted. 'There were surly expressions. Men stayed later than formerly in public houses. There were threats, whispers, and hints when the lower classes were drunk or angry of revenge upon enemies'. The road to revolt perceived by Handcock was widened at harvest time. An organisation whose reputation alone spelled menace seeped into Wexford.[17] It was known as the Orange Order. The Orange Order was formed in Armagh in 1795 following a murderous riot between Protestants and Catholics. Called after King William of Orange, its reported aim was the 'extermination of the whole race of Catholics out of the County of Armagh.' Branches of the society multiplied nationally and its aims were expanded, but the factor which inspired fear on a nationwide scale was the oath allegedly taken by all recruits to the Orangemen. The words of this oath, published later in pamphlet form, distributed across the land and accepted by Catholics as the truth, went:

> In the awful presence of Almighty God, I, *A.B.* do solemnly swear that I will to the utmost of my power support the king and the present government; and I do further swear that I will use my utmost exertions to exterminate all the Catholics of the Kingdom of Ireland.

Very few documents in the entire century inspired as much fear amongst Catholics as that did, and the fear was created whether the document was genuine or not. Following the introduction of the Orangemen to county Wexford, the Order made control of the armed yeomen a priority.

The priests of north Wexford met Bishop Caulfield in Rudd's Inn at Enniscorthy in the same autumn. The bishop arrived, torn between rage and disappointment. Another Catholic priest, whom he had already denounced for 'incapacity and a riotous temper', was involved to the hilt in the United Irishmen's plans and operations.[18] He was Fr. Michael Murphy of Ballycanew. Caulfield was thoroughly briefed on the political and ecclesiastical situation all over his diocese. The clerical meetings provided him with a further supply of intelligence. When the information from his priests was totted, the total confirmed that the United Irish poison had penetrated the minds of his people. The delicate little man was on the brink of despair for he could well visualise chaos and more. He could visualise his own fate and that of his priests were the French Revolutionary system given free rein. That nightmare was not a figment of his imagination. That nightmare could well materialise, and well he knew that his own flock were working towards that end. As the situation stood that autumn, they had little of the material world to lose and, as it appeared to them, a country to gain.

Amid all the intriguing strands of life and endeavour which surrounded Fr. John Murphy as he gravitated towards the maelstrom of 1798, his relations with Bishop Caulfield are most compelling. Caulfield shrank from no phrase of vituperation to lacerate the curates who so readily defied him and threw in their lot with the United Irishmen.[19] His written words are scarifying to this day, and they specify transgressions: 'for drinking, dancing and disorderly conduct suspended' and 'active in the accursed business of Uniting for which I interdicted him and suspended him' – (Fr. Thomas Dixon); 'notorious agitator' who did 'much mischief', 'prone to excessive use of spirits' – (Fr. Edward Sinnott); 'a most beastly drunkard and unfit for duty, was suspended ... and remained so' – (Fr. Thomas Clinch); 'Another reptile, ... deprived and suspended – (Fr. Bryan Murphy); 'An idiot' – (Fr. John Keane); but of the curate of Boolavogue, the 'most notorious' of all his curates, the severest adjective Dr. Caulfield employed was 'giddy'. In Caulfield's judgement 'giddy' meant impressionable. No indictment for immorality or drunkenness is attached by the well informed bishop to Fr. John Murphy, and he is specific on the matter of immorality when reporting to Archbishop Troy of Dublin. The image of John Murphy is rather that of a rigid puritan who was later to breathe fury on followers found in drinking bouts.

Caulfield had comprehensive knowledge of all his priests, their family backgrounds and circumstances, and must have been conscious that there were conflicting pressures between the call of home and land and the discipline of the Church. Many of his most loyal priests had brothers and relations in active leadership positions in the United Irishmen.[20] In Fr. Murphy's own case the pressures of the day were magnified on his visits home to Tincurry or to his mother's homeplace, Whittys of Tomgarrow. Both homes were anti-government, possessing sworn United Irish members, both had pike-bearing rebels in the field eventually, while before the outbreak Murphy's bacon-curing business gave them contact right up to United Irish headquarters through the Dublin carmen.

It is not difficult to reconstruct the scene of a Sunday visit home by Fr. John that autumn, or a visit to his mother's family, the Whittys, across the Slaney river. There could have been nothing but anger and bitterness in the air, with shattered incomes adding to the list of woes. The reception in both places for a peace-preaching brother or nephew, even if he was a priest, is no matter for speculation. He and the Church were the butts of ridicule. The censures, arguments and debates on the times that were in it raged in every home and haggard. The Irish lust for land was renewed afresh, and the likelihood of a chance to wrest it back from the landlord and planter was examined with intensity. All these issues grew in crescendo as the circumstances on the farms became more desperate.

There can be no doubt that John Murphy heard, as every caring pastoral priest does, the constant whisperings of the grass roots. Questions coming to his mind requiring decisive replies were simple enough. Who were the United Irishmen? What were their motives? Were they bitterly anti-Catholic? Were they wild peasant ruffians, mad for blood and robbery? Or were they decent men, women and families, force-fed on humiliation, outraged by the long memory of the Cromwellian and Williamite theft of their families' lands? And what about Caulfield, the ordinary of the diocese to whom was due his most solemn obedience, how was he regarded in Tomgarrow, Tincurry or Boolavogue?

Caulfield, by comparison with his predecessor, Bishop Sweetman, was looked upon as an upstart and was regarded bluntly by the United Irishmen as 'a paid government man,' 'bought for a few guineas', an episcopal loyalist, in gratuitous collaboration with the mortal enemies of his people. So widely accepted was this concept of James Caulfield that he had later to refute it by pastoral letter from every altar in the diocese, and the smear survived down to the middle of the twentieth century in the folk memory.[21] The epitaph, 'a government man' was the one brief judgement of Caulfield by which he was popularly recalled. Fr. John nevertheless had the benefit of listening to his bishop for over a decade in council and of measuring him. It is evident that there was a bond of mutual respect between the two men.[22] In those contrary and opposing magnets lay the terrible dilemma of John Murphy. The contending loyalties which swayed the curate of Boolavogue first one way, then the other, created a myth of the man that confused the folk memory no less than the enemies who reviled him, and to the confused may be added his devoted followers who in defending him could not explain him.

The meeting of the clergy with the bishop in Rudd's after the harvest of 1797 debated not only the ecclesiastical and civil politics to which they were heirs, but also the catastrophe on the farms, the collapse of incomes, crippling debts and bankruptcies, the entire debacle as sudden as it was disastrous. It was against this background of new misery that other perils in north Wexford demanded notice. The bishop was plied with questions easier asked than answered. Catholics had been dismissed with insult from the yeomanry. What was to be done if armed and uniformed yeomen attacked parishioners and destroyed their property or winter fodder? All that they had to do was harass and ruin any of John Murphy's people, have them evicted and have one of their own kind take over the farm.

Fr. John's major supply of information came from Tom Donovan, a sworn United Irishman, now more aggravated than ever before, while he himself was placed in the middle of the old Irish and planted lands, with a much sharper insight into the people than Caulfield had from his High Street mansion. Nonetheless he was vulnerable. He now had a blot upon a clean ecclesiastical record and a question about his judgement as far as the bishop could estimate. Despite that, the overall view of Caulfield was questioned by Fr. John. Deference to a distant London monarch and the preached benefits of his government appeared as vacuous nonsense to the curate of Boolavogue and his parishioners. Even as bishop and clergy debated, fifteen of these parishioners sweated in the packed jail of Wexford, several of them in danger of the gallows, and for what? Their rights as men in their own country! Fr. John took their part, but he was roundly denounced for his attitude by the unflinching bishop. He was reproached and reprimanded again, and it was under that cloud of episcopal disapproval and suspicion that he returned home to face the long winter nights.[23]

The governments in London and Dublin realised well that preparations were far advanced for the landing of the French. In north Wexford the magistrates and landlords were aware of accumulating incidents which could no longer be regarded as coincidental.[24] They knew that there was unaccountable activity at night time. Dogs kept barking from dusk to dawn. Estate trees vanished. Blacksmiths were working around the clock. The conclusion was inescapable. In the government's view north Wexford teemed with pike-making units, making ready the arms and equipment for revolution aided by French help.

All reports and military intelligence were assessed by the Government with one new factor in the forefront. On 26 October 1797, Napoleon Bonaparte was appointed General Officer commanding the French army being assembled on the Atlantic coast.[25] It took until mid-November for alarm to overtake the magistrates and landlords of Wexford. Meeting at Gorey on 20 November[26] they examined the most up-to-date reports and deliberated upon them. They finally passed by an overwhelming majority the proposal to proclaim sixteen parishes, including Monageer-Boolavogue, under martial law. Mountnorris, whose property and lands included the parishes to be proclaimed, was vehemently opposed to the measure. In this he was supported by only seven other magistrates.

Overnight the dread of what was proposed reached all quarters, and Fr. John had to contemplate for the first time military violence approaching Boolavogue. Caulfield was immediately informed in Wexford. In a short space of time, John Murphy had an urgent letter from the bishop delivered to his lodgings, a letter which made clear what proclaiming a district under the Insurrection Act meant:

> Rev. Sir,
> In the present critical state of this country, the most alarming and perhaps the most distressful that it has experienced for ages past, we feel it an indispensable part of our duty to repeat to those of our charge our admonitions and exhortations to return to their duty, to warn and caution them against the most imminent and most dreadful dangers to which they are exposed, viz; in the first instance a military force to be sent on them, on free quarters, who will be warranted to commit the greatest excess; to burn their houses, to destroy and consume their stock, their corn and hay and every article of their substance.

Now while they have the means and time to avert these impending and dreadful calamities, they should not lose a moment, they should come in immediately and bring in and surrender to the magistrates their arms, guns, muskets, pistols, blunderbusses, swords, spears, pikes, and any and every warlike, offensive or hostile weapon in their possession; they should renounce and abjure with sincere contrition any and all unlawful oaths of combining or conspiring with United Irishmen, (which are only bonds of iniquity); they should disclaim for ever more all attempts of disturbing the peace of the country and give solemn and satisfactory assurance to the magistrates of their loyalty, submission to the established laws and constituted authorities, of their inviolable fidelity and attachment to his Majesty, to his government and the constitution.

Caulfield concluded his letter with an urgent exhortation:

You should hasten to repeat, to inculcate, and impress on their minds these awful important considerations, and exert all your industry and zeal to bring back those of your flock, who have been led astray, to their country, and to the best of kings. You should where necessary go from town to town, from village to village, and if possible accompanied by a magistrate to speak these things and to exhort your people in Christ Jesus.

I remain in haste and truth,

Revd. Sir,
Your faithful serv. in Christ,
James Caulfield.[27]

There was no time to be lost. The Catholic clergy of the threatened parishes adopted a carefully composed letter for the attention and use of Lord Mountnorris whose hand undoubtedly facilitated its composition:

My Lord,
We the parishioners of Kilcormuck, having heard with astonishment and concern the very extraordinary result of the meeting at Gorey, the twentieth of this month, beg leave to assure your Lordship, that we are unconscious of having incurred the stigma so ungenerously thrown upon us, of disloyalty and disaffection; we therefore appeal to your lordship, as our neighbour, as a magistrate, and as a friend to humanity, to receive our oaths of allegiance, and to assure his excellency the Earl of Camden, that we are as firmly attached to the constitution as any other members of the community, whatever our enemies may insinuate to the contrary.

We further entreat your lordship's interference with government to avert a compliance with the prayer of the memorial, agreed to

31

on Monday last, as being unsupported by evidence, and therefore ill-founded. A striking proof of the tranquillity of this peaceable county appeared at the convention at Enniscorthy, when, after the strictest investigation, there were not the slightest grounds for any parish in this district being proclaimed.

Allow us to ask your lordship, whether any act of outrage had been committed to justify or palliate so cruel a measure? Should your lordship's exertions prove abortive, we mean to beg of you, as one of our governors, to call a meeting of the county; and we trust that the sense of that meeting will evince how unwarrantably we have been pointed out as proselytes to defenderism; for the congregate body will always protect the individual's good name, which is as dear to him as his life. Before we take leave of your lordship, we humbly request you will accept of our tribute of gratitude for your opposition to the determination of the twentieth; and you will add to the obligation by conveying our acknowledgements to the seven other magistrates who so liberally stepped forward to justify us from an imputation which we reprobate as unprovoked and unmerited.

Signed: John Murphy,
Curate.[28]

Mountnorris of Camolin Park collected the letter from the several priests on his estate with relief. A last opportunity had presented itself to avert calamity. The implementation of martial law as planned was no less a shock to the liberal landlord than it was to his tenants. He had loudly protested his liberalism, a stand which was contemptuously opposed by the extremist faction in the county. His entertainment of 'popish' priests like Fr. John and Camolin's Catholic curate Fr. Redmond, was derided. Now with insurrection detected on his own patronised enclaves his postures would be treated as deceit bordering on high treason. His reputation was, however, of lesser consequence as he contemplated the commercial havoc that would accrue. His great north Wexford property would be devastated and, worse than that, the capacity of his tenants to pay their rents would be undermined for a long time to come. He took rapid action. He arranged a suitable day with each priest on which he would address their congregation and administer an oath of loyalty composed by himself.

Mountnorris started his visits to the parish chapels on his estate, accompanied occasionally by a magistrate. One by one he collected the signatures, the signed oaths of loyalty from each chapel congregation, following his preliminary address advocating conciliation. Boolavogue was the last chapel to be visited by the respected landlord and no difficulty was expected there from either the congregation or the mature clergyman whose piety and learning he had found worthy of respect.

Fr. John introduced his lordship to the packed and uneasy congregation. Lord Mountnorris, buttressed by his successes in previous days, exuded optimism. He pointed out to the men in the crowded benches and the rear of the chapel:

> the happiness resulting from the constitution under which they lived; that a man of any persuasion whatsoever, though his descent were ever so mean, who should advance himself by honest means in the world, and from nothing acquire abundance, would be protected by it, and that it was very wicked and ungrateful to attempt to destroy those protectors of our persons, rights and freedom; that the laws of the realm protected the poorest cottager from the cruelties of a rich oppressor; and that there was no such thing as wanton barbarity in their land.

He entreated them to surrender the weapons of their rebellion and invited them to come and take the oath of allegiance. He proposed to give them certificates of the same, and expressed the wish that they would return to their duty. He had upon his person that day an oath which would reassure him and the Government that such measures as were proposed were quite misdirected. It had been taken by the pastors and parishioners all over north Wexford already. It was:

> I do sincerely promise and swear, upon the Holy Evangelists, that I will be faithful and bear true allegiance to his majesty King George the third, and to the succession of his illustrious family to the throne. That I will, to the utmost of my power, support the constitution as by law established. That I will use every possible exertion to prevent and suppress all tumult, riot, or secret conspiracy. That I am not an United Irishman, and that I never will take the oaths of the United men. That I will give up all kinds of arms or offensive or defensive weapons in my possession, and that I will inform against any man keeping arms without being registered. All the above I most solemnly swear in the presence of the Almighty, and as I hope to be saved through the merits and mediation of my blessed Lord and Saviour Jesus Christ, without any equivocation of mental reservation whatsoever. So help me God.[29]

John Murphy and his congregation listened to their landlord as the oath was read out. The effect, however, was not that experienced in other chapels by his lordship. This time, responses came in unison from priest and men which clearly showed that no oath would be taken by them at all. Mountnorris was aghast. He demanded to know why they would not. The reply in Boolavogue understatement was 'It was too strict!'[30] Mountnorris lost his composure as his whole project seemed to collapse due to the intransigence of one half parish. A flood of rage wrenched the words from his lips. He promised them of steps he would take himself. He threatened them that if they did not take the oath he would quarter the military in their countryside, and that it would then be so strongly defended by the soldiery that 'they would demean themselves as peaceable subjects, through fear, if they would not now take the oath for love'.[31]

In the ensuing silence, the angry words took effect. Soldiers on free quarters over the winter were to be avoided at all costs. John Murphy signed the formula of the oath and was followed in turn by the whole congregation. By noon the mollified landlord withdrew with Boolavogue's sworn oaths of loyalty and assurances of compliance with the law. Mountnorris communicated his triumph to the government and the momentum towards martial law was stopped. It had, however, been a very close call and the stand of Fr. John and his congregation, differing dramatically from all the rest, drew further uncomfortable attention on Boolavogue. It was known to the clergyman magistrate, Thomas Handcock and was certainly reported to Caulfield.

John Murphy was reprimanded again and then threatened with the most severe penalty that the bishop could impose, specifically, his suspension from priestly functions and dismissal from his office in Boolavogue.[32] This ultimate threat to Fr. John's vocation and profession had a chastening effect. Fr. John, in obedience to his ordination promise, accepted the reprimand and carried out his superior's policies and instructions through Christmas and into the following spring. Painful though it may have been, he too, like his bishop, was regarded in many quarters as 'a government man'.

In the north of the county throughout the remaining days of December and the early days of 1798, the preparations of the United Irishmen went ahead.[33] Already the French Directory had nominated April as the month for their assault and the Wexford United Irishmen understood that the coming spring had been finally fixed for the simultaneous rising. Miles Byrne of Monaseed remembered the preparations:

Nothing could exceed the readiness and good will of the United Irishmen to comply with the instructions they received to procure arms, ammunition, etc., notwithstanding the difficulties and perils they underwent purchasing those articles. Every man had firearms of some sort, or a pike; the latter weapon was easily had at this time, for almost every blacksmith was an United Irishman. The pike blades were soon had, but it was more difficult to procure handles for them and the cutting down of young ash-trees for that purpose awoke attention and caused great suspicion of the object in view.

Climatically, 1798 was splendid. There was a fine spring, the harbinger of one of the finest, sunniest years the country had ever seen. Despite the drop in prices, food production went on. The crops were in early in Wexford. Potatoes, turnips, barley and wheat were all safely in the ground as if nature contrived to offer time for war. Virtually under John Murphy's gaze, the United Irishmen were completing their preparations for the expected French landing. There was to be a simultaneous nation-wide uprising.[34] An adjutant-general was nominated to inform United Irish headquarters of strength and dispositions. From a strategic point of view, Wexford county was itself like a plateau open to the sea and defended by river and mountain. The Scullogue gap, the Bunclody gap and the Arklow gap were the only major exit or entry points through the mountains which rimmed the county. Every road, vantage point, rallying centre and strategic eminence was noted. Instructions were issued for joint operations and the provision of supplies for the French when they landed. The Government was informed of the entire situation at home and in the French Atlantic ports. Camden decided that he could no longer stay his hand.

On 12 March 1798, the county Wexford delegate of the United Irishmen, Robert Graham of Inch, had an appointment in Dublin, one of the most vital of his life.[35] It was a meeting of the Leinster directory of the United Irishmen. The venue was the premises of Oliver Bond of Bridge Street, a woollen merchant and a United Irishman. Graham had on his person documents relating to the membership and state of preparation of the Society in county Wexford. Robert Graham was late for the meeting. When he arrived, it was to discover that the entire Leinster directory, with the exception of Lord Edward Fitzgerald, had been surprised by officers of the Crown at Oliver Bond's and were all under arrest. Two members of the Supreme Executive were seized along with their papers and during the morning five others, the cream of the National Directory, were also arrested. The venue, the business and purpose of the meeting, with the addresses of the national officers, had been supplied to Camden by another trusted friend, turned informer, Thomas Reynolds. The United Irishmen's faces and operations were as open books to their enemy.

Had conditions of normality existed, this would have spelled the finish of revolt. But it did not. Spasmodic and spontaneous eruptions occurred all over the country. The rural United men strove to keep the fabric of their society in cohesion. 'The country is now so bad,' reported Sir John Carden from Templemore, 'that it should be declared in a state of absolute rebellion'.[36] On 30 March 1798, powers were given to the armed forces which went beyond the restrictions of martial law. The 'disaffected' were to be treated with the most summary measures unless they surrendered their arms. The entire country was declared, by a signed proclamation of the Privy Council in Dublin, to be in a state of actual rebellion. At the outset the men available to the government for this campaign numbered almost 100,000, consisting of about 20,000 regulars, three corps of German dragoons, the Lowenstein, Hompesch and Waldstein plus Hompesch reinforcements; 50,000 yeomen and almost 22,000 militia.[37] The yeomanry, under their local landlords and magistrates, combined with their zeal an overwhelming fear that if they did not rapidly gain the upper hand, they themselves would be victims within a very short space of time.

It was in this atmosphere that John Murphy went to Enniscorthy on 16 April 1798.[38] Caulfield arrived there, bringing with him the holy oils for distribution to the clergy. There was no latitude for compromise in Caulfield, and his outlook was shared by the assembled priests. The only hope of averting destruction was to conform to the established regime. 'Render to Caesar the things that are Caesar's, and to God the things that are God's.' They each reported on the position in their parishes. The Orange dominance of the yeomanry and the disarming of Catholic members was recounted. Bishop Caulfield again warned that only the most determined opposition to tumult and oathbound societies was to be entertained. There was no other way. Fr. John Redmond's stand in Camolin was an example. He had refused to hear the confessions of United men and had turned them away from his knees. 'You cannot serve God and Mammon. The masses of the people are hopelessly deluded and if they persist will bring death and destruction upon us all.'

Mountnorris again intervened. He organised another round of addresses with the help of the priests. A new formula was composed for presentation to the Lord Lieutenant and the parishioners were expected to sign it. The curate of Boolavogue turned to the task.[39] He concluded that if he was to make any impression on the obstinate in his congregation he would have to take extreme steps. It was Passiontide, and during the ceremonies of that solemn Christian commemoration Fr. John summoned all the resources of persuasion that he could muster. He bade them attend at Boolavogue chapel on the following Easter

Monday to sign an address to the Lord Lieutenant, the very last chance they had of escape from the rigour of free-quartered soldiers. He outlined the wrong in the French Revolutionary system and its proponents. Then he took a hard step, the most extreme a priest can take. Easter or not, from that day forth, he, John Murphy, would refuse the sacraments to all United Irishmen in the parish who refused to abjure their oaths and business. And that is what he did.[40]

On Easter Monday a packed congregation assembled once more in the thatched chapel of Boolavogue. Fr. John read the address composed for Lord Camden to all of them:

> We, the Roman Catholic inhabitants of the parish of Kilcormuck, in the barony of Ballaghkeen, and county of Wexford, do think it our duty to come forward at this crisis of internal disturbance, thus publicly to declare our unalterable attachment to his sacred majesty King George the third; and we do hereby declare, and in the most solemn manner pledge ourselves, to support with our lives, fortunes and influence, his majesty's happy government established amongst us, determined as we are to exert ourselves for the suppression of rebellion and sedition. And we do likewise solemnly pledge ourselves, should any person attempt to disseminate amongst us seditious or levelling principles, all of which we hold in the utmost abhorrence, that we will use our utmost endeavours in bringing such miscreants to condign punishment. And we do further assure all our Protestant brethren of our sincere affection for them and our absolute determination to co-operate with them in every means in our power, for the support of this happy constitution, the suppression of rebellion, the welfare of his majesty's government, and in love and loyalty to his sacred person.
>
> And we do request of the right honourable the Earl of Mountnorris, and Sir Thomas Esmond, baronet, to present these our declarations to his excellency the lord lieutenant.

Both the terms of the address and his own harangue may have gone against Fr. John Murphy's grain, even against his own family's hopes and instincts, but the end result was that the curate of Boolavogue signed the address and was followed by a huge number. There were seven hundred and fifty-seven signatures to the address by the end of the forenoon in the curacy of Boolavogue. A mere one hundred and fifty-four had signed in the chapel of Castlebridge. One way or another, the impressive testimony, along with the signatures from ten other parishes in Mountnorris's area, was presented to the Lord Lieutenant, the earl of Camden, in Dublin Castle on 18 April 1798.[41]

Chapter 5

The Explosion

The signed protestations of loyalty to King and government from the Catholic parishes elicited contempt from the authorities. One week after the presentation of those loyal addresses, twenty-seven of the Wexford magistrates met in Gorey. Their determination was stiffened by two proximate developments.[1] The first was the ill-concealed joy in Monageer and Boolavogue when the fifteen Boolavogue men arrested the previous autumn appeared before the April assizes in Wexford courthouse and were acquitted by the jury. The second development was the arrival in the county of government reinforcements. It was resolved that the whole county should forthwith be proclaimed under martial law.

The proclaiming of Wexford took place two days later on 27 April. In the meantime, the public face of imminent punishment appeared with the arrival of the North Cork Militia to Wexford town.[2] The North Corks marched in with deliberate pomp emphasising their military aggressiveness. The drums beat, the banners flew and the officers and ranks had themselves extravagantly decked out with Orange favours, devices, colours and ribbons. Their women and children came with them, while at the head of the loyalist pageant rode their commanding officer, the Earl of Kingsborough. The officers of the regiment were all men who, with the apparent connivance of the authorities, promoted the extension of the Orange Order. Some of the rank and file were of like affiliation, while finally, as leaven, there was a proportion of Irish-speaking Catholics in the ranks. Three companies of the regiment were posted to the Wexford garrison, one company was detailed to Enniscorthy, another to Gorey and the last company to Ferns. Their open flaunting of Orange emblems instantly promoted tension, but it had a quite different effect upon Government loyalists. Those in the county who hitherto leaned toward Orange extremism now became Orangemen themselves.

Having done so they, too, publicly displayed the emblems of the Orange Order upon their persons and when appropriate rode out with the Orange favours on their horses' tackle, 'in the face of the whole world' as one of them defiantly boasted.[3]

There was an added goad to the North Corks visible even as they marched because young French sympathisers had adopted the fashion of short cropped hair. They became instant targets for the North Cork Militia.[4] The North Corks made wide use of a system of torture called pitchcapping, and in Wexford they took the opportunity to judge its effectiveness in large-scale application. They had in their ranks a non-commissioned officer who was their torture expert. He was a sergeant, Thomas Honam, known in Wexford as 'Tom the Devil', the man who perfected the pitchcap torture.

The pitchcap took the shape of a conical cap like a clown's. It was made of the nearest materials to hand, whether those were hard brown paper or stiff linen. Into this cone, boiling pitch was poured and the receptacle was then upturned and pressed down on the prisoner's head. The boiling liquid ran down the face and into the eyes and mouth. Sometimes the prisoner was released with his arms still tied behind his back. His resulting convulsive run, together with the efforts to loosen the torment, made spectacular sport for the militia. On reaching a wall, many victims severely injured themselves dashing their heads against it. The victim was on occasion held and when the pitch had cooled the militia men wrenched the pitchcap off. When militia man or victim pulled the pitchcap off, it was accompanied by the hair and most of the scalp. Suspects whose hair was long had their hair cut by shears which the North Corks maintained for the purpose. Little finesse was employed in that operation and ears were frequently sheared off.

'Tom the Devil' was inventive. He practised applying moistened gun powder to the close-cropped scalp and then he set the mix on fire. It would in many cases have been kinder if they had killed the 'croppies' outright. It certainly would have been more politic. Almost up to the 1860s and recounted with living memory was the spectacle in country chapels of men self-consciously huddled at the back of the chapel, out of the public gaze, not bareheaded, but with knotted white handker-chiefs covering their heads. They were pitchcapped croppies who had survived.[5] Sex, age or station provided no shelter from the North Cork Militia. 'Many women had their petticoats, handkerchiefs, caps, ribbons and all parts of their dress that exhibited a shade of green torn off, and their ears assailed by the most vile and indecent ribaldry ... Gentle loyal ladies who like their Irish sisters donned green in innocence were not spared either. Many women of enthusiastic loyalty suffered outrage in this manner'.[6]

The magistrates, the yeomen and the recently enlisted supplementary yeomen now unleashed their pent-up hatred on the people.[7] If the North Cork Militia set the trend, the yeomen followed and their local knowledge of likely rebels was of immense value. If a man had no weapons, then he would know of someone who had, and he was there and then flogged in front of his neighbours and family. Father and son were flogged together. Brothers were whipped, pitchcapped and half hanged. Half hanging was a process whereby the victim was dangled until life was almost extinct, then he was lowered, revived and the process started all over again. Blacksmiths were marked men as the yeomen knew the fund of information they possessed. Up, down and across Wexford the industrious interrogators travelled. The guilty, the innocent and the elderly were flogged to extract information or disclose the whereabouts of weapons. Men were taken up when passing through the market place, walking along a road or at their private business. Previous character or absence of animosity was no protection. They were taken up 'in consequence of military whim or the caprice of magisterial loyalty.' These were instantly stripped and publicly flogged. The details of the exhibitions were brought far and wide by the beholders, so that people shrank with fear from the mere thought of the scourging. Men were afraid to leave their homes or women, especially in the areas where the North Corks operated, for rape was common. Provisions became scarce and dear because the farmers were afraid to go into the towns with produce. This in itself brought more suffering, for the military went out to the country and took what they wanted. A farmer so visited was glad to give all he had and survive without flogging or pitchcapping.

For John Murphy there was still only one remedy. If it was weapons they were looking for, then all the concealed weapons should be handed over to Mountnorris or some other convenient magistrate of known liberal disposition like Isaac Cornock in return for a written guarantee of protection. He worked ceaselessly amongst his people to this end, and succeeded in getting many of them to hand over newly forged pikes of varied quality. An arsenal of surrendered pikes was assembled at Mountnorris's in Camolin Park and the man who surrendered a pike received a written guarantee of protection. Although it was not appreciated at the time, that man was then not only deprived of self-protection, but he was also an identified suspect. As one rebel, Peter Foley who refused to surrender his pike, said, 'A written protection in our hands is only a death warrant. It will be evidence of our disaffection.[8]

Nonetheless, Fr. John relied on the power Mountnorris possessed. He remained convinced that this man would secure the life and property of any who surrendered his weapons to him. This was his solution, and he strove tirelessly to get every weapon in his own parish area handed over to the proper authorities' arms dump in Camolin Park or, if it suited, to Ferns or Oulart. Fellow priests from the neighbouring parishes were of similar mind. It was, however, well noted that yeoman patrols increased in areas where weapons had been surrendered, and the more the weapons flowed to the magistrates the more vindictive the nightly yeoman patrols became.[9] Houses were vacated at night for fear of the yeos, and since this was against the regulations empty houses were burned down. The yeoman operations were next provided with support by regular military units that were put on 'free quarters' in north Wexford. This meant that the people were compelled to support and fully provide for all the needs of their armed occupiers. In addition to three corps of German Hessian dragoons, there was also a corps of Welsh fencible cavalry, the 'Ancient Britons', already blooded in Ulster and now let loose in a system described by a later viceroy, Lord Cornwallis, as 'comprehending universal rape and robbery throughout the whole country.'

Dublin Castle officials were not unaware of the latent danger which lurked in Wexford. After the April assizes in Wexford town, Sir Jonah Barrington, the Dublin attorney, attended a party in Lady Colclough's residence in Georges' Street, Wexford.[10] Among the gathering were several members of Wexford's Grand Jury and it also included Cornelius Grogan of Johnstown Castle, his brother Thomas of the Castletown Yeoman Cavalry, Captain Matthew Keugh, a former British army officer, John Colclough of Tintern Abbey, Dr. John Henry Colclough of Ballyteigue Castle, the lawyer John Beauman, Beauchamp Bagenal Harvey of Bargy Castle, William Hatton, one of the United Irish Directory in county Wexford, and several others, numbering about seventeen and almost all of whom were members of the Established Church. After dinner, the wine and port worked their spell and tongues loosened. The conversation reached so radical and disloyal a pitch that Barrington begged them to desist. Next day he compared notes with Beauman and they drew up a list of those whom they considered most likely to end up hanged. William Hatton was on the list. His passion for revolt so impressed Barrington that he never could comprehend how Hatton escaped the gallows that summer.

A jovial Harvey insisted on Sir Jonah joining him in Bargy Castle the following Monday night to discuss matters with some congenial company. That company included John and Henry Sheares, both lawyers; Captain Matthew Keugh of Wexford town, Dr. John Colclough of Ballyteigue Castle, John Hay of Ballinkeele and William Hatton. The party was cheerful, even boisterous, but as the night wore on and the

41

wine flowed, Barrington was given confirmation, in the midst of Protestants and men of property, that conspiracy of the most radical and far-reaching potential was well developed, despite the dispersal and arrest of the United Irish Leinster Directory the previous month.

Sir Jonah wrote immediately to Secretary Cooke in Dublin Castle. He was careful not to mention names, place or source. He outlined the substance of the danger and assured Cooke that there was not a doubt that an insurrection would break out, and at a much earlier period than the Government expected. He desired that the State Secretary ask him no questions, but that he might depend on the facts he had written, and he advised the instant dispatch of a commanding force to garrison the town of Wexford. His information was considered but the counter measures he advised were ignored.

The patrols, raids, burnings, floggings and pitchcapping intensified. Fear reached the stage where people began to bang out crude iron pikes in order to have something to surrender and receive a protection. Fr. John still advised that the surrender of arms was the only way to safety.[11] Without arms, they posed no threat. There would be no cause to persecute them. He insisted on the surrender of arms. He appeared to be certain that Mountnorris would protect his own tenants as he had done in the past. Fr. John's instructions were proved timely when, on Monday 23 May, the Wexford Grand Jury issued a last warning, which at the same time provided a fourteen-day leeway. A breathing space for everyone concerned seemed to have been bought:

> NOTICE – We, the high sheriff and magistrates of the county of Wexford assembled at sessions held at the county court-house in Wexford this 23rd day of May 1798, have received the most clear and unequivocal evidence, private as well as public, that the system and plans of those deluded persons who style themselves, and are commonly known by the name of United Irishmen, have been generally adopted by the inhabitants of the several parishes in this county, who have provided themselves with pikes and other arms for the purpose of carrying their plans into execution. And whereas we have received information, that the inhabitants of some parts of this county have, within these few days past, returned to their allegiance, surrendering their arms, and confessing the errors of their past misconduct. *Now we, the high sheriff and magistrates, assembled, as aforesaid, do give this public notice, that if within the space of fourteen days from the date hereof, the inhabitants of the other parts of this county do not come in to some of the magistrates of this county, and surrender their arms or other offensive weapons, concealed or otherwise, and give such proof of*

their return to their allegiance as shall appear sufficient, an application will be made to government to send the army, at free quarters into such parishes as shall fail to comply, to enforce due obedience to this notice.[12]

The price of a pike soared. Homemade pikes were manufactured, of so useless a craftsmanship that they scarcely were fit to cut melted lard. Pikes came into the authorities so fast – mock pikes and the genuine article – that the magistrates and yeomen were amazed. If this mighty arsenal was an indication of the dispositions of the Catholic mob and their organisers, then there was no doubt left at all. They were all, it was concluded, to have been murdered in their beds. The entire overthrow of their realm and society accompanied by slaughter was not just an aspiration. It had, they now assumed, been a carefully prepared project.

The yeos intensified patrols, shootings, burnings and pitchcapping in the areas which had surrendered weapons. Hysteria escalated. In a time when outrage was the norm, only the most ghastly cruelties were items worth telling to strike terror to deeper roots. The reports that the Protestant prebendary of Camolin, Rev. Roger Owen, a magistrate, personally pitchcapped victims, swept through the north of the county.[13] The reports were verified, although the activities of this man can only be understood if the possibility of insanity is admitted. All the while, suspected rebels, the finest of men, were being shipped out of New Ross and Duncannon for the penal settlements of Australia. Above all, the merciless attentions of militia, Hessians and yeos continued, day and night, as the third week of May was endured. And still John Murphy urged the surrender of arms.[14]

It was in this phase of near anarchy that the United Irishmen's arrangements for revolt in Wexford suffered catastrophe. Their leading organiser, Anthony Perry of Inch, a Protestant, had remained in his local yeoman cavalry unit as a matter of deliberate policy after Catholic members had been dismissed from the ranks. By mid-May he could no longer stomach the ruthless severity of the yeomen patrols and in an open display of protest he withdrew from the ranks while on parade at Fort Chester. In so doing he had as much as signed his own death warrant. He was arrested by the North Cork Militia on 24 May and brought into Gorey. 'Tom the Devil' was on hand to extract information.[15]

Perry was bound and his hair closely sheared. Gun powder was mixed through it and set on fire. The process was repeated until every atom of hair was pulled out by the roots, and still 'Tom the Devil' had not exacted satisfactory responses from Anthony Perry – so a lighted candle was applied to the head continually until it was one total blister. Perry's endurance gave way at last after two days of agony. On 26 May

43

he signed a detailed confession of his activities in which he gave specific information of the organisation, as well as the names of his closest associates.

The signed revelations by the tortured United chief meant that the administration and government of the United Irishmen in Wexford were betrayed. Bagenal Harvey, John Colclough, Robert Graham and Thomas Howlett were amongst the several named along with one of the most popular and dominant figures in the county, Edward Fitzgerald of Newpark. The civil and military executives of the conspiracy were exposed; they were now wide open to arrest, prosecution and conviction. Within hours named United leaders from Inch on the borders of county Wicklow to Ballyteigue Castle on the southern coast were being hustled into custody and in some cases were to endure merciless flogging so that more information could be extracted.

In the third week of May, there commenced a strange interaction of seemingly unconnected events in the vicinity of Boolavogue. An incident as inconsequential as straying May cows combined with local family animosities to ripen into calamity.[16] Together these local developments contributed in uncanny fashion to complete the moulding of a revolutionary leader. One afternoon in that very troubled week, Fr. John's three cows broke into a field of growing barley in the townland of Tomnaboley. They were seen by a Protestant neighbour, Clement Gough. Gough shared with John Donovan the delicate distinction of being native Irish and having transferred from the Catholic Church to the Established Protestant Church. He was, however, popularly regarded as a decent neighbour. Clement Gough elected to perform a good deed. Since there was no one else around, he turned Fr. John's cows out of the barley and drove them into Thomas Donohue's haggard at Tomnaboley where Fr. John lodged.

The cows were very likely obstreperous after dismissal from a juicy green field, and Clement Gough was undoubtedly experiencing difficulty – a situation well known to all stockmen. He was sighted at the end of the haggard, struggling with the frisky cows by Fr. John's helper, the 'priest's boy' Quigley. Quigley's reaction was violent and immediate. He went at once to the place where he had a gun concealed. He loaded it and in his stated belief that he thought Clem' Gough was 'stealing the priest's cows', he fired at him. Gough fell wounded and to the consternation of Fr. John and all in the neighbourhood, he later died. Apart from the certainty that Fr. John himself was compromised in this tragedy by his own helper, there is no record that any development arose from it, beyond the shocked regret of all the neighbours. Very likely the week's acceleration into terror and warfare removed the killing from detailed attention, whatever about later retribution.

The Donovan families of Tobergal and Boolavogue were shortly to inject a further dose of fear into the atmosphere.[17] The fever of the time had driven the Protestant yeoman, John Donovan of Tobergal, to greater spasms of drinking than ever. His situation, domestic and political, was producing intolerable distress. John Donovan had spent three entire days that week drinking in public houses between Camolin and The Harrow, ranting and belligerent. His local knowledge was such that both his loose tongue and accurate knowledge were feared. On the other hand, reciprocal knowledge of him and his personal affairs was so total that his possession of an Achilles' heel was skillfully exploited. In neighbourhood gatherings, a nuance, a gesture or a wink sufficed on the crossroads or in front of a bar counter. When the camouflage of time is penetrated, John Donovan's pathetic circumstances become clearer. Because of his marriage to a Catholic woman, allied to his own native Irish background, he would not have enjoyed the trust or esteem of the ascendancy faction. He was never promoted beyond the rank of private in the yeoman cavalry. At home the ambiguity of his situation was no better, while his constant heavy drinking was a permanent goad to misery.

John Donovan employed a young farm labourer who became a favourite with his Catholic wife.[18] The full story of the Donovans of Tobergal was banished from folk tradition by the engulfing conflagration which followed but it is clear that the farm worker in question was a son of John Boyne of The Harrow. He was a Catholic and a sworn United Irishman.[19] He could be heartily disliked for any one of these properties by his employer but the quality for which he was most despised was that which captured the affection of John Donovan's wife. The situation in Tobergal was too entertaining a plot to be ignored by bitterly antagonistic neighbours, not least the Catholic neighbour whose farm and fields were back-to-back with the Donovans at Tobergal – James Gahan. In those days of violence John Donovan left a personal trail of terror. In the middle of drinking men, he had that very week loudly forecast pitchcaps for three farmers in the townland of Ballyorley.[20] Towards the end of his alcoholic binge, he found himself drinking in haste with a group of Catholic neighbours in The Harrow's sole public house. It was the evening of Thursday.

The men gathered in The Harrow tavern were all infected by the vicious hatreds of the week and they had no difficulty in 'rising' John Donovan. In the whiskey talk, one word borrowed another. Donovan's home situation was the obvious theme for the double-meaning remark, the sophisticated taunt. And if an insinuation of impropriety in a Tobergal farm yard could be floated, however vaguely, or the faithful service of the Catholic worker to the farmer's wife be given air, then the public house in The Harrow was the fittest forum in which to do it. The insinuations grew to sneers and the sneers spawned jeers. The inevitable climax arrived and John Donovan was lashed with insult. Shaking and hysterical with passion he stormed out but then turned back to face his tormentors. As he roared at them, he invoked the vivid memory of massacre. He swore that the following night there would be 'more blood spilled than in Cromwell's war'. One of the men present was a member of the pitchcap-threatened trio from Ballyorley named Murphy. He reported all that had transpired to Fr. John at his lodgings in Donohues.[21]

What did the curate make of the threat? Was it a retort to insult from an inebriated and sorely vexed man? Or was it a significant straw in the wind? Later that night, John Donovan's own next-door-neighbour, James Gahan of Tobergal, arrived at Fr. John's lodgings in fear of his life, family and property.[22] John Donovan had arrived at his door on a formal visit that same night as a member of a uniformed yeoman cavalry patrol. He there and then accused Gahan of being a sworn United Irishman and declared his intention of returning the following night to pitchcap him. Gahan was so terrified that he determined to leave for the Barony of Forth to take refuge with friends until the madness subsided. Fr. John with great difficulty persuaded him to stay where he was. The first words publicly recorded to associate Fr. John with the option of armed resistance were uttered. 'Don't go, Jim,' he said, 'it's their turn tonight, it may be ours tomorrow.' For the first time, he mused aloud to James Gahan on the better choice of dying like men than being shot like dogs. James Gahan decided to remain at home with his family and face the consequences as best he could.

There are several versions of John Donovan's involvement on that particular evening. All of them agree that he was drinking in Camolin and The Harrow that Thursday, and that Fr. John was informed of danger.[23] A warning also came from another and more sinister source. One of the maid servants at Lieutenant Bookey's seat, Rockspring, two miles from The Harrow, was brought to Fr. John's lodgings late on Thursday night. She informed him of a conversation she had overheard taking place in Bookey's drawing room after dinner. Bookey of the Camolin Yeoman Cavalry had agreed on a punitive expedition to Boolavogue and The Harrow. All the reports concurred that John Donovan was vehemently advocating the raid. On hearing the last piece of evidence, Fr. John sent his man, Quigley, over to Tom Donovan at Boolavogue with a message acquainting him of the charges accumulating against his cousin and the Camolin Yeoman Cavalry, Mountnorris's own corps.

By morning of the next day, Friday 25 May, it had become clear even to Fr. John that deliberate killing and raids were being carried out over a wide area. It was hard for him to sift fact from fiction, rumour from reality. On the one hand, there were rumours that the counties of Kildare, Carlow and Wicklow had taken the field in open revolt. The matters of immediate preoccupation related, however, to the people of his own curacy. To Fr. John Murphy's personal concern, there was added the grim determination of the United Irishmen in Boolavogue to meet steel with steel. The last restraints on rebellion and defiance were being rapidly whittled away. There was but one apparent stumbling block as far as the United Irishmen were concerned and that was the exertion expended by Fr. John Murphy to get his parishioners to hand over arms in exchange for written guarantees of protection.[24] A meeting was arranged by Tom Donovan for Friday morning between Fr. John and the men of the parish, amongst whom were several sworn United Irishmen. The subterfuge employed by Tom Donovan was to utilise the annual turf-saving job at the turf bank outside Boolavogue. Catholic men of the parish came together on an agreed day each year to save the winter's fuel for the priest. The men assembled with Fr. John at about ten o'clock on Friday morning. Tom Donovan and James Gahan were amongst them, as the urgent exchange of views and information carried on in tandem with the turf cutting. About eleven o'clock the noise of galloping hooves was heard. It was a detachment of the yeoman cavalry and they came careering forward in full rein. They saw the priest and the working men, so they pulled up and faced their horses around to inspect the group. After a minute or two they wheeled around and trotted away again.

Relief was scarcely registered when Fr. John and his helpers saw them returning. This time they drew forward and as the horses flicked their tails the yeomen gazed intently into the group, examining the priest and the men who were with him. Their attitude conveyed imminent danger. Not one word passed and after another few threatening moments they again cantered off. For the first time, John Murphy showed openly that he was aware of the awful conditions accumulating in the land. He reached the only possible conclusion and declared that it was dangerous for them to remain there together any longer.[25] They parted.

On that night few, if any, slept in their homes. The nights were dry and hot, and furze brakes and reaskes provided more secure blankets. Many spent the night hiding their belongings, repeating what loyalist families had been doing for the previous week.[26] It was as if fate was tidying up an arena for combat and that the time-table was fixed and known. That night John Murphy also took precautions.[27] He removed from the chapel anything that was vulnerable to desecration. He put the vestments that he most required into a bag and, along with some clothes and effects, hid them in a hastily dug pit at the back of his lodgings in Tomnaboley. Included in the bag were his diploma and reference from the Dominican College in Seville. He then left Tom Donohue's home and sought the shelter of his sister's house. He spent that night with her and her family, the Walshes, at Effernogue.[28]

The precautions taken did not necessarily imply belligerent intent. The instinct at work was self-preservation, for the yeoman corps patrolled unremittingly throughout the nights, diligently seeking out and inflicting trouble. Despite the fourteen-day respite, magistrates led the night patrols themselves. Of all the yeoman patrol commanders in Wexford, four men were notorious, especially as they were believed to have embraced the Orange Order's bigoted zeal.[29] Hawtrey White hunted with his corps in the east of the county; Hunter Gowan reached refinements of selection in the north; he released chosen prisoners of his who could pay substantially for mercy. Archibald Hamilton Jacob never left Enniscorthy without an executioner, hanging ropes and cat-o-nine-tails; while James Boyd of Rosslare prosecuted the wide area around Wexford town. It is in that atmosphere of protracted fear that the enigma of John Murphy remains at its most baffling, the more so in view of his subsequent role.

As the morning of 26 May moved from dawn to bright sun, news of the greatest horror to date reached Fr. John at his sister's house.[30] Twenty-eight fathers of families, prisoners, had been taken into the ball alley in Carnew on the previous day and shot by the yeomen. One of them, William Young, was a Protestant already under sentence of transportation. Even more devastating in its impact was the report that Reverend Cope, the Protestant rector of Carnew, a magistrate, had presided over the executions. Prior to the slaughter, fourteen men had been flogged and pitchcapped in the town. There was no room to doubt or dispute the news, for the men were familiar faces at the fairs of north Wexford. The awesome news was shortly added to with even greater effect. Thirty-four yeomen from the Narraghmore and Saundersgrove Corps were made prisoners as suspected United Irishmen by their captain, Saunders, taken to the fair green of the Wicklow town of Dunlavin, and shot dead by their yeoman colleagues, without preliminary, trial or compuction. Whatever shock these tidings gave to Fr. John, there was no concealing the horror it created when the news was confirmed. Men who had already surrendered their arms became sullen and silent. It was accepted that there was a fate to be met and soon, but there were men determined to meet it now with whatever means of defence they could hold in their hands.

Fr. John did not alter his instructions to the men that morning.[31] They were to surrender their pikes to the presiding magistrates, Isaac

Cornock and Reverend Francis Turner, that Saturday afternoon as arranged in Ferns. John Murphy's obstinacy on this vital point was as well-remembered as it was found incomprehensible, but there is one aspect of the day's events which will admit of no dispute. Whatever the cause, whatever his motive or reasoning, Fr. John trusted Captain Cornock.

In the midst of conjecture about Cornock's established record for fair play or his amiability in company with Fr. John on social occasions in the Mountnorris mansion, there is one shaft of insight found in the folk tradition. Cornock was so liberal in his politics that he had been under suspicion by the government of having United Irish sympathies, if indeed he was not under suspicion of being a United Irishman himself.[32] Whatever the case was, Fr. John succeeded in his stubborn efforts to get men and their weapons to Ferns. When the last batch of his hearers had left for that ancient power base he decided to follow them and so at midday he viewed the distant hulk of Ferns Castle from the high road at Milltown near the townland of Coolatore. Here he was compelled to pull up his mare abruptly. His men were coming back home. They were indeed unarmed but were retreating in headlong flight before a mounted group of yeomen cavalry, clothed in the red of King George, armed with muskets which they discharged at will and with yelping jeers into the cowering groups.[33] The yeomen were Isaac Cornock's men, local men, designated to this day as the 'black mob'. They recognised Fr. John Murphy and pulled their horses up. Nothing more is remembered beyond the fact that on his appearance they halted their rout, turned their horses and galloped back to Ferns.

Fr. John now accompanied his disarmed parishioners back toward The Harrow. They gave him a full description of the scene in Ferns with breathless detail. Captain Cornock and Reverend Turner had supervised and signed certificates of protection to each man as he tendered his weapon. As each man dropped his weapon on the growing pile, the attending Ferns yeomen loudly hooted and cheered. When the last pike was dropped they completed the proceedings by driving the 'protected' like herded cattle before them in a procession which developed into a gallop as the Boolavogue men decided to take to their heels. When Fr. John was asked 'What now?' his reply showed that a drastic process of change had taken place inside him.[34] 'I know they have me marked out,' he said. 'Look to the inhuman slaughter in Carnew, and if the report of the butchery in Dunlavin is true, it is worse. Our jails are full of the best of our people and it may be our own lot to be in company with them before tomorrow night.' He began to speak his mind openly and admitted it would be better for them to die like men defending themselves than to fall with folded arms under their enemies's swords. As the hours of foreboding went on several of the men he had spoken to volunteered to stay with him and take the consequences of the night patrol which all now expected.[35]

Fr. John spent hours considering his position and the full implications. He was not yet a rebel in arms. Nevertheless, there were many around him who heartily wished he were, and that quickly. There were men such as Tom Donovan, a well-connected and fully informed United Irishman who had accurate knowledge of the immediate situation not only in the vicinity of Boolavogue but countywide.[36] The local information available to him and for that matter to Fr. John was that John Boyne's home, about a quarter of a mile from The Harrow, was to be one of the main targets for the yeoman patrol that evening.

Later that evening Fr. John joined a muster of men, numbering about thirty, who went around the homes of the area in a protective strategy.[37] They were so indifferently armed that they would scarcely qualify for the definition of vigilantes. However, Tom Donovan had not been so easily persuaded by his breakfast friend to hand over his arsenal to the authorities. Both he and his brother-in-law, Paddy Roche, resurrected guns that they had buried and brought them with them, while a few of the neighbours carried pikes, slash hooks or pitchforks.[38]

John Donovan of Tobergal determined on revenge, especially on his farmhand. He was out for blood and had no hesitation in informing his wife of what was on his mind. His wife succeeded in getting word across to Boynes and the youthful object of affection and venom slipped quietly away.[39] At Camolin barracks, John Donovan persisted in advocating a raid into The Harrow area. The captain of the Camolin Yeoman Cavalry, Sir Frederick Flood, opposed the proposal. It was his firm opinion that The Harrow was none of their business. It was the concern of Captain Isaac Cornock of Ferns. Nonetheless Donovan had firm information on the rebels in the countryside, information which demanded more vigorous measures than Isaac Cornock had the stomach for. Donovan was so vehemently supported in his proposals by Lieutenant Bookey of adjacent Rockspring that in the end Flood conceded to them. He was deeply apprehensive of the outcome. 'I will not see you alive again,' were the last words he spoke to Bookey as they parted.[40]

Fr. John and his group completed a careful inspection of all the houses on the Boolavogue-Harrow roads and at ten o'clock in the long evening's twilight they turned towards the house they left until last, the one singled out as the main target of yeoman attention, John Boyne's of The Harrow.[41] Fr. John went into the house himself and spent sometime in conversation with the family. He then left and with his band of neighbours went back towards The Harrow. Not far from The Harrow there is a bend in the road. It is a blind, but not a sharp bend. At the same time twenty well-armed men of the Camolin Yeoman Cavalry walked their horses quietly towards that bend from the opposite direction. Both parties approached it at the same time. Towards the bend they burst upon one another's vision. The yeomen perceived armed men marching towards them. The Boolavogue men recognised the Camolin Yeoman Cavalry, outside their area and John Donovan among them. 'We're a night too late!' John Donovan roared, but the yeomen opened fire with a volley. Some of the unarmed men jumped over the nearest bank for safety but John Murphy concentrated their minds with his first shouted command, 'Take to the stones!'[42]

A shower of small rocks and stones was hurled at the yeomen but, determined on their business and quarry, John Donovan and Bookey forced their horses through and galloped on to Boyne's house. They had the dry thatch on fire immediately and the house was a blazing beacon within minutes. With the house ablaze and the Boyne family terrorised, they then turned about to help their comrades write finish to a riotous assembly; they found instead that their well-armed comrades had fled. Tom Donovan raised his gun, took aim and fired. His yeoman cousin fell dead. The officer, Bookey, was piked in the neck. He fell forward, wounded, on the horse's mane. A second pike lunge went through his body. The third pierced his horse's flank. The agonised horse plunged with such fury that it jerked the pike from its attacker's hand. Riderless, it galloped to The Harrow before the pike fell from it.[43]

Fr. John looked down. Two warm and bloody corpses lay at his feet. John Donovan, the object of so much bile and scorn throughout the curate's twelve years in Boolavogue, was a mere private. Bookey was, however, of a different caste. He was one of the gentry, owner of a mansion at nearby Rockspring, a commissioned officer in the yeoman cavalry, prominent and landed. Fr. John's life, station and loyalty were forfeit. They were now rebels in arms against a monarch to whom they had taken an oath of loyalty; rebels without the means of defending themselves, for he had persuaded his people to surrender arms in return for guarantees of protection that were now not only worthless but, in the nature of the situation, signed death warrants.

Chapter 6

Battle of Oulart Hill

John Murphy saw that the prospect was altered beyond redemption. The surviving yeomen would be reporting to Ferns and Camolin. Within hours every available redcoat would descend on them for vengeance. There was no time for further thought about the dead. He was then asked what was to be done. 'It would be better for us to die like men,' he firmly repeated, 'than to be butchered like dogs in the ditches. If I have any men to join me,' he added, 'I am resolved to sell my life dearly'.[1] Everyone of the men cheered support. He made them rouse their neighbours at once. This was not difficult, since almost every man, woman and child was sleeping out in the open.

John Boyne's home continued to flame brightly in the night. As soon as the yeos streamed out for revenge they put the houses of the adjacent countryside ablaze. The rebels followed suit. They descended immediately on the nearest yeomens' houses and burned them to the ground.[2] At midnight the whole country seemed to be on fire. Fr. John had little time for a firebrand operation, for his urgent need now was arms and he sought the nearest arsenal. He knew that the surrendered arms were stored at Camolin Park with Lord Mountnorris; at Oulart; at Ferns; and at Bookey's mansion in Rockspring where there was an armed guard. His resolve grew. Though he had tirelessly preached against crossing the bridge of revolt, once across, with every passing moment he seemed to be shrugging a burden off his back.

The first objective was Camolin Park about four miles away.[3] It was a most urgent objective and the rebels had to get there before the yeomen. Speed was essential. They marched hard, passing Rockspring on the way. They crunched across the gravel avenue at Camolin. Theirs was no furtive approach. There was no time. Fortune favoured them for Mountnorris was away in Dublin. The house was still unguarded, not a yeoman in sight. It was searched from roof to cellar. From everywhere more men appeared. The word had spread. Those whom Fr. John had sent to recruit men had turned up with volunteers. Pikes were there, the best of pikes and a hoard of the mock pikes. Newly delivered carbines and sabres for the Camolin Corps were also discovered. They took as much as they could carry away and their new commander buckled on a belt and sabre. Then he tongue-lashed his men from mansion and cellar where the corks were already popping. Pat Murray of Crane emerged with a magnificent banner. It was a banner adorned with harps and green emblems from a Wexford Corps of the 1782 volunteers. Back then to Bookey's of Rockspring, halfway between Camolin and The Harrow, as hard as men could travel.

At Rockspring mansion the raiders were expected by Bookey's servants. They were met by a fusillade of musket fire. A demand to surrender brought another volley. The insurgents opened fire with their Camolin carbines. Stones were showered through the windows. A sledge was procured from an outhouse and with four blows the entrance door was in bits. Fr. John and his men strode in. Two defenders at the head of the stairs ceased firing and John Murphy, now for the first time with drawn sabre in his hand, ordered his men to find out who they were. Two of the insurgents raced up the stairs and were blown back by defending muskets. It was decided that the mansion would be fit company for the thatched houses that were lighting the night. Rockspring was burned to ashes.[4]

The unswerving zeal which Fr. John had brought to bear on the surrender of arms was now transformed to the prosecution of war. Tom Donovan, his friend, was not able to influence events, for tough though he was, he was in shock after shooting his yeoman cousin. It was his son Jerry who stepped into the breach. Jerry, a youth of nineteen, was already established as spirited and daring even though he was lame since childhood. He was chosen for a special and vital mission, for now Fr. John was certain that the time to rise the country had come.[5] Jerry Donovan was dressed in a yeoman's uniform obtained at Bookeys. He was mounted on a good horse and sent off with bogus dispatches that showed he was a servant of Bookey. He carried letters written and addressed to Lord Mountnorris. In reality, his orders were to summon Shelmalier's United men to meet the men of Boolavogue near Oulart Hill. Fr. John's men knew where the dependable United Irishmen were located and their instant recruitment was sanctioned.

Jerry Donovan rode south through the night. Oulart people remembered a horseman shouting as he galloped in the direction of Wexford. 'Get up and fight,' he shouted, 'or you will be burned or butchered in your beds! The country is in a blaze all round you!'[6] He met and escaped danger, for he passed through yeomen from Glynn with some of whom he had gone to school. He carried on with his mission as far as Castlebridge, three miles from Wexford town, until finally he laid his message before a very extraordinary man, a sergeant in Captain Le Hunte's Shelmalier Yeoman Cavalry. He was Edward Roche, miller and prosperous tenant farmer of Garrylough, a sworn United Irish officer.

There was now assembling around Fr. John's band a collection of frightened women and children and he decided that if they wanted to follow their men they would have to march along with them south towards Oulart about six miles away. Oulart is a long hill which straddles central Wexford east of the river Slaney. It is a strategic eminence with a panoramic view, an ideal point for assembly and observation. The straggling village of Oulart at its base was an important cross-roads and stagecoach station on the Wexford-Dublin road with a well-known hotel, McCauley's, situated near the Catholic chapel. At this time of hurried consultation and rapid decision the local United Irish network was coming into play, although the Boolavogue group was not then aware that the authorities, acting on Perry's confession, were busy arresting the county's United Irish leaders.[7]

Early on Whit Sunday morning, 27 May, Fr. John led his party into the village of Oulart. There he was informed that Rev. Burrows, Protestant rector of Kilmuckridge, who lived at Kyle Glebe outside the village, had assembled a collection of weapons, including not just pikes but also guns, pistols and muskets. The elderly gentleman had a popular reputation for kindness and his personal possession of such a quantity of arms was unexpected. Nevertheless, firearms were lacking and the volume of recruits was growing as word of The Harrow spread. Rev. Burrows had garrisoned his house with nine or ten well-armed yeomen. Fr. John was told this in Oulart and his men understood that the house was prepared for defence. They made for Kyle Glebe, but Fr. John insisted that they were going there for the arms only. There was no debate on the point, for hostility to the agreeable clergyman was unknown in those parts.[8]

On entering the lawn before Kyle Glebe they were greeted by a volley from the upper windows of the house. Mr. Burrows was not in command nor did he give the order to fire. When the firing ceased he opened the hall door and came out on to the step, greeting Fr. John in distress and starting to parley. Fr. John explained their business and guaranteed protection for the rector and his family on condition that they surrender the arms. The yeomen upstairs concluded that if the mob before the house caught them they would be torn to pieces. As Mr. Burrows proceeded to parley, they fired another round of shots into the rebel ranks. One of Fr. John's men, James Redmond, turned to his brother alongside him and saw his face opened and gushing blood. Incensed with fury and crying aloud he rushed forward with his pike towards Burrows. The old gentleman ran from him down along the square of the lawn but before anyone could intervene Redmond had driven his pike into him.[9] The affable minister of the gospel fell down dead.

Pandemonium broke out and Fr. John lost control for the first time. Burrow's son was also piked but not mortally wounded. Fr. John shouted command and the tumult ceased. In rage he again promised protection to the family. They emerged, shocked with grief and terror. They were taken to McCauley's Hotel in Oulart where everything possible was done to alleviate their anguish. One of the rebels later wrote of Robert Burrows: 'One thing is certain. He was not a tyrant.' His wounded son was borne on a door by the rebels to the hotel in Oulart and a couple of days later the family was taken to Castle Annesley, five miles away, where they were minded in safety throughout the rebellion. Seven yeomen in Kyle Glebe were piked to death and the house was set on fire. The members of the household who were not engaged in the firing were allowed to go free but in the confusion two yeomen contrived to escape and bear the grim news to loyalists across the land.

As his mare bore him down the tree-lined avenue from the sorry scene, Fr. John must have contemplated his identification with revolt. In the space of twelve hours he had become an outcast and a rebel. No doubt remained but that the charge of murder of an innocent clergyman would be the least that would be laid at his door. But if the death of Burrows put a brake upon fever, the temperature was not allowed to subside for long. One side's outrage would complement the other's. Fr. John was proven correct in his belief that the yeomen had him marked out. That day his youngest brother, Patrick, joined him with news. The previous night, their mother, the family, including Pat and their married brother, Mogue, with wife and child, John, had taken to the furze brake on top of the hill above the house. It was fortunate for them that they did. The first place the yeos made for that night was the family home-place in Tincurry. It was burned to the ground in revenge for Bookey and everything they possessed in the farmyard was burned as well. It was 'the first house that was burned in the rebellion of 1798 by the King's army', recorded a loyalist.[10]

The few who did not know what had transpired during the night turned up at Boolavogue for Mass the following morning. There was no priest and there was no Mass. Soon there was no chapel, for the yeomen burnt it on Whit Sunday morning.[11] They then entered the priest's lodgings at Donohue's and discovered the shallow pit that contained his personal effects. There they found the sack with the vestments concealed in the ditch. They kept his papers of reference from Seville, left the vestments but burned the house. 'Punish the man,' the yeoman captain was quoted as saying, 'but do not mock or insult his religion.' The man was to be punished, for now having discovered his deliberately hidden possessions they had evidence of premeditation.[12]

Edward Roche of Garrylough answered Fr. John's call promptly. His motives in gambling life and fortune upon revolt were amongst the most fascinating.[13] He was not merely a tenant farmer and maltster. Nor is it sufficient explanation that he was a permanent sergeant in the Shelmalier Yeoman Cavalry commanded by Captain Le Hunte of Artramont. To add that he was an educated man with a sure instinct for the right word in speech and letters would still not clothe him with all his credentials. Edward Roche was the lineal descendant of the first Flemish mercenary hired by the deposed King of Leinster, Dermot McMurrough, to fight in his wars in August, 1167. That mercenary's wages consisted of a large grant of fertile land in Shelmalier on the east bank of the Slaney almost opposite Wexford town and land at Drinagh south of the town.

This once powerful family had made an immense impact on the scene. They built Artramont Castle, Drinagh Castle, established the abbey of Selskar for the Augustinian Order, were created knights, appointed sheriffs of the county, and enjoyed the style and title of nobility until dispossessed after the Cromwellian war in 1650. Their lands and castles were used by an impoverished English Parliament to pay one of their officers, a man named Le Hunte. Despite expulsion, the Roche family worked its way back and accepted the role of tenants on their own ancestral lands. Edward Roche of Garrylough was keenly aware of who he was, and he knew who Le Hunte was. In his estimation, Le Hunte was descended from a Cromwellian thief, but had to be called 'Sir'. He fattened on the Roche ancestral land, tolerated the head of that family as a sergeant in his corps, regarded him as a peasant and addressed him as 'Roche'. Edward Roche rounded up six of his best and trusted comrades from the Shelmalier Yeoman Cavalry. Morgan Byrne of Kilnamanagh was one of them. They set out towards Oulart well mounted, armed and in full regimentals.[14]

As Kyle Glebe flamed and smoked, Fr. John and his party of rebels, somewhat better armed and equipped, marched to Castle Ellis about three miles to the south. There they were joined by more recruits summoned from the Macamores and Blackwater under George Sparks, a Protestant United Irishman, highly popular in an area almost exclusively Catholic.[15] Sparks presented himself dressed in his uniform of yeoman cavalry sergeant, a trusted and dependable fighting man. The number willing to fight was now an estimated 400 men. They carried on together a mile further south to the village of Ballynamonabeg, where the assembly grew further.[16] There Fr. John Murphy's force was joined by Edward

56

Whittys of Tomgarrow, the homeplace of Fr. John Murphy's mother,
The modern farmhouse incorporates
the older Whitty one. *(J. B. Curtis).*

Bishop Nicholas Sweetman. *(Whelan,*
Wexford, *p. 239).*

The farmhouse of the Hall family, Boolavogue, incorporating the 1798 home of
Thomas Donovan. The modern Catholic church is a few yards to the west of Fr.
John Murphy's thatched chapel. *(J. B. Curtis).*

The room in which Fr. John Murphy breakfasted with Tom Donovan, as it is today. *(J. B. Curtis).*

The gable end of the now derelict farmhouse of Donohues, Tomnaboley, in which Fr. John Murphy lodged. *(J. B. Curtis).*

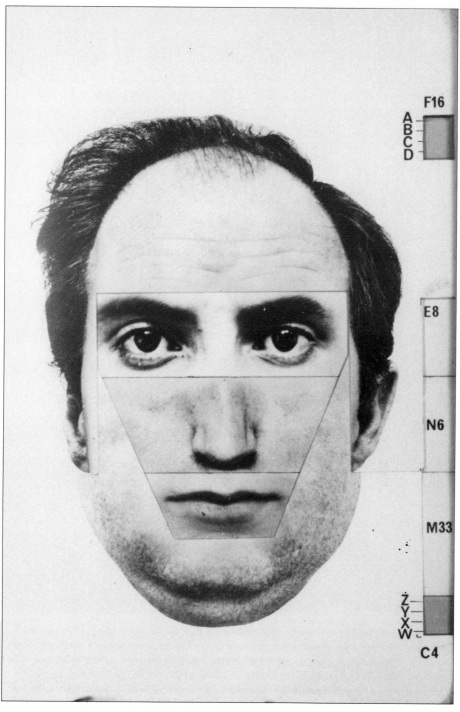

An identikit likeness of Fr. John Murphy from contemporary descriptions, assembled at the Garda Technical Bureau by courtesy of Chief Superintendent Anthony McMahon. The identikit was compiled by Detective Sergeant Niall Heron.

Fr. John Murphy (by courtesy of Mrs. Margaret Hall, Boolavogue). This portrait was made in the mid-nineteenth century by a Dublin artist from a contemporary black-and-white line sketch. The sketch had been preserved in the lodgings of Fr. John Murphy at Donohues, Tomnaboley, Mrs. Hall's home before her marriage. The redrawn portrait has an unwarranted clerical collar and the original sketch was never subsequently found. This portrait was carried at the head of the Monageer-Boolavogue contingent at the '98 commemoration in 1898, 1938 and 1948. It is carefully preserved in the Hall home at Boolavogue, which incorporates the home of Fr. Murphy's friend, Tom Donovan.

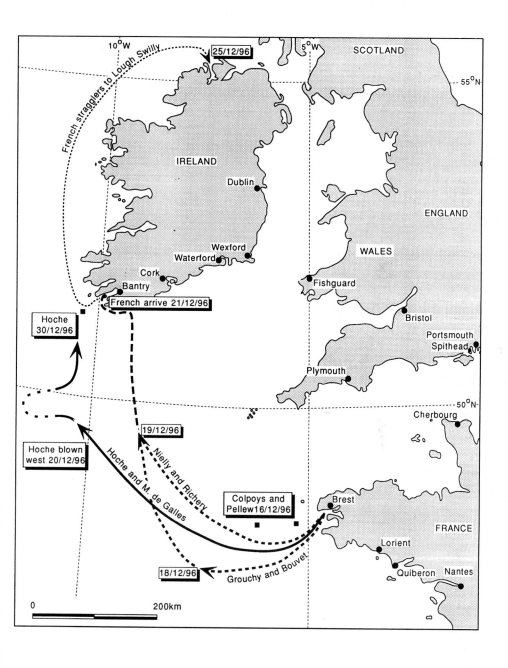

The French expeditions to Ireland Christmas 1796, based on the work of
Marianne Elliott. *(Mathew Stout)*.

The Chapman residence at Tobergal which incorporates the 1798 home of John Donovan. *(J. B. Curtis).*

Bookey's residence at Rockspring as it is today. *(J. B. Curtis).*

The ball alley at Carnew, in which the prisoners were shot without trial, was behind the wall where the 1798 memorial was erected, adjacent to Carnew Castle. *(J. B. Curtis).*

The Battle of Oulart Hill. *(From a photograph by J. Hayes of a painting by Fr. E. Foran 1898).*

The '98 commemoration, 1938. Abbey Square, Enniscorthy, where the marchers assembled for the parade to Vinegar Hill (in the background).

Enniscorthy in May 1857 (photograph by Strangman Goff). The scene shown had changed little from 1798. The Slaney is festooned with gabbards, which carried the grain of mid-Wexford downriver. Rudd's Inn (later the Portsmouth Arms Hotel) was directly opposite the bridge on the east side of the river.

Roche with his well-armed and mounted troop in bright yeoman uniforms. Another experienced soldier and United Irishman clinched his link with the rebel ranks there as well. He was Jeremiah Kavanagh, a veteran of George Washington's army. It was in his hostelry that the leaders of revolt now conferred and it was there in Ballynamonabeg, close to the Newpark home of Edward FitzGerald, that the arrests of the previous hours were assessed and the gravity of the situation absorbed. Edward FitzGerald, maltster, United Irishman, a friend of Fr. John and the outstandingly popular figurehead in central Wexford, had been taken under guard to Wexford jail by Captain James Boyd's cavalry. The significance of FitzGerald's arrest may not have been immediately apparent to Fr. John, but there is little doubt that the gathered United Irishmen realised that a vital senior authority of their organisation was in the hands of their enemies.[17]

There was little time for Fr. John Murphy to assess men or developments in depth, although a conference was arranged. The new meeting of minds, the fierce pressure of events, the understandable indecisions, all may have swallowed vital time at Ballynamonabeg, but cohesion was abruptly injected into the gathering with the appearance to the north of a large force of redcoated cavalry. When these cantered within sight it was found that Hawtrey White rode at their head.[18] They were two hundred strong and consisted of corps from Gorey, Ballaghkeen, Camolin, Castletown and Coolgreany. All Fr. John controlled was an indifferently armed crowd with no conflict experience at all. The men with him trained in the trade of war numbered no more than ten but from a defensive point of view their position was excellent. The fields were small with strong hedges, well covered by furze. It was an infantryman's battlefield. Edward Roche grasped the issue quickly and made a move with the best-armed men to outflank the cavalry. Hawtrey White, astonished to see fight in front of him, had second thoughts about the day's business. He wheeled and with his well-armed yeomen retreated out of sight up the Gorey road, finding time to indiscriminately shoot about twenty people on the way.

By the early Sunday afternoon Fr. John's summons to Shelmalier had swelled the rebel ranks to almost a thousand. Some were fugitives from the yeomen, most had no arms, having surrendered them the previous day in Oulart, and those who had no other weapons came with reaping hooks or hay forks. Fr. John took the mixed crowd of insurgents to the summit of Oulart Hill which provided a superb view of the surrounding country side. They waited there as, little by little, men reached their ranks and joined them. At about two o'clock in the afternoon, the evidence of a major offensive was identified when a cloud of dust arose from the direction of Wexford and drew ever closer. It was the Wexford garrison troops with yeoman cavalry in support.[19] Fr. John was ignorant of formations, units and detachments, but he now had a man at his side who was not. Edward Roche knew that in addition to yeomen and the Wexford Militia there were three corps of the North Cork Militia in Wexford town.

There were between four and five thousand people on Oulart Hill. There were about one thousand fighting men. The rest were women, children, the elderly, all having abandoned their homes. Fr. John had this mass of targets to consider and also the realisation that Hawtrey White and his yeomen were somewhere behind them to the north. The North Cork Militia were the pitchcappers. Not a man, woman or child from Wexford to Gorey was unaware of what the words North Cork Militia meant. There were two reactions when it was learned who would spearhead the assault against them. There was fear and resolve. But as the red column came nearer and its drumbeat thudded out, resolve was at breaking point. At three o'clock the North Cork Militia could be seen clearly on the road, crossing nearby Boleyboy Hill little more than a mile away. Edward Roche recognised his unit, the Shelmalier Yeoman Cavalry and their Captain Le Hunte, spreading out across the hill. Everyone could see the officers consulting.

Fr. John pointed to the different corps of cavalry below them and told his men what they would do.

> They will wait to see us dispersed by the foot troops so that they can fall on us and cut us to pieces. Remain firm, together! We will surely defeat the infantry and then we'll have nothing to fear from the cavalry.[20]

Behind a high ditch on the brow of the hill Fr. John had his best-equipped men stationed. Most of these had good pikes now, the rest had scythes and pitchforks, and there were between forty and fifty with guns or muskets. He directed Edward Roche and George Sparks to place the gunmen.[21] These were positioned on the right of the main body, facing south to the North Corks and Le Hunte's cavalry. It was well that the formation was made before fear escalated, for as the confident redcoats entered Oulart panic seized the poorly armed men. Fr. John harangued them to stand fast. Edward Roche lashed spirit and orders into them, but the honours of the hour were won by Morgan Byrne of Kilnamanagh.[22] A yeoman himself with Le Hunte's cavalry, he addressed his wavering comrades with the language of the fields, the language they understood. He rode through the furze until the blood ran down his knees. He shouted, abused, cursed. 'Shame on you!' he roared, 'are you afraid of redcoats? They're only men like you, and not half as good!' He tore open his coat and shirt and showed his chest.

58

'They're like me and you inside! If you met them in a fair, man to man, would red coats frighten you? Not at all!'

The rebel lines strengthened again, to a great extent due to a hostile move behind them to the north. Hawtrey White and his cavalry had reappeared on the northern side of the hill. The rebels would have to fight or be slaughtered. The yeomen and the North Corks in front now seemed to be appraising the location for the best method of operation. Fr. John and the waiting insurgents stood, on edge with anxiety, under the hot sun. It was while they waited that John Murphy remembered the length of time it took to reload a musket. He went across to the line of gunmen and told them to fix their hats on the barrels and raise them a little above the ditch when the soldiers came near.[23] If the soldiers fired at the hats, they would have to halt to reload. That would be the time to send in the pikemen.

Edward Turner the magistrate was recognised amongst the Crown troops. Their officers decided to lure the rebels down by burning houses. Turner was seen to undertake this task. On the hill no one moved. Some of the badly armed started to shift north, until they halted at the approach of Hawtrey White's cavalry. At once the action commenced.[24] The militia men started to trot towards them. At a distance of thirty perches they saw the hats above the ditch and began to fire. The balls whistled over the rebel's heads. The North Corks came within twenty yards in clear striking distance and the first rebel went into action. He was a Macamore man armed only with stones and he cut the musket clean out of a militia man's hands. The rebel guns belched. Every pikeman from Fr. John down the line cheered and ran along the ditches to outflank the North Corks on both sides. The pent-up hate was let loose. The North Corks were consumed. Pikemen were now amongst them ripping them open. Gunmen leaped into them using breech and barrel.

Suddenly the North Corks saw their fate in the merciless faces. They started to turn, spilling down the hill, running, looking over their shoulders as pikemen spitted them. One group in a lane found the pikemen up on the ditches over them, ready to strike. They begged for mercy. They took out rosary beads, prayer books, scapulars. They begged for mercy in Irish. They blessed themselves and shouted out Catholic prayers. It made no difference. The only thing the pikemen appreciated was that they were the very men who flogged, raped and pitchcapped.[25] The pikemen jumped down and gutted them to death. Some of the North Corks crossed the road near the chapel and gained a bog, but no matter how fast they ran they could not outrun the pikemen. Ten of these were piked. Five others raced for the asylum of Sinnott's house at Oulart. Three were overtaken and impaled. Two gasped on for another

59

mile through the fields running alongside the road. They were two miles from the field of battle itself when Tom Cullen and Jim Reilly, both powerful men, caught up with them at a ditch and cut the life out of them. Another redcoat was seen hundreds of yards ahead. They overtook him too. He was drunk and drunk he died. He was the militia drummer. One of the Shelmalier men on the hill brought his long-barrelled gun to his shoulder and blew a Le Hunte yeoman off his horse.

Fr. John, covered in sweat and dust, watched as Le Hunte's Shelmalier Yeoman Cavalry galloped in hasty retreat from them. At the other side of the hill, Hawtrey White and his corps vanished northwards to the safety of Gorey. Two hours later a wounded officer, Colonel Foote, a sergeant and three privates staggered back across Wexford bridge, scarcely able to report the calamity that had befallen them. They were the only surviving remnants of the garrison that had marched out of Wexford in the morning to scatter the rabble on Oulart Hill.

The corpses lying in the sun, scarlet and buckled, looked far less fearsome now. Fr. John gave orders that every weapon was to be collected, and every scrap of ammunition. His men gathered up over a hundred muskets and over fifty rounds of ammunition per redcoat.[26] The first of his men to lay down their lives in arms were reckoned. There were six.[27] One of them was his companion and breakfast host for twelve years in Boolavogue, his faithful friend, Tom Donovan, the man who in firing the first shot the previous day had killed his yeoman first cousin, John Donovan. Tom Donovan had never recovered from that bloody episode. He had a presentment of death and had been overheard to say that morning that he would never return to Boolavogue again.[28] Inside twenty-four hours both principals in a family saga had been wiped out. The other dead men were Humphrey Crowley of Kilpierce, John Dunphy of Monavulling, Somers of Finchogue, a weaver from Courtclough and young Murphy of Kilcotty. Murphy was in very poor circumstances and had been wearing the redcoat of a cavalryman for a waistcoat. Wounded at an early stage, he lay face down on the ground. His companions mistook him for a militia man and piked him. All six were buried together in the churchyard of Oulart.

In the turbulent exultation that swept around Fr. John, it was impossible to assess the significance of what had happened. He did not know who the redcoat slain were. Edward Roche was able to enlighten him. There were over one hundred dead militia men.[29] Amongst the dead officers were Major Lombard, the Hon. Captain De Courcy (a brother of the Earl of Kinsale), Lieutenants Williams, Ware and Barry and, an Ensign named Keogh. As Fr. John thanked Edward Roche by calling him 'General', and as his morale and that of his men grew, the waves of shock spread rapidly from Oulart in all directions. When the news and its implications had been digested, there was one frequently repeated question pressed forward, 'Who was this popish priest Murphy?'

Few if any outside his own local and church circles had ever heard of him.

The North Cork Lane, Oulart Hill, 1898. The lane, now overgrown, was then still highly evocative of the 1798 battle. *(The '98 Centenary Album).*

Chapter 7

The Taking of Enniscorthy

Despite the excitement, Fr. John stirred his men into purposeful action. While some made off to acquaint their neighbours with the extraordinary news, his immediate concern was to move back north to protect the people and property left in the places of major yeoman strength. He decided upon the hill of Carrigrew, three miles north east of Ferns, as the best assembly point for fugitives and volunteers.[1] As he and his followers marched, the smoke from burning thatch as far as the eye could see gave evidence that the military were on active duty throughout north Wexford, but not one yeoman or militia detachment came near John Murphy's men. He detailed a group from Crossabeg to reconnoitre Boolavogue and report back to him at Carrigrew.[2] When they returned they were carrying a chasuble belonging to him, charred and torn. It was a vestment used in funeral masses, black with a white cross design on it from collar to knee. They carried this macabre and well-noted vestment as a banner throughout the entire insurrection. John Murphy's other belongings – his papers, personal items, his documents from the Dominican College in Seville – were all gone. His thatched chapel, they told him, was a smoking, ash-filled ruin.

During that day, in unconnected actions, scores were being settled. An enthusiastic Ferns yeoman officer, Charles Dawson of Charlesfort, was shot and his home looted.[3] The home of Reverend Francis Turner, magistrate, had been attacked, defended, overwhelmed, looted and burned. The leader of the raid against him was his own Catholic tithe proctor, Michael Keogh, a man whose skill in his profession had 'raised him to a state of comfort and affluence from downright poverty'.[4]

John Murphy spoke at length with his closest collaborators in the days' activities. The certainty of a general uprising with the backbone of United Irish help took substance. The thought kindled many questions before weariness overcame all of them. What if the enterprise were to grow? What if they carried the challenge to the enemy? What if they were successful? They posted newly arrived, fresh men on watch and the men who had been through thirty-six hours of upheaval fell into an exhausted sleep on Carrigrew Hill. During the night the fresh men made arrangements for the provision of food and though bread and vegetables were scarce at first there were other commodities which were not.[5] The remnants from the 1797 harvest were still in surplus supply and the insurgents carried pocketfuls of grain until a better provisions system was organised. They were able to get milk, too, because, throughout the night, cows which had not been milked that Sunday were loudly indicating not only where they were but that they wanted badly to be milked.[6]

John Murphy was up and about at dawn on Monday morning, 28 May. Edward Roche was established as chief military consultant. He was a few years younger than Fr. John, probably a little over forty. Roche was a practical man with a clear idea of the business afoot, who consistently drew a distinction between religious differences (which he regarded as of no consequence) and national differences.[7] Fr. John explained the situation north of Carrigrew to Roche and it was decided early on Monday morning to strike for the heart of the yeomen's activities and wipe out the redcoats if they could be caught. The centres selected for attention were Camolin and Ferns and it was only necessary to shout these words to get insurgents on the road.[8] They hoisted their two banners, the black, white-crossed vestment, and the old volunteer flag. Fr. John sent men ahead of the main body to act as an advance guard. Already that morning the ranks were swelling for the word had spread for miles about Oulart that Fr. Murphy from Boolavogue was leading the revolt.

The reconnoitring party crept towards Camolin, the straggling village that lay astride the road to Dublin. To their amazement, they found not a redcoat, horse or guard in sight. There was silence. The village was deserted except for a few elderly Catholics and some dogs. The yeoman garrison and the loyalist inhabitants had fled to Gorey. In the unreal silence of empty Camolin, Fr. John arrived at a conclusion which would have been unthinkable for him twenty-four hours previously. He decided to attack and take the garrison town of Enniscorthy without delay. He grasped the likelihood that the initiative lay with them.

Facing south once more, the body of rebels entered the grounds and mansion of Lord Mountnorris at Camolin Park.[9] Some arms were collected by men who had none, but the visit there ended with an unhappy personal confrontation. Although it was early in the morning, Camolin's curate, Fr. John Redmond, a friend of Mountnorris and like Fr. John an oftentimes guest of his, arrived at the mansion. He angrily denounced the rebels and with scant regard for the cascade of events which had altered the entire circumstances he showed dismay at the presence of a Catholic priest in a leading role. There is no account of the verbal exchanges between Redmond and Murphy. A balanced exchange of views was likely impossible but the mansion and its contents were left intact at Redmond's persistent pleadings. He was poorly repaid for his anxiety. Mountnorris's men hanged Redmond, an entirely innocent loyalist priest, on Gorey Hill on 22 June and the Earl personally fired a brace of bullets through his dead body.[10]

Fr. John got his men with speed down the road to Ferns. Ancient Ferns was also empty of enemies. There were no yeomen there to harass or jeer now. The English Bishop, Euseby Cleaver, was gone. His magnificent palace, one of the finest in Ireland, was entered and looted.[11] Library leathers were taken and used as saddle covers. The palace was about to be burned to the ground, when an original idea gained currency. It would be an appropriate residence for John Murphy when the present business was concluded, so it was left intact for that purpose. The men around Fr. John were now being openly hailed and described as 'United Irishmen', not that the distinction mattered to him any more. One member of a Christian sect in Ferns was greeted with particular affection. He was Joseph Haughton, a Quaker merchant.[12] Haughton had refused to sell rope to Government forces to hang a United man, notwithstanding the danger he risked. He could have been hanged himself for the refusal alone.

Once more Fr. John had to bully some of his men whose vengeful assaults on the houses of Orangemen was delaying the march. He shouted at them until every man was under way again. The objective of their march was the hill of Ballyorril outside Enniscorthy town. By this time he and Edward Roche realised that a full-scale fighting campaign was the certain outcome, so there would be a problem providing food for the growing throng of rebels. They ordered a field of strong cattle to be collected and herded along at the rear of the column.[13]

The assembly point at Ballyorril was to provide further stimulation to Fr. John's own morale and self-determination. It introduced him to remarkable men and cemented comradeship with others. Shortly after their halt on the hill, he saw a new body of volunteers approaching. They were led by another priest, Michael Murphy from the north Wexford village of Ballycanew.[14] Michael Murphy was a man who, despite bishop and censure, had worked at an intense rate in the cause of the United Irishmen. The new arrivals bore the signs of hardship and were badly armed, many coming with sickles, slash hooks or scythes to do the work of the pike.

Fr. Michael's followers were the lucky survivors of a massacre on the previous day. The priest from Ballycanew had been informed of the victory at Oulart Hill. He then went into Gorey to report to the United Irishman with whom he lodged, James Kenny, but Kenny had been already taken by Camolin Yeomen and shot dead. The fearful fever of insurrection and counter-insurrection was spreading, so he returned to Ballycanew only to find that the yeomen had been there before him. Having failed to find him, they wreaked havoc on the Catholic chapel and drove the families suspected of United Irishman sympathies out of their homes. All of these people abandoned the village and led by Fr. Michael sought Kilthomas Hill close by, where thousands were gathering in the hope of joint security. That afternoon they were surrounded by the Carnew Yeoman Cavalry who opened fire on them. The crowd fled in all directions but one hundred and fifty were shot dead or cut down by sabres. The yeomen then sought more targets. By nightfall they had burned up to one hundred farm houses and cabins and for good measure added two more Catholic chapels to the flames.

Michael Murphy and his men were welcome recruits to the business underway at Ballyoril. He had enrolled two of his nephews on the way while he himself was a well-connected United Irishman, fully committed to the gathering revolt. Despite Fr. Michael's established credentials as a United man, it was Fr. John who was confirmed in the role of rebel commander.[15] Over the previous twenty-four hours a strange reality had been developing. John Murphy was being placed by the men around him in a position of moral authority. Despite his public stance of the past, he accepted the role with alacrity. The vacuum created by the unexpected arrests of the top United Irish commanders and administrators in Wexford was being filled by a previously obscure, unexpected but successful candidate, Fr. John Murphy, and the United Irishmen of all ranks and motives in his company fully supported him.

John Murphy's words of welcome to Father Michael's band of men were scarcely spoken when into the camp rode a young man of mature physique. Superbly mounted and well armed, he appeared to be the officer in charge of a body of armed men. He carefully eyed the curate of Boolavogue in studied curiosity, for the one and only thing the newcomer knew about John Murphy was that 'he was one of the priests who had used their pious assiduity and earnest endeavours to keep the people in thralldom.' He knew of John Murphy's successful campaign to have pikes handed over, he was aware that United men had been refused the sacraments but he had heard too about John Murphy at the Harrow and Oulart Hill. He announced himself to be Miles Byrne of Monaseed, a sworn United Irishman. He introduced his men, all of them obviously older than himself, one old enough to be his grandfather: Ned Fennell, John Doyle of Ballyellis, Nick Murphy of Monaseed, Michael

Redmond and Matt Mernagh from Little Limerick, and many others whom this young man grandiloquently described as 'the best, most independent and respectable farmers in his district'.

Fr. John took stock of the brash young United officer and expressed satisfaction with his bold sentiments, but he had an important question to return to him. Would he, Miles Byrne, and his men do what they were told to do? With little debate on the point, they one and all agreed to obey him and have his orders strictly executed. Miles Byrne and his men crowded around Fr. John, fascinated by the man. They pushed forward their opinions on the way the war should be waged. Fr. John listened patiently. Byrne confessed that he found the priest to be a courageous and simple man and from that day on regarded him with uncritical affection. Fr. John enjoyed the enthusiastic exchanges with Byrne and the Monaseed contingent. In the light of their military submissions he agreed to accept the role of General-in-Chief, but he added that he would only do so 'provisionally'.[16] In his use of the word 'provisionally' Fr. John signalled his understanding that his role was not going to be permanent.

Byrne's group was followed by others. The army on Ballyorril Hill was again strengthened with the arrival of the Kiltealy United Irishman contingent led by the brother of Fr. Mogue Kearns. Inevitably, the party included the suspended priest himself, Fr. John's boisterous hunting companion.[17] The surge towards battle had become inexorable.

The march against Enniscorthy was formed and started to move out at half past one in the afternoon.[18] Edward Roche was in joint command with Fr. John. The insurgents numbered some 5,000 and the entire force made a column a mile long on the Bunclody road. A couple of hundred were armed with muskets or fowling pieces and raids had provided them with a modest supply of ammunition. Behind them came the pikemen, followed by those with only farm implements for weapons. At the rear of the column, Fr. John had arranged experienced cattle drovers to bring the cattle along behind them.

The tradition in Wexford county holds that the rebels had been goaded into such fighting fury and determination that they entered battle with unflinching spirit. Nevertheless, it is difficult to conceive that amongst the men about to attack the strong urban maze of Enniscorthy there were not many who were facing 'the red maw of war' with justifiable fear. None except the survivors of Oulart Hill had battle experience and none of them at all with the solitary exception of Jeremiah Prendergast, the American war veteran, had an inkling of the close combat ferocity of street-by-street warfare. How they would prevail against a well-equipped and armed enemy was now a matter of biting anxiety for their leaders. The test was shortly to be put to them all.

The garrison of Enniscorthy was prepared and waiting for the crowd of rebels. It consisted of infantry and cavalry units of the North Cork Militia, the Enniscorthy Yeomen, the Scarawalsh Yeomen and many hastily recruited supplementary yeomen, young and old, numbering about 500 well-armed men. The commander was Captain Snowe of the North Corks. Fr. John ordered forward about 200 men with firearms flanked by some pike men to attack the Duffry gate's defenders on the steep western approach to the town. They recognised the local yeoman units, horse and foot, waiting for them – the first time yeomen had stood and faced them.

Captain Joshua Pounden of the Enniscorthy Yeomen was in command on the open ground before the Duffry gate. As the attack intensified, Captain Isaac Cornock, who had accepted the surrendered arms from the Boolavogue men in Ferns the previous Saturday, was sent forward with the Scarawalsh Yeoman Cavalry. The cavalry rode out upon the insurgent advance party, attacked with vigour but was thrown back by the rebels with shot and pike. The insurgents then leaped over the hedges and ditches on both sides of the road to deal with another charge by the regrouped force. The cavalry, however, withdrew to the ground held by their infantry who were in a strong defensive position. The nature of the battle ground made matters difficult for rebels without any idea of urban warfare. The town centre was flanked by the Slaney river on one side and on the other by solid buildings, from the windows of which a devastating hail of musket fire issued from redcoat guns. Fr. John saw many of his irreplaceable gunmen being levelled and he realised immediately the peril of a massed pike attack against such strongly held positions.

It was at this juncture that the battle for Enniscorthy was won and lost, although hours of bitter hand-to-hand fighting remained. Fr. John remembered a stratagem that had successfully turned the tide of battle in other times.[19] He told Miles Byrne and Edward Roche of the plan to create chaos. It was by the simple means of a cattle stampede. He ordered the rounding up of forty of the youngest and wildest cattle from the rear of the column. They were then goaded and pike-prodded by scores of yelling pikemen. They started to trot and then to rush in a mad headlong gallop towards the yeomen infantry, whose muskets were useless against the onslaught of the crazed animals. Through the lines the cattle burst, heaving upturned carts aside like chaff and tossing redcoats into helpless disorder and confusion. Then they stampeded bawling through the Duffry gate and down into the town, the pikemen racing behind them, roaring at their heels. Most of Enniscorthy's houses outside the Market Square were thatched so Edward Roche ordered the burning of Guttle Street, an additional move which instigated havoc as the roofs burst into flames, spreading from house to house.[20] Soon the entire high ground of Enniscorthy's western side appeared as one gigantic furnace. Irish Street was added to the conflagration, while across the river infiltrating rebels set the houses at Drumgoold on fire.

For four hours the battle for Enniscorthy raged in the narrow steep streets. Snipers firing from upstairs windows shot down rebels at will. Smoke filled the air, doors crashed, battle cries were roared, steel slashed on steel and terrified women screamed. The newcomers to battle, the rebels, compensated for their military ignorance by an enthusiasm which turned them into fighting machines who charged muskets without care for consequences. As Fr. John led from the front, his opposite number, the Protestant rector and magistrate of Kilcormuck, Thomas Handcock, was in the battle also, fighting with the Government forces. Handcock was using a blunderbuss with a spring bayonet, firing at the men he had described the previous Christmas as 'quiet and industriously employed'. The world had indeed been turned upside down, not least for Handcock. It had been reported to him that John Murphy, the popish priest in Kilcormuck, was the man in command of the rebel forces.[21]

The final phase of resistance was reached when Thomas Sinnott of Kilbride, sixty years of age and of 'very independent property', led his group of several hundred pikemen across the Slaney river at Blackstoops under heavy fire.[22] That action was decisive. Templeshannon on the east bank of the river and then the vital bridge of Enniscorthy itself rang with the clash of steel and resounded to musket fire and battle cries. Only a few of Sinnott's men had muskets but the pikemen fought with fury while their redcoated North Cork Militia enemies fought for their lives.

Suddenly in the late afternoon, the retreat of the Government forces was ordered by Captain Snowe. In the collapse of resistance, every yeoman and militia man had to look after himself. They ran like deer to reach safety, through St. John's Wood on the low western bank of the Slaney and from there to Wexford port. Some threw off their redcoats in the hope of escaping identification. Officers ripped off their epaulettes and any insignia which might betray their rank. Others turned their coats: despite their rout and terror, they fired on every man who showed on their way.[23] A number of loyalist families also fled with the troops in scenes of unparalleled confusion and panic. Even as they fled, violence overwhelmed Enniscorthy. It was as if the outburst of war was still at boiling point in the rebels' blood. Pikemen raked every house and hovel for enemies. An enemy was an identifiable Orangeman, a rank or supplementary yeoman. Once found they were piked. Instant suspicion was enough. Outrage fed the hunger for revenge. An elderly

Protestant clergyman who was a tithe proctor and middleman for the Earl of Portsmouth's estate, Rev. Samuel Hayden, was piked to death before his wife's eyes by a butcher named Beaghan.[24] Loyalist property was broken into, looted and plundered as Enniscorthy burned around the living, the dead and the dazed.

Fr. John walked his horse through a ruined town. The blistering heat and the long drought lent flame to anything that could catch fire. There were corpses everywhere, lacerated redcoats, dead pikemen, wounded rebels. Fr. John saw dead Boolavogue men, Shelmalier men, rebels of a few hours from Ballycanew. There were men lying down in the streets worn out. The smoke with the unaccustomed stench of gunpowder wafted about in swirls. Shocked townspeople stumbled around looking for children and neighbours or just hopelessly watched their smoking and collapsed homes. No satisfactory tally of the losses in dead and wounded on both sides, combatant or civilian, was arrived at. Miles Byrne estimated the number of defending troops killed at over one hundred, but the officers killed included powerful establishment names in Wexford — Lieutenant John Pounden of the Daphne, a magistrate; Lieutenant Hunt and Lieutenant Carden of the Scarawalsh Yeomen. Captain Cornock himself very narrowly escaped death. Byrne estimated the rebel dead at about one hundred as well, and that both attackers and defenders lost around the same number of killed and wounded. The casualties amongst the civilian population have never been satisfactorily computed.

Byrne, seemingly tireless, was ready for instant pursuit and filled with admiration for the priest he had only heard of as an effective anti-United Irish preacher. Now he had seen him marshal men, lead them and fight at close quarters. Not yet twenty but a leader himself of the Monaseed contingent, he became satisfied to follow and obey John Murphy without question. John Murphy had been very lucky to survive. After the battle he showed where more than once his hair had been shaved by musket balls.[25] With the town now firmly in their hands, he organised a force to remain on the streets to restore order. He then left with the leaders and the main body of the insurgents to set up camp on the rock outcrop above Enniscorthy, Vinegar Hill. Insurgent horsemen then raced in all directions carrying news of the Government's calamity at Enniscorthy. No one within twenty miles of the town was left in any doubt about what had happened. No explanation followed the shout of 'Victory', for the roar of battle, the flames and smoke had proclaimed what was afoot that afternoon under Vinegar Hill.[26]

Chapter 8

Leaders and Plans

John Murphy knew nothing of the impact he had made on friend and foe. The unlikelihood of his being involved with the insurgents, after all that he and most other priests of the diocese had preached, extended his fame. The panic he created at Oulart was magnified to justify the flight from battle by Hawtrey White and the retreating yeomen. Gorey was abandoned by the loyalists.[1] The North Cork detachment in the town shot their prisoners in the street and left them writhing. Anthony Perry escaped their fate for, in consideration of his 'useful information', he had been released to stand subsequent trial.[2] He was being nursed as well as possible in a safe house. A sight of war familiar in all ages, the refugee column, this one of loyalists, choked the road to Arklow. Most of the refugees had spent the night in the ditches outside the crowded town.[3] Dublin was in a state of alarm. Although Fr. Murphy did not realise it at the time, the country lay open before him. What he and his men expected immediately, however, was the arrival of substantial Government forces to put them down.

All through the late evening and night, volunteers and fugitives, armed and unarmed, kept arriving at Vinegar Hill. Some came in lamentation and more came begging the new liberator to protect their own area from the King's troops.[4] One man simply stood before Fr. John and silently pointed to his head, branded with the fresh scars of the pitchcap. Another bared his flogged back. Others told how their homes had been burned, how their belongings had been plundered or destroyed, their wives and daughters ravished by the Hessians and militia. They begged Fr. John for a force to protect their families from the Orangemen. More demanded that he help them get revenge. All this cacophony of woe surrounded him as he conferred with Edward Roche, Miles Byrne, Fr. Michael Murphy, Thomas Sinnott, Morgan Byrne, Mogue Kearns and others he knew as group leaders. In Miles Byrne he

70

had at his side a comrade fully briefed on United Irish affairs, a sworn United Irish officer and a near relative of the United Irish delegate for Wexford, Robert Graham.[5] Byrne was fired with ambition for the United Irishmen, the cause and the arrival of the French. By nightfall he had briefed Fr. John on the strength of the United movement in the county, the situation in the country generally and the leading personalities involved in Wexford. Edward Roche, Fr. Michael Murphy, Thomas Sinnott, all with countywide connections and similar involvement, corroborated.

Next Fr. John was joined by Fr. Thomas Clinch, a curate from the remote peninsula of The Hook.[6] Fr. Clinch, a cousin of the United Irish captain in Kilrush, had given Bishop Caulfield little solace. The bishop had denounced him as a beastly drunkard. Clinch reciprocated the contempt. His grandfather had fought for James the Second at the Battle of the Boyne, so Clinch, like Bishop Sweetman who ordained him, was an unrepentant Jacobite. The week before the outbreak, yeomen had murdered his mentally retarded nephew at Scarawalsh. Now he was prepared to exact retribution. He was to become one of the most conspicuous fighting men, of formidable stature, riding a great-hearted white horse throughout his time in action.

The next day on Vinegar Hill above the smoke and stench of smouldering Enniscorthy, Fr. John was joined by further talented United Irishmen of diverse backgrounds, some of whom had military experience in Europe's finest regiments. The first of these was William Barker, a brewer and general merchant in Enniscorthy town.[7] He had been an officer of Walshe's Regiment in the service of France. The celebrated John Kelly of Killanne, the blonde giant, a United Irish officer, marched up at the head of a body of men he had drilled in secret for months.[8] He was followed by another young man of stature and respect amongst all classes and creeds, Thomas Cloney of Moneyhore, who brought with him a large body of men who had assembled in west Wexford's barony of Bantry.[9] Michael Furlong, Templescoby, of the senior branch of another once powerful but dispossessed family, joined them. Parties of tens and twenties began to arrive from the Wicklow Hills. Garret Byrne of Ballymanus, member of an aristocratic Gaelic family, arrived with a party of followers. Fr. John sent out posses to bring in more men and inform the countryside that they were at war.

Another experienced military officer recruited was John Hay of Newcastle who had served in Dillon's Regiment in the Irish Brigade of the French army. John Hay joined the rebellion reluctantly, a reluctance which had at least two aspects.[10] He was a man thoroughly aware of the United Irish plans for Wexford and Ireland, an intimate friend of the movement's leaders and without doubt a sworn United Irishman fully informed of the week's events. He was also keenly aware and likely dismayed at the arrests of the leaders more particularly his cousin, the outstanding Edward Fitzgerald. The other cause of his reluctance was his own military experience. With military and administrative cohesion seemingly lost to the United Irishmen, he was now summoned to the side of a new priest leader who had trenchantly opposed armed revolt. At Vinegar Hill he emphasised to Fr. John the fragile nature of their military situation. He told him bluntly that because of the lack of warlike stores, ammunition, and, more ominously, preparation, the insurgents could not possibly stand against regular military for, as he said, 'any soldiery knowing their duty must cut them to pieces.' But there was no turning back for Fr. John and the possibility of French help began to dominate his mind.

A general uprising and French intervention which Miles Byrne knew was advanced in preparation were the logical developments. Such considerations were imperilled by a chaotic situation on Vinegar Hill that Tuesday morning. There was no order as pikemen and fugitives calling bitterly for extermination attacks on yeomen and yeomen property in their own home areas proposed private wars of revenge.[11] Excited arrivals argued that the most important place to attack was their own parish and barony. There was no single director with full authority over the growing numbers gaining the hill. Thomas Cloney's first reaction was one of consternation. The hard-core United Irish leadership cadre was under arrest. An acceptable commander with decision-making authority was an issue which caused confusion amongst the senior United Irishmen present, for the situation as it had developed was one they had not expected. In that unplanned state of affairs, the authority of Fr. John Murphy grew with each episode. Nonetheless, for a half day Fr. John was overwhelmed by disputes and he lost the initiative. At one stage it seemed that the insurgent army would break up into guerrilla bands.

William Barker proposed an immediate march to take New Ross in the belief that the people of the adjoining counties of Kilkenny, Waterford and Tipperary would join the rising *en masse*.[12] He was supported by Miles Byrne but not by the other leaders. As the day wore on, indecision grew and conflicting ideas multiplied: at four o'clock in the afternoon, as groups of pikemen were already leaving to take revenge in their own areas, a development took place which had the remarkable effect of binding the strands of revolt once more.[13]

The rebel outposts at St. John's wood spotted two gentlemen riding towards them bearing a white flag. One of them was instantly recognised as the widely known Edward Fitzgerald of Newpark.[14] Fitzgerald was of a small emergent class. He was a Catholic of education and property. The relaxation of the penal code had enabled him to attend Trinity College, Dublin, and he had been called to the Irish Bar. His father, a wealthy maltster, had amassed a considerable acreage of rented land. Edward, who came home to manage the family business on his death, was held in extraordinary affection by his neighbours, rich and poor alike, amongst whom he enjoyed an impeccable reputation for integrity. He was a founder member of the Wexford United Irishmen and a first cousin of two other political activists, John and Edward Hay of Newcastle and Ballinkeele. He had the easy bearing and appearance of an aristocrat, a characteristic which led to his being known as 'Lord Edward' throughout Wexford. Like so many others, he faced bankruptcy with the collapse of the corn and malting industry, but beyond all that was the factor of his rank in the United Irishmen. It had been expected that he would take the commanding military role in the planned revolt. It was his arrest particularly which sowed confusion in the United Irish ranks.

A joyful reception for Fitzgerald spread like a wave over the town. The news of his arrival was shouted from man to man as he was given the welcome of a hero. The greetings reverberated through the devastated streets and across the bridge as he rode to the hill. The tumult was so great that it was heard by groups of insurgents who had left Enniscorthy to pursue their own vendettas. They returned to find out what was causing such a thunderous acclamation. Edward Fitzgerald and his comrade were escorted to the summit of the hill surrounded by excited men. There Fitzgerald renewed his acquaintance with Fr. John and he introduced his companion, Dr. John Henry Colclough of Ballyteigue Castle. Both had been arrested and lodged together in Wexford jail, charged on Anthony Perry's confession which betrayed the identities of the leading United Irishmen in the county. They were released on bail by the notorious James Boyd, magistrate, having raised and lodged £1,000 bail money with the authorities. The most important condition of their release was, however, that they would act as envoys from the Crown garrison in Wexford to prevail upon Fr. John and his insurgent army to hand over their arms, disperse and return peacefully to their homes and lawful allegiance.[15]

When that condition was stated, Miles Byrne erupted. 'Imagine telling a victorious army to disperse, to go to their homes and wait until they be shot in detail!' He reckoned that there were about 16,000 rebels then in Enniscorthy, some 3,000 of whom had firearms. He correctly interpreted the envoys' mission as a sign of panic by the military in Wexford and concluded that the 'cowardly garrison should be captured there and then'. Drive and purpose claimed Fr. John and spread to leaders and fighting men alike. At once the attention of all concentrated on the garrisoned county seat and port and its nearby landing beaches.[16] It was decided to march on Wexford town. The insurgents insisted on keeping Fitzgerald with them in Enniscorthy. They sent Dr. Colclough back to Wexford with a demand for the surrender of the town. No other terms would be entertained.

As Dr. Colclough departed the insurgents sprang to action. A committee was established for Enniscorthy with William Barker as the senior officer.[17] He was entrusted with restoring some vestige of normality. An officer was appointed to each parish to arrange supplies of provisions for the fighting men and each of these officers had a number of pikemen under his command. Vinegar Hill was designated as headquarters and also made the principal assembly point and reservoir of food. The women were to manage the cooking and baking. A garrison placed in Enniscorthy was to be relieved at regular intervals by men from Vinegar Hill. When these arrangements were put into motion, the main body marched south on the Slaney's banks towards Wexford, gathering numbers as they went along.

Vinegar Hill became a symbol of defiance. It also became a dreaded symbol of revenge.[18] William Barker could not contain the people's recourse to the 'oldest arbitrament in the world – blood for blood'. Every day, yeomen were sought out and done to death. Anyone even suspected of being an Orangeman was shown no mercy. A number of Quakers were arrested and taken to Vinegar Hill camp for trial. All were discharged and sent home again. Luke Byrne of Oulartard became principally involved in the prosecution, persecution and execution of loyalists. He, too, was a maltster and owned a brewery in Enniscorthy. It is recorded that on one occasion he asked how many persons were condemned to death. On being told that there were twenty-seven he declared 'if anyone can vouch for any of the prisoners not being an Orangeman I have no objection they should be discharged'.[19] Thirty-two loyalists were put to death on the evening that Fr. John and the fighting insurgents left to attack Wexford.[20]

Success brought hundreds of volunteers to the camp on Vinegar Hill. Every United Irishman fit to march was alerted, Protestant and Catholic. They had been awaiting the call to arms. The revolt which had exploded from an action of self-preservation on a country road was gathering momentum and there were many far-sighted enough to realise that in the event of military success the political management of the aftermath would need to be in appropriate hands. Some men came unwillingly to the camp, fearful if they did not join the insurgents. Many more had merely been waiting for an uprising and a definite point of assembly; they came in to be allocated to an area where they could strike the most effective blow. Vinegar Hill also attracted a multitude of worn-out refugees and fugitives, male and female, old and young, impoverished, pitchcapped and flogged, all crying out aloud for retribution and keeping the orchestration of vengeance at full volume.

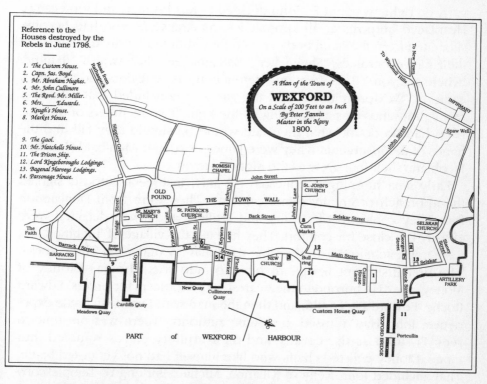

A plan of the town of Wexford, 1800, by Peter Fannin. *(Redrawn by Stephen Hannon from Musgrave's **Memoirs**).*

Chapter 9

Wexford

Fr. John led his column to a shoulder of the Mountain of Forth called the Three Rocks.[1] Two miles from Wexford town and situated at the junction of five roads, it offered a panoramic view of the rest of county Wexford, north, south and west as well as the Irish Sea and Atlantic Ocean off Wexford's coasts. Miles Byrne wanted to attack the Wexford garrison right away but Fr. John decided to rest his men and form camp. He placed outposts at all approaches. As stragglers who had become separated from the main body arrived they shouted loudly the names of their native baronies, 'Shelmalier', 'Ballaghkeen', 'Scarawalsh', 'Bantry', 'where are you?'[2] This went on intermittently as stragglers and new men came in. Wexford citizens and the garrison concluded that a host of many thousands was assembling by the hour. Two members of the garrison had no doubt what their fate would be should they fall into the hands of the insurgents. They were James Boyd and Archibald Hamilton Jacob and their fear grew as the night wore on.

Early next morning, Wednesday 30 May, insurgent outposts sighted the approach of enemy reinforcements. They were from Duncannon fort. They consisted of cavalry and artillery and when detected were already too close for comfort. They had left the village of Taghmon and were approaching Wexford on the road that lay under the Three Rocks. The first insurgent leader to be informed was Thomas Cloney of Moneyhore.[3] He hurried to the nearest senior officers for orders. Edward Roche, Edward Fitzgerald, and then the man with European battle experience, John Hay, refused to assume authority. There was not time to seek Fr. John as the cavalry and their artillery pieces rumbled into range. Cloney enlisted chiefs who like himself had not yet tasted battle. They included John Kelly of Killanne, Michael Furlong of Templescoby and Robert Carthy of Birchgrove. Within minutes they had their men collected and placed on the height directly above the road. Silence was

76

imposed on the camp as Cloney took the initiative.

The reinforcements under the command of Captain Adams consisted of an advance party of sixty-six men of the Meath Militia, three officers, and sixteen gunners of the Royal Irish Artillery Regiment with two how-itzers. The howitzers were short-barrelled canons which fired shells at a high elevation. Cloney maintained tight control of his men until the mili-tary were immediately under their position. On his order to attack, his men rushed on the troops with a burst of shouts, leaping over fern, ditch and furze, firing and piking. The astonished militia men fired as many rounds as they could at close quarters but in vicious hand-to-hand fighting the pikemen overwhelmed them. In the exchanges and noise of gunfire the horses plunged uncontrollably in terror, unused to such havoc. This added to the consternation of the infantry. It was all over after a quarter of an hour's frenzied assault, carried out, as Cloney said, 'with more of irresistible impetuosity than military skill.' Seventy of the redcoats were piked to death along with three of their officers. Four gunners were killed. An officer, a corporal and eleven gunners were made prisoners. One officer and four or five of the militia escaped and fled back to Taghmon as fast as they were able. Not long afterwards the insurgent outposts learned that the main body of the reinforcements, commanded by General Fawcett, had evacuated Taghmon and were in full retreat back to Duncannon fort.

Cloney took charge of an officer who had surrendered. He was Lieutenant Wade of the Meath Militia and he begged Cloney to save him from the rebels at the Three Rocks. Cloney conducted him up the hill to the camp, organised refreshments for him and kept him carefully under his own protection. Cloney next had the two howitzers hauled up the hill and placed, one of them to fire over the approach road to Wexford town.[4]

Next day General Fawcett reported on the action and the rebels to his commanding officer, General Eustace: '... any attempt that was not next to a certainty of succeeding against them should never again be attempted. Believe me they are no longer to be despised as common armed peasantry. They are organised and have persons of skill and enterprise among them'.[5]

Since the disaster at Oulart, Lieutenant-Colonel Jonas Watson, a retired officer, had taken charge of Wexford town's defences.[6] He had barri-cades built and in the belief that the insurgents had no artillery he utilised the town walls and the old narrow gates. He had rough block-ades of masonry put at the gates with room only for patrols to get through. Loyal citizens were issued with muskets. Scouts were organised to reconnoitre outside the town. The house burning in Enniscorthy was not to be repeated. All thatched houses were stripped of their roofs.

Bakers were forbidden to heat their ovens. Watson achieved a good level of morale. It was not an easy task and it was made all the more difficult by the lamentations of the North Corks' widows and orphans, embittered because only the bodies of officers were brought back from Oulart Hill.[7] Nonetheless Watson was quite contented that the garrison had the strength to hold Wexford town and port until government reinforcements would arrive.

The garrison was commanded by Colonel Maxwell who, the previous day, had arrived with the Donegal Militia, fresh men, new to the area.[8] The Donegals, the remaining North Corks, five detachments of yeoman cavalry – the Wexford, Enniscorthy, Taghmon, Healthfield and Shelmalier – with 200 men of the Scarawalsh Yeoman Cavalry under Captain Cornock, made up the bulk of the Wexford garrison, which was augmented by urgently enlisted supplementary yeomen. Colonel Maxwell had no reason to doubt the arrival of the reinforcements from Duncannon fort under General Fawcett. They were to join together in an encircling and destroying manoeuvre. He was not aware of General Fawcett's retreat, of the seventy corpses which littered the road under the Three Rocks, or that the rebels had captured artillery men along with their howitzers in perfect working order. In pursuit of their plan, several hundred men of the garrison rode out confidently from the ancient walls under the command of Colonel Watson.[9] One of their number was not convinced that their enterprise would have a happy outcome. Archibald Hamilton Jacob elected to leave the contest to his fellow yeomen. At an appropriate moment at the slopes under the Three Rocks, he contrived to desert, and by keeping to the byroads escaped across country to New Ross, thence to Waterford port, a ship and England.[10]

Outposts reported to Fr. John and the other leaders at the Three Rocks the approach of the enemy column from Wexford. Preparations to deal with it were effected at once. Cloney had his howitzers at the ready. One of his men, an artillery veteran, was put in control of the howitzer overlooking the road to Wexford town.[11] Colonel Watson rode forward to observe the insurgent positions. A Shelmalier long-barrelled gun was aimed and fired. Colonel Watson was blown dead from his horse.[12] Cloney ordered his artillery man to fire. The howitzer roared once and the King's troops did not wait for a second round. They retreated as fast as they were able. As the garrison gained the sanctuary of Wexford, surprise was quickly replaced by terrible fear in both defender and loyalist populations.[13] There was no question of another sortie by the troops. The insurgents had artillery and knew how to operate the guns. They had muskets and thousands of pikemen. Wexford was no place for yeomen or militia. Further danger was threatened on another front. A crowd had collected at Ferrybank on the country side of Wexford bridge. The crowd watched, threatened and waited in anticipation of the last resistance by loyalist Wexford.[14]

If ever a situation required decisive action, it had arisen for the insurgent chiefs at that moment. Miles Byrne saw with the luxury of hindsight that the garrison should have been instantly pursued and annihilated but the peculiar circumstances surrounding the actual outbreak in Wexford continued to create indecision amongst the leaders. It could be claimed that the arrests of the United Irish leaders in Dublin, followed by the betrayal and undermining of the Wexford leadership in Gorey by a thoroughly informed (if unidentified) senior officer had robbed them of their dynamism. That dynamism was now absorbed by an enthusiastic country curate who had captured the loyalty of insurgent fighters, a man who, at the same time, was totally untrained in such a role. The enemy was not pursued and it was a grievous mistake, for neither Fr. John nor the other leaders were aware of the panic that gripped fortified Wexford. They did not know that already the town had been won. At that very time a trained military brain in Wexford proposed a ruse which bought vital time for the garrison. Wexford was to be abandoned forthwith, but emissaries were to be sent to the Three Rocks camp at the same time to negotiate terms.

The first person invited to act as an emissary on behalf of the authorities was a prisoner in their custody. He was the United Irish chief, Bagenal Harvey. Harvey refused, claiming to his captors that he would be unknown to those in the camp. They finally persuaded two brothers, natives of the town and members of the Wexford militia, Loftus and Thomas Richards, to undertake the hazardous task.[15] As the brothers reached the rebel outposts on the steep approaches to the insurgent camp, they were surrounded by what Loftus Richards described as 'many thousand vagabonds'. They asked whom should they address as their leader and the reply they got was 'Fr. John Murphy of Boolavogue or Lord Edward Fitzgerald,' as Edward Fitzgerald of Newpark was styled.

Fr. John, riding on horseback through the camp, heard his name shouted along the line from the Wexford end of the hill. As he turned the mare towards the commotion he was told that two militia men had come out from Wexford to speak to him. Fr. John rode forward to meet them and a collection of pikemen went with him alongside his horse. The envoys who had a white flag and bore arms, were surrounded by an angry mob of his men. They introduced themselves and then produced a letter, composed at the authorities' directions, from county Wexford's senior United Irishman, Protestant, landlord and magistrate, Beauchamp Bagenal Harvey of Bargy Castle:

I have been treated in prison with all possible humanity and am now at liberty. I have procured the liberty of all the prisoners. If you pretend to Christian charity do not commit massacre or burn the property of the inhabitants and spare your prisoners' lives.

B.B. Harvey,
Wednesday 30th May 1798.

'Pretend to Christian charity!' Fr. John studied the words. And what did the two gentlemen propose? They had been sent on behalf of the garrison and the inhabitants to negotiate terms, they told him. Fr. John looked down at the two redcoated militia men. The armed forces of the Crown in Wexford were wanting terms from him! 'I do not know what terms they can expect from me', replied John Murphy, 'not after the treatment I have received'. The memory of all that had transpired moved him to anger before the two militia envoys, and 'from his savage aspect,' Loftus Richards reported, 'they had very great reason to be alarmed'. John Murphy addressed them in bitterness. 'They have burned my house and burned my property,' he declared. 'I was obliged to take shelter in the ditches.' He looked at the throng of insurgents around him. 'They have put me under the necessity of rising the whole country.' His men cheered. Many of them wanted to pike the envoys, whose arms were taken from them. The Richards were in a situation of mortal danger but the approach that moment of Edward Fitzgerald brought calm. He knew the men. One was a chemist in North Main Street, Wexford, the other a member of the legal profession. Fitzgerald ordered the belligerent insurgents to leave them alone.

Robert Carthy of Birchgrove suspected treachery for he feared the arrival of reinforcements from Duncannon fort at their rear. Both the Richards brothers told him that the 13th Regiment had advanced as far as Taghmon but had retreated back to the fort. Carthy refused to believe them, so it was agreed that Edward Fitzgerald should go with the two brothers and make a swift reconnoitre towards Taghmon. If they found the 13th Regiment moving up they were to instruct its commander that terms were under negotiation. The three had ridden to within a mile of Taghmon when they encountered a band of Fr. John's foragers on their way to the Three Rocks with cart loads of supplies. These cheerful rebels confirmed that the 13th Regiment was in full retreat back towards Duncannon Fort.

By the time that Fitzgerald and the Richards returned to Fr. John, a trail of smoke and flames was clearly visible, edging through the barony of Forth beneath them to the south. Carthy became convinced of treachery by the Richards, while the Richards were completely unaware that they were pawns in a strategy. Loftus Richards instantly proposed as evidence of their sincerity that his brother and Fitzgerald go into Wexford to provide proof of their commission and to present before the authorities the insurgents' conditions. He himself proposed to remain as a hostage against their safe return. This was agreed and the conditions demanded by the insurgents were outlined by Fr. John in consultation with Fitzgerald. Lives and property would be spared only if the arms and ammunition of the garrison were surrendered.[16] Edward Fitzgerald and Thomas Richards spurred their horses towards Wexford. They were expected back in about an hour. Even as they left and as time wore on, the smoke and flames to the south spread further west in an easily identified line. It was the smoke from the houses being set alight by the Wexford garrison in their retreat towards Duncannon fort.

Loftus Richards was lodged under guard in a hut by Cloney. Inside it lay some of the badly wounded insurgents from the Three Rock's battle. Richards watched through a hole in the wall as insurgents drilled and carried on what he interpreted as superstitious popish practices. Fr. John meanwhile ordered a body of insurgents to the outskirts of the town near the Windmill Hills, to be ready there to receive the arms, ammunition and other military stores which in accordance with the capitulation terms he had made he expected to be surrendered.

An hour, two hours passed and there was no sign of Edward Fitzgerald or Thomas Richards. When Fitzgerald had not returned after three hours, the insurgents concluded that they had been betrayed, that he was probably killed or being tortured for information. They decided to pike Loftus Richards. John Hay burst in on him in the hut to tell him he was to be killed. Richards pleaded for his life with such heart-rending eloquence that Hay successfully argued his innocence to the leaders. John Hay, the man with French Army experience, was now distraught with the inactivity and the hopeless waste of time. His training and instincts told him that the smoking columns stretching in a line from Wexford south-west through Mayglass for over fifteen miles was a military action. He begged to lead a party to intercept and attack, but he got no support from the other insurgent chiefs. No sense of vulnerability or desperation or revenge spurred the leaders to descend and wipe out their bitter foemen. The belief persisted that fortified Wexford was the place where the maximum opportunity lay. After another half-hour's wait without Edward Fitzgerald's return, it was decided to march and attack Wexford.

The insurgent army, which to Loftus Richard's apprehensive eyes numbered 'not more than fifteen thousand banditti', was called to attention. Fr. John's order was sent to the rear by the captains and the now familiar cries of 'Bantry, come to your colours!' 'Shelmalier, to your colours!' were called in the bright summer evening. The green flag was hoisted by Pat Murray and the Shelmaliers carried their black chasuble with the white cross. Fr. John rode at the head, the unquestioned leader amongst men who had only sampled independence. He sent Cloney and a party ahead on horseback in order to protect the townspeople and their property. He also gave general orders that respect was to be shown to females of every class and party.[17]

The scenes on the entry of the insurgents into Wexford defy description.[18] For Fr. John Murphy it was the experience of a triumphant general leading his men and accepting the adulation of his people. The garrison had fled. As he rode through St. John's Gate and down into the Cornmarket, the streets erupted in shouts of welcome. The cheering was returned by the insurgents. Musket shots pealed into the air from insurgent guns. It appeared that his entry in triumph was expected, for green flags, green handkerchiefs and the accepted emblem of the insurrection, green boughs, decorated every window of almost every house. 'Respectable ladies' waved from the windows as he rode his mare at walking pace, flanked on both sides by a bodyguard of pikemen. Girls were wearing green cockades and shortly were giving them as gifts. Soon every rebel sported a green cockade. Houses that had no green decorations had ornaments displayed, all contributing to the effect of celebration. The town was intact and open. No doors were closed. Townspeople smiled and waved. Most astonishing of all to the new masters of Wexford was that several men they knew to be yeomen were greeting them and smothering them with embraces. The enthusiasm of these men was almost hysterical and they even outdid the rebels in jubilation. Their redcoats were gone. On the shirts were green favours and anything else which would convince the insurgents that they were enthusiastic United Irishmen.

Refreshments of all kinds, whiskey, ale, milk, food were offered to Fr. John and his men as if available in double surplus. Long tables, weighed down with food and drink, were laid out in the bright streets. The refreshments, fairly distributed, convinced a great many rebels that if vengeance was to be visited on anyone it was not to be here amongst the hospitable townspeople. Drink from known loyalists was suspect and a few insurgents asked these people to have a precautionary sup first. Some as usual got too much too soon. A millinery shop was raided and soon revelling rebels were making their fury fade in laughter as they appeared in such unaccustomed wear as ladies' hats and feathers, caps, garments, bonnets and tippits. To Fr. John and a great many more, it was the best day of their lives. Wexford was won. To the loyalists and the establishment, the French Revolution, the terror included, had gained the land. To military strategists, the situation meant something else. On 1 June, Edward Cooke, the Under-Secretary, wrote from Dublin

Castle to Admiral Kingsmill:

> A rebel force has taken possession of the town of Wexford and there is reason from private information to believe that a French succour of frigates is expected there. You are to send a force to prevent any assistance from France on that coast and I am to suggest that gunboats are calculated particularly for that harbour.

Across the Irish Sea a new name was presented for entry into the newspapers and published. John Murphy, the popish priest, leading an army of rebels against the King, had emerged from obscurity.[19]

Bagenal Harvey, the senior United Irishman in the county, was released from custody as soon as the first insurgents could race down to the Stonebridge and Wexford jail. On his liberation he was paid the deference due to high rank by the other members of the organisation who had joined Fr. John's ranks, a deference to which the mightily relieved Harvey responded in a euphoria of good fellowship.[20] Restored to his town house at the junction of Georges Street and Selskar Street, he not alone entertained fellow United Irish officers including the hero of the Three Rocks, Thomas Cloney, but also loyalists of proven antagonism, with the gestures of the magnanimous victor. One class absent from the streets' receptions and celebration dinners was the Wexford clergy of all denominations. No Bishop Caulfield, priest, friar or parson showed head, for they were out of their wits with fright.[21]

Despite the celebrations, some of the insurgents kept their minds on the serious business in hand. They began to search for the stores, arms and ammunition they expected to find in quantity. Gradually the truth began to filter through to them. With the exception of three barrels of gunpowder found after a meticulous search of every room, store and vault in Wexford barracks, a few hundred cartridges with some odd casks and pounds of gunpowder found in shops and the townhouses of prominent loyalists, there was nothing. They found to their helpless fury that all the military stores had gone with the garrison from the town. On being informed that boatloads of loyalists had been sailed across to Wales, they decided to search the remaining ships and colliers riding at anchor off the quay. They found a small quantity of arms and ammunition but, strange to relate, they also found men with stubbles in women's clothes, wearing the shiny black boots of the yeoman cavalry underneath their skirts.[22]

There were two types of yeomen in Wexford apparently, yeomen welcoming them in the streets and disguised yeomen on board ships in the harbour. The conclusion was that the disguised yeomen were those guilty of the worst excesses. These were brought ashore, marched down along the town and lodged in the jail at the Stonebridge. The jail became full to the point of suffocation, so two sloops were designated as off-shore prison ships. One man identified on board ship was compelled to bear the sins of his infamous brother. He was John Boyd, brother of Captain James Boyd. He was recognised by many of the insurgents as soon as he was landed on the quayside. When he saw the hunger for revenge in their faces he burst free of his guards and ran for his life down the Custom House Quay. He was overtaken by the furious mob and piked but he was not killed outright. Left to die, he survived in agony until the following day.[23]

Another redcoat officer discovered on board ship was Captain Philip Hay of the Light Dragoons, brother of John and Edward Hay and a first cousin of Edward Fitzgerald. The insurgents did not pike or shoot him. Instead he was encouraged to join them. 'A spit was put to his throat by some of the rebels whilst others of them girt a sword upon his side'.[24] Throughout the evening, however, one serious question agitated many of the insurgents. What had happened to Edward Fitzgerald? He was nowhere to be found. It subsequently transpired that on arrival in Wexford from the Three Rocks with Richards, Fitzgerald found to his amazement that the town had been abandoned by the military.[25] Whether his reaction was rage or relief was rendered of minor interest when a new intimation of havoc was presented. The Mayor of Wexford, Dr. Ebenezer Jacob, took him to Wexford Bridge. At the far side of that bridge, the Shelmalier side at Ferrybank, a vast crowd of people from his own and Edward Roche's home countryside were gathered, giving every indication that they were waiting to level loyalist Wexford to the ground. In case Wexford was in any doubt about their intentions, groups of them kept marching and counter-marching in full view, up and down on the hill above the bridge entrance. The portcullis on the bridge had been hoisted as part of the town's defences, but the toll house at Ferrybank as well as the first span had been burned down by the vengeful crowd with the help of pitch and tar. They had later procured planks to make the bridge somewhat passable and were poised to give vent to their hatred on Wexford.

Mayor Jacob begged Fitzgerald to use his undoubted influence and popularity to calm the mob. Fitzgerald crossed to the country side of the bridge where again his paramount stature as a local leader proved a decisive factor. He calmed the huge crowd, the hostile and spectators alike and they crossed cheering into Wexford to celebrate but not destroy. Fitzgerald then rode on up the road to his own home at Newpark about seven miles away. He left no message of reassurance for the insurgents. Noises of menace were soon being made against his person by mystified United chiefs as the evening grew to dusk.

It also came to notice that one of the insurgents' prime targets for retribution, Captain James Boyd, had made a prudent and early escape.[26] He had noted the disappearance of his colleague, Archibald Jacob, early that morning. He galloped his horse down to Paul Quay where he badgered a ship's captain. Passage to Wales he beseeched. Too late. She was loaded to the gunwale with refugees. Despite his pleas and stature, he was brushed aside. He rode off down the South Main Street, and those aware of his flight and its significance joined him. He careered from the walls of Wexford to Jonah King's house, fifteen miles away on Bannow Bay. With a few fellow fugitives he succeeded in crossing the Scar river by boat and so to Duncannon fort. One of the many who did succeed in getting passage to Wales for themselves and their families was the Reverend Handcock. Refused passage at first, he presented arms to the fishermen and forced them at pistol point to set sail.[27]

It became a night of revels in Wexford. There was some looting but unlike Enniscorthy, surprisingly few people were killed. A search was made for Archibald Hamilton Jacob. As he had escaped to England his Georges Street town house had to absorb the fury of the crowd who wrecked it from slate to pavement.[28] There was a mighty influx into the town, camp followers, supporters, new fighting volunteers, refugees and spectacle seekers as well, for here indeed was spectacle. There were also those who exult with the winner and torment the loser. It was in a special way Fr. John's occasion. A loyalist, Mrs. Brownrigg of Greenmount, kept a diary. She would not have known him, but what she saw as he rode from one crowded street to the next coincided with her concept of popish idolatry among the 'lower elements'. 'Often the people stopped, knelt down, wiped the ground,' she wrote, 'then set up their hideous yells and followed their priest'.[29]

At this stage a priest under severe censure, Fr. Philip Roche, had linked up with Fr. John and the insurgents. Bishop Caulfield had already suspended him from all his ecclesiastical functions, having noted that, though he was 'a proper man and would be useful,' he had become a United Irishman agitator, 'and became abnoxious'.[30] Fr. Roche was a voluble and gregarious character, a good-hearted man who had nevertheless a ferocious appearance, with the additional misfortune of being an alcoholic. He was a native of Monasootagh, four miles from Ferns and John Murphy knew him to be, as his bishop once did, a man of energy and potential. Once more in the company of United Irishmen, now active insurgents, he was attached to the Bantry men amongst whom he had worked as curate and 'agitator'. From the moment of his arrival he took a leading position alongside Cloney and John Kelly.

Insurgents who were senior United men reported to Bagenal Harvey on the events of the previous four days. The organisation in county Wexford, shattered after the betrayal by a high-ranking but still unidenti-

85

fied member, was recovering. Before long Harvey, the veteran leader of the movement in the county, was presiding at meetings, interviews and even trials in Wexford jail or in the Selskar town house of his cousin, Mrs. Lett.[31] The formalities and etiquette of an embassy were observed. Sentinels were placed outside, green flags were hoisted and appropriate dignity was maintained. Those available to confer with Harvey on that night were the most influential United Irish leaders in the town, including John Kelly, Edward Roche, Captain Matthew Keugh, Nicholas Gray, Thomas Cloney, George Sparks, Michael Furlong, John and Edward Hay and Miles Byrne. The unexpected origin of the outbreak and the prospects were under consideration. Undoubtedly, the dominant position of a Roman Catholic priest from an obscure country chapel, who was the executive of victory at Oulart and at the capture of two garrison towns in three days was examined. There is no report of Fr. John attending any of Bagenal Harvey's or Captain Keugh's house meetings. His presence might not have been welcome, as his own involvement, its usefulness and drawbacks, was under scrutiny in the debates.

Fr. John went unattended by any officers through the main thoroughfares of Wexford. On reaching the southern end of Main Street where the jail was situated at Stonebridge, he entered the jail and at the back of the jail yard saw a firing squad in readiness for an immediate execution.[32] Facing the squad was a prisoner from that morning's engagement at the Three Rocks. He was Corporal Sheppard of the Royal Irish Artillery and he was a whisper away from death. Something instantly alarmed Fr. John. He loudly cried 'Stop! This man has longer days to live yet!' He dismissed the squad's truculence with another rough shout. Sheppard was reprieved and taken back into the jail. Fr. John then resumed his lone inspection. Sheppard was persuaded by Edward Roche to serve in the insurgent army and the next day he marched north with the division led by the curate of Boolavogue. There is no tradition that Fr. John sought out his bishop in his High Street residence or met him at any time after the capture of Wexford. There is, however, little doubt that had Dr. James Caulfield, bishop or not, been rash enough to put in an appearance on the streets amongst those who had suffered the worst attentions of militia and yeomen, his very life would have been in danger. His anti-United Irish diatribes were known to them all, heard only a few days previously from the windows of McCauley's Hotel in Oulart.[33]

The evening did not fade without another dramatic event. Into the south end of the town through the Bride Gate came scores of men, some on horseback. They were armed mostly with farm tools and fowling pieces. At their head rode one of the most distinguished Protestant landlords and magistrates in the county, widely connected and on intimate terms with his peers in the south Wexford United movement, Cornelius Grogan of Johnstown Castle.[34] He was a major shareholder in the new Wexford toll bridge and a brother of Knox Grogan, Captain of the Castletown Yeoman Cavalry. He was over seventy, corpulent and plagued with gout.

Grogan's personal appearance at the head of an angry body of new rebels was stimulated by the vicious retribution visited on his tenant farmers by the Wexford garrison in their retreat. Despite their panic, in which many cut off their epaulettes and buttons and tossed them over the hedges for fear of identification, the retreating redcoats set the thatched houses on either side of the roadway ablaze with musket shot. Any man foolish enough to be a spectator at the military's humiliation was shot. It was this progression of fired houses which was visible from the Three Rock's camp, but in the vicinity of the retreat route itself the reaction of the roadside families was of uncontrollable fury. The menfolk affected by the devastation at Whiterock, Moorfield and Rathaspeck, went in anger to the popular local landlord, Grogan, and reported the destruction. He refused to believe that it could have happened on the scale they presented. They insisted that he go with them to see for himself. He did so. Aghast at the casualties and burning homes, he came to Bagenal Harvey with a throng of United Irishmen and new recruits to join the insurrection. Amongst them was their United Irish captain, schoolteacher Patrick O'Brien, grandnephew of Bishop Nicholas Sweetman.

That night Wexford town quietened as tired occupants were overcome by exhaustion. Early next morning, Thursday 31 May, the streets were alive with activity. Thoughts settled on the missing chief, Edward Fitzgerald.[35] Anger that he might have betrayed them grew amongst the suspicious insurgents. The threat of execution was dispatched to his home by messenger. Shortly afterwards the debonair Fitzgerald rode back across Wexford bridge, up into the Bullring, and so effective was his authority and charm that animosity melted as rapidly as it had grown. He resumed without question his position as a senior United Irish leader.

It was decided to take the active insurgents off the streets and set up camp at the Windmill Hill above the town. It was a macabre site, the place of public execution, but it was chosen as the vantage point and venue to hold the most representative and crucial conference of the Wexford insurrection.[36] The conference provided Fr. John with his first taste of political manoeuvre, his first opportunity to express an opinion at a fully convened council of war, and it certainly presented him to a United Irish leadership segment who until that week may never have heard of him and if at all it was as a pulpit-pounding enemy.

Undercurrents surfaced when the leaders met. Thomas Cloney remembered the embarrassment caused by the presence of the Boolavogue curate: 'He was the least likely of any other priest in the county to appear in arms.' Many faces new to Fr. John were there, and he may well have been surprised at the broad spectrum of people and locations represented, particularly from south Wexford.

No complete list of those taking part in the Windmill Hill council of war exists, but so vital was its purpose that we must assume the presence of others than the recorded leaders. Bagenal Harvey very likely presided over the disparate strands of revolt now gathered. Leaders already known to Fr. John included Edward Fitzgerald, the Hay brothers, Edward Roche, Thomas Cloney, Miles Byrne, the Furlongs of Templescoby, the Byrnes of Ballymanus, George Sparks, John Kelly and the suspended clergymen, Mogue Kearns and Philip Roche. Fr. Michael Murphy was not at the conference. He had remained out at the camp on the Three Rocks.[37] Men representing another dimension to the insurrection included liberal Protestants like Captain Matthew Keugh, Henry Hughes of Ballytrent and his brother-in-law, Nicholas Grey; John Boxwell of Kilmore, William Hatton of Clonard and Cornelius Grogan of Johnstown Castle. Dr. John Colclough of Ballyteigue Castle, Harvey's life-long friend and companion, was present, and more than likely men intensely active in the decade's campaign for Catholic rights, like John Devereux of Shelbeggan, Richard Monaghan of John Street, Wexford, Walter Devereux of Ballybrittas and Nicholas Sweetman of Newbawn.

The presence of Fr. John Murphy created one source of strain. The spectre of unexpected betrayal presented another and could not be exorcised from the minds of Harvey, Fitzgerald, Colclough, Roche, or anyone who appreciated the significance of the arrests. No one knew who had betrayed the leadership. For all they knew, the spy might be in their midst. Now, in the foreground of their enterprise, a new and eager convert to arms had appeared. Hitherto unhelpful but now strong in the position of leadership, with the imagination and loyalty of his men secured, the forty-five year old priest presented an unsought dilemma. The unexpected course that events had taken was reflected at the Windmill Hill conference. It was a long and acrimonious meeting; the opposing sides have never been revealed, but Thomas Cloney, still disturbed by the memory after three decades had passed, named the position of Commander-in-Chief as the item upon which the 'cabals and jealousies arose which omened badly for our future prosperity'. There was a protracted dispute over the position of supreme commander in the light of recent treachery from within and over the appearance of a new leader. There was no likelihood that Fr. John Murphy could have become overall commander, no matter how much it was regretted many years later.[38] The probability is that the final selection lay between Edward Fitzgerald and Bagenal Harvey. Eventually the majority decision placed Bagenal Harvey as the Commander-in-Chief, an outcome which bore the appearance of compromise.

Miles Byrne deplored the indecisions and lack of bold purpose. As for the election of Harvey as over-all military commander, he complained that although a gentleman of integrity, zeal and liberal patriotism, he did not possess the military talents or qualities necessary for such an important rank. 'His very delicate constitution', Byrne added, 'rendered him quite unfit for such a command.' Thomas Cloney expressed an identical verdict. Yet Harvey was the majority choice and from then on the conference was occupied with the business of direction and administration. Despite disagreement, the eventual strategies bore the audacity of confidence. The conference decided that their forces would be divided into three divisions which would advance in separate directions with separate objectives in the short term. The first objective was determined by the expectation of substantial French help and the provision of adequate facilities for their ships and army's maintenance. It was decided to take New Ross, march south to obtain control of Waterford harbour, port and city, and then extend the revolt in Munster. Duncannon fort was to be ignored, for United Irish infiltrators had discovered its guns to be defective, information which had been passed on to the French.[39] The second division's objective was to advance north to secure county Wexford, take Gorey and Arklow, and then march on Dublin. The third and smallest division was expected to take Bunclody, raise the midlands in support and wheel around on Dublin from the west.

Bagenal Harvey had personal command of the division that was to break out of county Wexford through New Ross and march on towards Waterford. This division was given the artillery pieces along with insurgents experienced in their use, like John Boxwell. Harvey's associates in command included Fr. Philip Roche, Thomas Cloney, John Kelly of Killanne, John and Walter Devereux, Nicholas Sweetman, Dr. John Colclough, John Boxwell, Henry Hughes and the Furlong brothers of Templescoby. Matthew Furlong was appointed Harvey's aide-de-camp. The men of this division were from the baronies of Forth, Bargy and Bantry.[40] There was but one fatal flaw with this division of high quality insurgents and that was a lack of necessary urgency on the part of Harvey. New Ross was ripe for capture but Harvey was in no hurry. At conference end, he returned to his town house in Georges Street to host friends and foes in entertainment.

John Murphy was pointed in what appeared to be the most daring direction with Edward Fitzgerald, Edward Roche, John Hay and Fr. Michael Murphy amongst the leaders at his side.[41] They were ordered to lead their division to the north, take Gorey and Arklow and join with expected insurgents from county Wicklow in an advance on Dublin. The timing was right. The whole government edifice was believed to be on the verge of collapse. With yeomen greeting them in the streets, militia desertions to their ranks were expected. Victory was possible even without French help. Fr. John was briefed on the imminence of landings by the French and the implications of the rapid enemy retreats all around them. The Midlands were in revolt. All that was lacking was co-ordination.

A third division was designated for a specific task and the choice of its commander indicated decided United trust in his dependability. This division, given about 2,500 men, was to take Bunclody, then known as Newtownbarry, on a pass through the Blackstairs Mountains.[42] The intention was to enter and co-ordinate the revolt in the Midlands, wheel towards Dublin and link up with Fr. John's division. The command of this division was vigorously sought by Fr. John's turbulent hunting companion, Fr. Mogue Kearns. He was then, to all appearances, promoted ahead of his brothers who were established United leaders in that mountain region. Miles Byrne and his men were part of this formation and they were given the additional aid of a brass six-pounder artillery piece, a howitzer and some ship swivels.

Captain Matthew Keugh was appointed military governor of Wexford town and port.[43] The main square of the town, the Bullring, was converted into an ammunition factory.[44] Every available blacksmith, gunsmith and carpenter with helpers went there to make and repair muskets, pistols, pikes and swords. Every forge in the town rang with hammer on anvil. The fort of Rosslare at the entrance to Wexford harbour was revitalised. Three old pieces of cannon were brought down from the fort, oiled and placed in position. In case any enemy ship should succeed in passing through the harbour entrance, four old sloops were placed in the channel, ready for scuttling. The Wexford sailors and fishermen joined the insurrection. Four oyster boats were fitted-out in the harbour, each manned by twenty-five seamen. They cruised outside the bar into the trade route of the Irish Sea and succeeded in arresting a number of Dublin-bound vessels laden with provisions.[45]

A press for printing proclamations and statements was commandeered by Harvey. Christopher Taylor, a loyalist printer, undertook the printing jobs.[46] A seven-man committee of public safety was formed and administration organised under the presidency of Harvey. Authority was comprehensively delegated. William Kearney became deputy to Captain Keugh, Dr. Ebenezer Jacob was put in charge of the sick and wounded, Cornelius Grogan assisted in the maintenance of provisions and supplies, and one of the Richards brothers agreed to serve in an administrative capacity.[47]

Fr. John was not prepared to relax and he had no time to provide for drink or celebration. He was absent from Harvey's dinner given in Georges Street that Thursday.[48] Harvey invited close associates but avowed loyalists also, amongst them the magistrate Edward Turner of Oulart repute. Turner was recognised as he entered Harvey's house and by the time the meal was over a lynching mob had gathered outside. Two of his guests, Edward Fitzgerald and John Hay's brother Edward, tried to reason with the crowd, who were insisting that Turner be put to death for burning their houses. Fitzgerald once more placated the protesters, the crowd left, but almost at once repented of their leniency and returned. Fitzgerald and Hay were informed that they would be killed themselves unless Turner was handed over. Turner volunteered to surrender then for the crowd agreed not to kill him on the spot but to lodge him in jail to go on trial. In his opinion jail was the only safe place 'when neither the house nor the interference of his friends or the chief commander could ensure him protection.' He was hustled along the Main Street into the jail that was already packed with loyalist prisoners.

Fr. John would have known that by this phase of his life he had, *ipso facto,* suspended himself from priesty duties. Knowing Bishop Caulfield, he was not in any doubt whatever about his attitude. Hiding behind closed doors, the bishop was informed, probably by Thomas or Loftus Richards, of the presence of a Catholic priest in the camp at the Three Rocks and that he was acknowledged by the rebels as their leader, by name Fr. Murphy. He must have queried the identification as he had already suspended Fr. Michael Murphy.[49] He never did suspend Fr. John, nor was Fr. John nominated for suspension at any stage during the insurrection, a fact recorded by Bishop Caulfield in a written report to his metropolitan, Archbishop Troy.[50] The insurgent priests continued to celebrate Mass at the camps. A loyalist prisoner reported that Fr. John and Fr. Michael Murphy celebrated Mass on different days during the insurrection. The bishop associated the United Irishmen with the godless ideals and practices of the French Revolution but rebel camps indicated that whatever their reputation they still maintained the public observance of their religion and equally firmly held that Bishop Caulfield and most of his priests were 'government men'.[51]

On Thursday 31 May, at midday, Fr. John gathered the men of his division for the march to the north. Accompanied by Fr. Mogue Kearns, Miles Byrne and the men to move on Bunclody, they made for the Three Rock's camp where they collected Fr. Michael Murphy and the remaining fighting men. Fr. John was now joined by two separate corps of rebels from Wexford town, the Faythe Corps, volunteers from Wexford's seafaring and fishing district, and the John Street Corps, whose captain was one of the insurrection's and Wexford's most colourful characters, Richard Monaghan.[52] John Street was a long street of small workshops and traders. It teemed with carpenters, tanners, butchers, blacksmiths, shoemakers, coopers, indeed every industry or service required in a busy port. It was also the street which had witnessed the shooting of eighty people by the military and Wexford Militia in 1793. It was the street of the Catholic chapel, the street of the indigenous Wexford people with generations of cunning, survival and intrigue as a tradition.

Richard Monaghan epitomised the brazen optimism of inner Wexford. He had been prominent in the Catholic movement for equal rights in the 1790s which denotes his political role in John Street. He recruited United Irishmen, probably when the grain trade which gave him his livelihood was crippled. Throughout all vicissitudes he was sustained by a razor sharp wit and humour which caused him to be bestowed with the title, 'Mayor of John Street' and the nickname by which he was known everywhere, Dick 'Monk'. Always active, alive, humane, he fought alongside Fr. John with his men to the last, and inevitably appeared in a tidying-up role where discipline was jeopardised. Monk as a rebel officer dressed somewhat as the Irish National Foresters of later years did. He wore a jacket of green with silver lace crossbanded in front, matching trousers with silver seams, and a green hat with a white ostrich feather. In a bitter period of warfare, he provided the few shafts of hilarity. That morning he had set himself up magisterially in Wexford jailyard where, to the awe of his town companions, he interrogated rural yeomen prisoners who were determined to conceal their identity. He put them through a question and answer 'catechism' session to decide if they were, as they claimed to be, United Irishmen.

Edward Roche of Garrylough had also changed from his previous redcoat of the yeoman sergeant.[53] He rode alongside Fr. John in a snuff-coloured coat, black waistcoat, corduroy breeches and a round hat. For distinction he wore two gold epaulettes, a silk sash and a belt in which he carried a pair of large horse pistols. He wore a sword by his side. Behind them marched the veterans of The Harrow, Oulart Hill and the men of Shelmalier, all from the east side of the Slaney along with the two Wexford Town Corps. The divisions set out, marching and on horseback, long columns of determined men with banners flying. They left behind them a garrison of guards at the Three Rocks as well as the fugitives and the elderly who could not keep pace with the fighting men. There was a long, rapid march ahead for Fr. John wanted to get as near to Gorey as possible before nightfall, aiming to reach the hill of

Carrigrew, north-east of Ferns.

The insurgents rested and were fed at Vinegar Hill. Then they divided forces. The division to attack Bunclody and break into the midlands made their farewells. An optimistic Miles Byrne and a complacent Mogue Kearns parted from Fr. John in full confidence of success and the expansion of revolt. Then the division heading north moved forward in haste again. That night Fr. John and his men set up camp on the hill of Carrigrew.[54] It was twenty-three miles from Wexford and seven miles north of Enniscorthy.

In Wexford town, Mrs. Brownrigg recorded in her diary:

> The rebel troops paraded twice a day on the Quay opposite our door. They had fiddles, drums and fifes. They were pleased to call it a parade. It was in reality a regular tumult. Everyone gave his advice and opinion. One said 'I will go and take Ross,' another 'I will take Newtownbarry'. Henry John listened one day with great attention and said, 'Dear Mama, are they everyone Kings?

The '98 commemoration at the Three Rocks Mountain. *(From the Rosslare Strand Hotel movie film, **Historic Wexford**).*

Chapter 10

The Novices of War

One enormous fire on Carrigrew Hill from dusk to dawn of June's first day gave notice that the insurgent army was assembling. They gathered there, though hampered by a harmful chemistry: courage without clearly defined authority. While the meeting of the chiefs in Wexford gave clear responsibility to Bagenal Harvey the division heading towards Dublin had what amounted to control by committee.[1] Fr. John, Edward Roche, John Hay, Edward Fitzgerald and Fr. Michael Murphy were equals in command, as if this solved the dilemma of the Boolavogue curate's unexpected surge to popular leadership. They were joined by another leader whose presence spurred lust for revenge. Anthony Perry arrived, a once proud man broken in spirit, carrying the secret that he had betrayed them under torture.[2] Perry came with a group of other escaped prisoners from Gorey. His face and head made a sickening sight and it was plainly evident that he was suffering. The torture had raised all the skin of his head and part of his face. He was in misery, but was determined to fight to the last vestige of his strength. That morning he had left the house where he was being nursed and marched south with the former prisoners, all resolved to join in the revolt. Perry was instantly accorded his rank of insurgent chief.[3] No one ever realised how acute his anguish was. No one in the camp suspected that under torture he had identified the leading men in the United Irish movement in Wexford, including his comrade in arms, Edward Fitzgerald of Newpark; Perry alone carried his terrible secret.

Perry was able to fill gaps in information. He reported that once the insurgents had left north Wexford to move on Enniscorthy and Wexford town, Hawtrey White and Hunter Gowan committed their yeomen corps to day and night patrols, burning and shooting. Many defenceless people were shot by them in the area where they operated unhindered. Gorey had been evacuated by its garrison, so there was nothing

94

between the insurgents and Dublin but Arklow town.

Despite Perry's report, Fr. John and the assembled chiefs decided that Gorey was an occupied strong point and a plan was devised to capture it. Fr. Michael Murphy was given an immediate assignment with a force of one thousand men.[4] He was to enter the village of Ballycanew and occupy Ballyminaun Hill, a commanding height between Ballycanew and Gorey. Fr. John planned to link up with him next morning in a combined move on Gorey. It was a task believed well within Fr. Michael's compass and Fr. John watched him go without anxiety. While he was away with his force, drill tactics and formations were organised on Carrigrew. The task of drill sergeant was taken on by a Dublin new-comer, Hugh Kennedy, a step-brother of Miles Byrne.[5] He showed the raw insurgent troops how to form a line and break into a column by platoons and sections. Everyone in the camp was anxious to be trained. Only the army officers, the United men and former yeomen had ever been drilled. The former yeomen who had resigned or been dismissed from Knox Grogan's Castletown Corps, Beauman's Corps and Hawtrey White's Corps also gave instruction. Some former members of White's Corps were employed to instruct the insurgents in the safe loading and priming of their firelocks. Those who had served in the yeomen cavalry, well drilled themselves, found their expertise respected and their instructions obeyed. At Carrigrew John Murphy's own amateur swords-manship was honed to a more professional standard.

In the afternoon, the noise of battle could be heard by everyone on Carrigrew. For one hour the sound of musketfire came from the direction of Ballycanew and further north, about three to four miles away. It was presumed that Fr. Michael and his men were fit to take care of the situation, for no party left Carrigrew to give support. Then, later in the afternoon, a sorry spectacle formed before them. Fr. Michael's shattered column, returning in small groups and singly, regained the safety of the camp.[6] They had been overwhelmed. Men who had set out on horse-back were now on foot. Where were the horses? What had happened? An exhausted Fr. Michael explained the debacle. Over 200 fully armed redcoat cavalry had intercepted them. His men decided to engage them with their own muskets and were hopelessly outgunned. Then the Camolin Yeoman Cavalry charged the retreating rebels and cut them down at will. How many did they lose? The total killed amounted to some 150. The horses and cattle Fr. Michael's men had commandeered on the way across country had scattered in the engagement and were lost. The wounded were left in the ditches around Ballyminaun hill. There was nothing the fit and able could do but scatter.

When the full implications of the disaster at Ballyminaun were studied at the camp, fear of the unknown prevailed. The art of politics was one thing, but it was evident that the waging of war was another profession altogether. How were they to deal with superior fire power? Instead of moving into attack, Fr. John halted. The following day, 2 June, his division remained paralysed on Carrigrew Hill.

Friday 3 June brought even worse news.[7] Fr. Mogue Kearns and Miles Byrne with their surviving men reached the camp at Carrigrew and reported to Fr. John that their objective, Bunclody, had been captured but lost within an hour. There is no record of John Murphy's reaction when confronted with this stultifying reversal by his hunting companion Kearns, a man who could be termed a veteran United Irish activist. There is little doubt, however, but that Miles Byrne blurted out the same story he detailed later in writing. As a fighting man Kearns was regarded by Byrne as a superb specimen who would have had a brilliant military career; but as a commander, his behaviour at Bunclody was little less than ludicrous.

Poorly equipped with firearms but bristling with pikes, Kearns' men halted on the rise of ground outside Bunclody on the Slaney's west bank. Byrne for the first time approached the column's commander,a huge man on a great horse. The eighteen-year-old United chief respectfully pointed out to Kearns how important it would be to have a similar military position on the other side of Bunclody. He was cut short. 'I have still more to say', proclaimed Kearns to all listeners. 'Tell all those you have any control over to fear nothing as long as you see this whip in my hand!' It was the only weapon he had. His strident reply brought grins of unquenchable confidence from his men. Byrne was dismissed. As he said, 'to speak to him of a rallying point in case of being forced to retreat would be worse than treason; his boats were always burned.'

Kearns put his men on their knees and removed his hat. The suspended priest beseeched his hearers to join him in prayer. He then gave the order to attack. The rebels descended on Bunclody with such enthusiastic vigour that the garrison of 500 regular infantry with yeomen cavalry support was soon compelled to retreat in disorder. Instead of pursuing their enemy, some rebels were diverted to besiege the landlord Maxwell's town house, still occupied by redcoats maintaining fire. More plundered the army's abandoned baggage, set fire to loyalist houses and in the enjoyment of rapid victory raided cellars and hostelries for drink.

When the retreating army concluded that it was safe to halt on the Carlow road, they realised that they were not being pursued. They regrouped and reconsidered their situation. They returned to survey the prospects and then arranged the counter-attack. They turned their guns and raked the packed Main Street and Square with artillery fire. The celebrating rebels were taken completely by surprise and consequently suffered terrible losses, estimated at not less than 250 fighting men. Bunclody was abandoned as quickly as it had been taken.

It took some time before Fr. John recovered from the news. Yet another day, the third, was lost, the most prodigious waste of time since the outbreak. and in the wasting of those days the enemy exploited opportunity. Government reinforcements poured back into Gorey. The time wasted was considered well used by Miles Byrne, although it infuriated insurgent sympathisers. 'The days were well spent in preparing for new combats', he wrote, 'and in acquiring accurate information as to the strength of the enemy and the respective positions and towns where they were concentrated.' This picture has been clouded by the disappearance from the folk tradition of Edward Fitzgerald, the French army veteran John Hay, and his brother, Captain Philip Hay, all of whom were present in the camp at Carrigrew. Debates between equals in command certainly contributed to indecision along with the uncertainties about their next move, while the terrible toll of dead at Ballyminaun and Bunclody haunted all of them. While Byrne stressed that a respite from constant action was necessary for the novices of war, their enemies moved to exploit that very weakness. The government initiated a two-pronged military movement to encircle and destroy the rebel threat.[8]

On 3 June the King's troops under Major-General Loftus reached Gorey. It was a mixed force of 1,500 men with five pieces of artillery. He ordered Lord Ancram to march from Bunclody to Scarawalsh bridge with the King's County Militia and a detachment of dragoons, a position which placed them advantageously between Carrigrew and the great rebel camp at Vinegar Hill to the south. Part of the garrison at Carnew was brought forward to occupy Camolin. On the morning of 4 June, the bulk of the troops in Gorey marched out with military precision. They were led by General Loftus and an officer of ebullient confidence, Colonel Lambert Theodore Walpole. They marched south and divided forces outside the suburbs of Gorey.

General Loftus with the Antrim Militia and his cavalry units turned left towards Ballycanew. At the crossroads south of Ballyminaun Hill, he posted a rearguard of 100 Antrim militia men, a force which would act as a reinforcement to Colonel Walpole if required. Walpole continued along the main road south from Gorey toward Enniscorthy. This movement was calculated to surround and annihilate the insurgents who would not be remotely able to match the fire power of the military.

Around 9 a.m. Fr. John and his lieutenants were roused by their outposts messengers. They reported that four regular detachments of Government troops with artillery, supported by several corps of yeoman cavalry, were advancing to attack them. The yeomen corps from Camolin and Carnew had been identified at once. The regulars and yeomen were coming from different directions and presumably all were to attack the insurgents at the same time. Byrne estimated the crowd on Carrigrew Hill at 'about ten or twelve thousand', a crowd with a very small supply of powder and ball since the disaster at Ballyminaun, and without cavalry save for a 'few gentlemen farmers who were still tolerably well mounted, as all the horses had not been taken by the Orangemen'.[9]

The time for analysing options was over. Fr. John Murphy consulted rapidly with the other insurgent chiefs and decided to attack the enemy at once. They chose to attack the forces directly in front of Gorey and if the day went with then to take the town. In this frame of mind, they started to assemble a formation as close as possible to orthodox military custom. The insurgents drew up in Donovan's of Ballymore underneath Carrigrew Hill. Their line was broken into columns and an advance guard of three hundred men was formed, some mounted. The orders were shouted to march upon the Gorey road and the advance guard, of which Miles Byrne was a conspicuous chief, set out in first-rate order. Flanked by sharp shooters, they preceded the main body by about a mile. They marched until they reached Tubberneering Rock where the road elbowed to the right. From that point they could see the redcoats drawn up for battle, their artillery ready to fire. A courageous rebel planted a green banner firmly into the ground near the Rock. A horseman was ordered back to tell the main body of the position and deployments but he had scarcely raised dust when the artillery roared and the muskets fired. A wave of insurgents was blown down.

The shock of this first artillery fire could have ended rebel pretensions there and then, for a great many of the advance guard were killed or severely wounded. Still, the rebels held their ground and then ran through a field towards a high bank which lay between them and the military. This brought them to within half a musket shot of the redcoats. The race to the ditch also cost them dearly for dozens were mown down by musket fire. Once into their new position, however, the rebels with firearms started to pick off redcoats, making each shot count.[10] They were now close enough and sufficiently protected to move the pikemen into action. While Byrne and the advance guard kept the army in front of them occupied, Fr. John with the main column of pikemen raced forward in support, their line of battle shaped like a half moon crescent.

Battle was joined with abandon on both sides as hatred contested with revenge to stimulate uncommon bravery. The military units now in action included the Londonderry Militia, the Armagh Militia, the Tyrone Light Company, the Suffolk Light Company and the hated Welsh regiment known as the 'Ancient Britons', along with local yeoman units.[11]

Colonel Walpole, anticipating active support from General Loftus to the south, moved forward into the main area of the fierce fighting, a conspicuous, almost theatrical figure, well remembered upon a grey horse, dashing furiously from side to side encouraging his troops. The rebels held their nerve to fight like men possessed.

Unknown to Walpole, Miles Byrne's fearless comrades had advanced upon the artillery. Before the drivers had time to lash the horses out of danger, Byrne's men had captured three pieces of artillery, cases of ammunition, gunners and drivers as well. As Walpole rounded the road bend to follow his troops, he was confronted by one of his own six-pounder guns planted in the middle of the road. Fire was opened on him and his astonished force by the rebel musket men and the artillery piece. As the battle raged in intensity, two rebel gunmen who were firing with deliberate aim from a rise of ground both took aim at Walpole. He received the first ball in the thigh. the second went through his head and he fell dead from his horse as the conflict carried on unabated.

Miles Byrne noted:

> Fr. John Murphy apparently with the simplicity of a child was a lion in the fight. In short he knew not nor cared, nor feared danger from the moment he was forced to take the field. He was seen in every critical situation encouraging the men and exposing himself to the greatest danger wherever he thought his presence could be useful. He was so well known that the moment he was perceived there was a general burst of joy and enthusiasm throughout the ranks of [our] army.[12]

Anthony Perry of Inch contributed a tactic that was terrifying to the enemy. He went into combat screaming at the top of his voice. To the redcoats and those who did not know him by name, he was referred to everafter as 'The Screeching General'.[13]

When the main body of rebels with John Murphy, Edward Roche, Michael Murphy and Anthony Perry realised that Byrne's men had captured the enemy artillery, their surge to victory was irresistible. Walpole's troops saw what they thought was the rebel line breaking. Instead, the two newly formed rebel lines set up a war whoop and made towards Gorey to cut off the redcoat retreat, now plainly imminent. An army soldier wrote:

> It was truly painful as we passed along to behold our cannon on the roads useless to us, also the groans of the wounded whose bodies torn and pierced by pikes while yet living rendered the scene altogether very awful. We fought and loaded while running and endeavouring to avoid the fire of our own cannon which were turned upon us by the rebels.[14]

The battle became a rout. Officers, privates, dragoons, cavalry, artillery regulars, yeomen fled from the insurgents. Fleeing enemies were pursued and shot or piked if overtaken. One of the sights was a redcoated black musketeer. Few of the insurgents had ever before laid eyes on a black African. Shouting to an officer in strange accents his words were remembered as, 'Sah, de army runaway! De Armagh [militia] retreat!'[15] The survivors of Walpole's force abandoned hope of recovery. They panicked and in their flight abandoned the town of Gorey, as well as Arklow, the last obstacle before Dublin. Nor did they breathe easily or slacken rein until they dropped down from fatigue in Wicklow town.[16]

The defeat of the government forces at Tubberneering had a much greater effect than was warranted by the military realities. Walpole's redcoats were demoralised when confronted by a captured redcoat gunner whose artillery piece roared grape-shot their way. Furthermore the withering blaze of musket fire with determined pike charges forced the conclusion that the insurgents were a superbly led force commanded by a competent general who knew his business.

While Walpole's troops were being overwhelmed, General Loftus moved his troops north-west toward Tubberneering from the Ballycanew side.[17] His force was composed of regular troops, the Dumbartonshire Highland Regiment and the Fifth Dragoon Guards. Loftus had heard the din of battle, assumed that the rebel rabble had been dispersed and that the business was over. His conclusion was that Walpole would be driving the routed insurgents right into his path to be exterminated. He soon discovered the facts. Startled, he halted his troops and approached the field of battle, picking his way through the tattered and bloody corpses of soldiers scorching in the sun.

Walpole lay sprawled in awkward death alongside his gored horse. Loftus ordered that wandering cavalry horses be shot lest they fall into rebel hands. Then he followed the path of war towards Gorey Hill which he approached with caution until he recognised the rebel army on the summit. He commanded 1,200 effective and well-mounted soldiers with artillery in support. If he did contemplate further action an unexpected round of grape-shot from the hill shattered his resolve and that of his men. He concluded that all was lost, that if attacked and surrounded they would be slaughtered. He ordered the retreat, a retreat across country which was facilitated by a loyalist guide, Brownrigg of Barnadown, who led them over the by-road to Carnew.[18]

Fear of slaughter gradually overwhelmed Loftus and the race to get further away commenced. He decided not to enter Carnew, fearing it would be unsafe. He and his troops sped past the town abandoning the countryside behind them to the insurgents. They did not stop until they had reached Tullow, nine miles past Carnew and almost twenty miles from the disaster at Tubberneering. No further effort by the King's army was to be contemplated other than a campaign fully planned and executed on a war footing. There was nothing now to prevent a massive landing in Wexford by the French.

The insurgents at Tubberneering knew that if time permitted all prisoners in Gorey would be shot by the retreating yeomen without compunction so the redcoats were very closely chased to the town. In the retreat, those who feared the most found time to turn their coats inside out.[19] Weapons and accoutrements were thrown away. Dozens of exhausted redcoats were captured in the fields on the way to Gorey by the fast running pikemen. The town was reached. With Miles Byrne in the lead, the insurgents gained the streets; even as they did, the yeomen were already shooting into the windows of the packed Market House in which over one hundred prisoners were crowded. The rebels reached the Market House in time to rescue the prisoners. Miles Byrne charged ahead in what he was long to recall as the happiest moments of his life, proud to save lives and set so many brave men at liberty.

One of the prisoners was a high-ranking United Irish officer, the greatest prize in their hands had the yeomen at Gorey realised it. He was Esmond Kyan a first cousin of Sir Thomas Esmonde and a former British army artillery officer.[20] When the yeomen opened fire, he ordered everyone in the Market House to lie down flat and had lost not a single man. He was a bluff, high-spirited character, about fifty, and member of a rare Irish eighteenth-century species, a Catholic landed family. A few years previously, he had fought a duel with a debtor and lost an arm. As a result, he had an artificial limb which he manipulated with good humour and dexterity. Though very different in background, he was to share with Dick Monk an impish sense of humour that made bearable the blackest moments. On his release from the Market House he strode into immediate action and authority. Within minutes, he was on his way to Gorey Hill to take charge of the captured artillery. It was Kyan's management of the artillery piece that induced General Loftus to abandon the field.

Fr. John rode alongside his men down into Gorey. Their rejoicing after two disasters was ecstatic. It became another day of welcome and celebration. Confidence was restored. More volunteers came in to join the insurgent army, many from Miles Byrne's area, and the greetings went on for a long time. A friend of Byrne, Denis Doyle, who was a timber merchant in Gorey, could scarcely contain his jubilation when Byrne told him how the battle had been won. Colonel Walpole had openly laid wager in Gorey that morning that the mob on Carrigrew could not resist for twenty minutes. Doyle himself thought it quite impossible that insurgents could prevail against the regular troops he had seen assembled to do battle.

The insurgents did not know how complete the victory had been or the full extent of the army's retreat, but Fr. John was not the sort of man to be swept away by the Bunclody-type counter-attack. The lesson of Bunclody lay heavily on his mind. Miles Byrne was instructed to mount an efficient guard. Assisted by Denis Doyle, Byrne placed guards at every approach into Gorey. A strong guard was placed on the Arklow road from where a counter-attack was likely. Byrne himself chose the men who were to be in charge of each post. He never slackened vigilance. After giving the watchword and the countersign, he made several rounds during the night and found all the men in charge doing their job perfectly well, even though none of them had ever previously undertaken such a duty. The possibility of attack from the most likely point ended when a body of Arklow men came down to Gorey to join the insurgent ranks. It was they who first reported to the insurgents that the survivors of Walpole's force had abandoned Arklow for Wicklow.

With chilling perception, a soldier of the Dumbartonshire Highland Regiment, Sergeant Archibald McLaren, writing of the defeat at Tubberneering and the retreat of the 'Flying Troops' at Gorey and Arklow, concluded with the observation that the day's events 'flattered the sons of rebellion with the fairest prospect of future success'.[21]

On 6 June, the Lord Lieutenant, John Jeffreys Pratt, Earl of Camden, appealed to Secretary Thomas Pelham in London for reinforcements and a competent military commander. 'I hope the spirit of the rebels is broken in the County of Kildare', he wrote, 'but the County of Wexford is a terrible example of their fury and licentiousness ...' Two days later, 8 June, Lord Castlereagh dispatched his estimate of the situation to Secretary Pelham. 'The Rebellion in Wexford has assumed a more serious shape than was to be apprehended from a peasantry, however well organised,' he reported. 'Their numbers are very great, their enthusiasm excited by their priests. I understand from Marshall you are rather inclined to hold the insurrection cheap. Rely upon it, there never was in any country so formidable an effort on the part of the people'.[22]

Chapter 11

The Difficult Road to Dublin

Although the immediate enemy was in disarray, Fr. John's triumphant division remained on Gorey Hill. On the morning after the battle of Tuberneering, Wednesday 6 June, scouts left the camp to reconnoitre. One party set out to burn and destroy all the property that Hunter Gowan possessed.[1] With no hope of laying hands on the magistrate himself, vengeance was taken on his mansion at Mount Nebo, its out offices, stables and barns. The residence with everything in it was burned to the ground, 'poor compensation and no consolation to the unfortunate relations of his victims'.[2]

Insurgents continuously patrolled the roads. Loyalists of significance and loyalists of no importance at all were brought back into Gorey to face examination. Inactivity again beset the leadership and while ten days of ferocity placed unaccustomed pressure on John Murphy, it is difficult to reconcile this dormant phase with his reputation for being 'terribly active' at all times. Frustration must have been growing. Silence also shrouds Fitzgerald, Fr. Michael Murphy, Kyan and the Hays in the days after the rout of their enemies at Tubberneering. Silence in 1798 often betokens unsavoury activity or dissensions. Byrne recorded another factor. The leadership had been told that General Loftus was re-assembling an army at Carnew for another assault on them. They were reluctant to march on Arklow for fear of an attack from their rear. In the meantime, parties of bitter insurgents continued to inflict as much damage as possible on the nearest and most powerful of the malignant ascendancy faction. Two mansions, the properties of extremist enemies, brothers Stephen Ram of Ramsfort, Gorey, and Abel Ram of Clonattin, were looted and burned to the ground.

When attention was brought to bear on the condition of guns, muskets and pikes, it soon became clear that they had not nearly enough gunpowder to tackle a well-equipped enemy. The military necessity of good supply lines and communications began to assume its role and the growing crowd of willing rebels aggravated the situation. The dilemma required urgent solution and the urgency was emphasised when one of the most active and useful leaders of Fr. John's division, Edward Roche of Garrylough, was selected to ride with a party all the way back to Wexford for a supply of gunpowder.[3] He left for Wexford on Wednesday 5 June. The following day was spent in Gorey at a time when Arklow lay deserted. 'This delay,' wrote the modern historian, Charles Dickson, 'was to lead to irretrievable disaster and the loss of many hundreds of lives'. With hindsight this is a valid military assessment; on Thursday, 6 June 1798, on Gorey Hill it was not a peril envisaged by John Murphy and his comrades in the leadership. In addition to the fighting men, refugees, fugitives, women and children, numbering twenty thousand according to Miles Byrne, were assembled on the hill. It was largely on meat that they lived, for it was with great difficulty that rations of bread and other victuals were procured. Offals and hides were left around the hill and in the hottest June of the century it is likely that many insurgents would have died from causes other than active service had it not been for the intelligent efforts of an elderly man, Barnaby Murray of Gorey, who drove into the camp with horse and cart every day and had the hides, bones and offals collected, carried away and buried.[4]

Late on Thursday afternoon, Miles Byrne was detailed to lead a reconnoitring mission to the north-west towards the Wicklow Mountains. Thirty mounted insurgents made up his party. At every village they secured a supply of provisions for the fighting men. Byrne told how they instructed the elderly men who could not bear arms to take the fat cattle off loyalist estates, have them killed, the meat boiled and then brought without delay to Gorey Hill. At the little town of Shillelagh they sighted a superior force of redcoats but Byrne decided it was not the right time for conflict and they returned to the camp. At the camp Fr. John Murphy had received confirmation that General Loftus was assembling an army near Carnew and making 'the greatest preparations'. Loftus had received reinforcements from Tullow, Carlow and other centres.

At last Murphy's urge for action surfaced again and a meeting of the insurgent chiefs was assembled. It was, however, at this stage that the frightful frustration of authority by committee was made acute and personal relations became strained. A man whose voice and thoughts had hitherto not been heard put forward forceful military propositions. He was Captain Philip Hay of the 18th Light Dragoons of the British army (later to claim that he had been forcibly conscripted into the insurgent ranks at Wexford), a brother of John Hay of Ballinkeele already with the rebels since the capture of Enniscorthy and of Edward Hay, a civilian

United Irishman, and thus a member of a leading old Wexford family.[5] Whatever Philip Hay's motives were, and they are in doubt to this day, he pressed for an immediate march on Dublin through Arklow. Despite Philip Hay's military experience, Fr. John Murphy vigorously opposed his proposition, arguing that the better course was to pursue Loftus through Carnew, wipe out his force if possible, take Tullow and open up the Midlands where there were organised United men in the most populous regions.[6] Fr. Michael Murphy supported Philip Hay with equal vigour and in the exchanges a chasm was opened between the two curates in arms. In the din of debate over the next and best objective, John Murphy's inflexible determination swayed the rest of the insurgent chiefs and the decision was taken to march west and engage Loftus at Carnew, without waiting for Edward Roche and his expected ammunition supplies. The march of the rebel thousands on Carnew was scheduled for early next day and in the minds of most was revenge for the vicious shooting of the twenty eight men by the Carnew Yeomen a fortnight earlier.

The insurgents were on the move early on the morning of Friday, 7 June, presenting a sight recorded by a loyalist prisoner:

> The rebel camp covered many acres of ground and their numbers were very great. It was very distressing to my mind to see their colours flying, drums beating and fifes playing, but no military force in the neighbourhood sufficiently powerful to engage them.[7]

The entire division marched against Loftus. Artillery under Kyan, forcibly served by royal artillery men captured at Tubberneering, well-greased muskets and hordes of pikemen packed the road towards Carnew. Miles Byrne had again been sent well ahead of the main body with a mounted detachment to probe as far as the town.[8] Having marched about two miles, Fr. John Murphy and the chiefs at the head of the division saw Miles Byrne's patrol returning. They pressed forward for details. Byrne reported that Carnew was abandoned by the Crown forces. Despite this information, the division still marched on to Carnew, propelled irresistibly by the wrath of the fighting men who had relatives and friends killed, flogged and pitchcapped in that detested loyalist stronghold. They occupied the town without any opposition.

In a short time the greater part of Carnew was in flames.[9] The malthouse of Robert Blayney was left intact, for his constant humanity and political neutrality were remembered. Not so with his publicly Orange brother, Ralph, whose property and possessions were burnt systematically to ashes. The remainder of the day was spent with insurgents wreaking vengeance on an empty town. No voice comes back to us from that day to echo protest from Fr. John, but it takes little deductive power to glean from the action that his authority over that mass of insurgents was of no avail. He was unable to pursue Loftus as he had so strenuously and vehemently insisted.

The insurgents eventually pulled out of Carnew and congregated on Kilcavan Hill outside it, leaving little to be seen except a giant column of smoke visible for over thirty miles. When one and all had gathered, a leadership meeting was hurriedly assembled. At once another new but authoritative voice proposed an alternative plan. It was offered by the Wicklow United Irish leader, Garret Byrne.[10] He proposed that he should set out and lead an advance force of six or eight thousand men and approach Dublin through the Wicklow mountain terrain he knew thoroughly, avoiding battle but keeping the approaches open and safe. This plan found immediate favour and was unanimously adopted, but it had scarcely reached the active orders stage when the situation altered drastically. Firm reports were brought to the leaders on Kilcavan Hill that Arklow had been re-occupied by the regular army, militia and yeoman units, and by reinforcements that had been rushed from Dublin with the greatest of effort in carriages, jaunting cars, carts, wagons and buggies.[11]

This news created consternation. In the new situation it seemed as if the government and loyalists had signalled Arklow as the vital bulwark against chaos. The question of their most urgent immediate objective was thrown open again and thrown open violently. The exchange of opinions became angry but most grievous of all was the antagonism which anger bred between John and Michael Murphy.[12]

Arklow was now a fortress astride the road to Dublin guarded by horse, foot and artillery. Fr. Michael Murphy strenuously pressed for a head-on assault immediately on this formidable obstacle. Fr. John Murphy insisted on the Garret Byrne plan, agreed unanimously shortly before. He hotly opposed Fr. Michael's line of reasoning and in the ensuing arguments, for and against, old ill-feelings may have surfaced. Fr. John, emboldened by success, was but a new convert to revolt; Fr. Michael was a veteran United Irish activist who scorned his bishop's authority while Fr. John toed the line; Fr. John handed over arms to magistrates while Fr. Michael recruited men to fight; Fr. John, hero of Enniscorthy and Oulart Hill, Fr. Michael the presiding officer at Ballyminaun's disaster; Fr. John, a rebel for a mere fortnight, now a dominant and domineering force who rushed away from an empty Arklow to follow the phantom army of Loftus. Spoken or unspoken, the fuel to fray nerve ends was there; the eventual result was that Fr. John Murphy was beaten down in the argument. He was outvoted by the other chiefs all of whom sided with Fr. Michael and although he remained convinced that it was the wrong decision, he was compelled to accept it.

The insurgents returned to Gorey to prepare for the hard battle which was now looming. Next morning, Saturday 8 June, they reassembled on Gorey Hill. Battle preparations were made but the day became riveted in the memory not as the eve of major conflict but as the day of Perry's revenge. Perry's local followers had scoured their own countryside in a wide sweep around Gorey and arrived back to the camp with prisoners of significance. How they were captured or why they were even in the vicinity is not clear, for the captured prisoners were identified as being amongst the most vicious yeomen in north Wexford. Among them was Reverend Roger Owen, Established Church rector of Camolin, a magistrate who had personally pitchcapped United Irish prisoners.

Owen was recognised and at once a rush of insurgents descended on him. Struggling with his guards were men who would have torn him limb from limb with pleasure, and no one was more aware of that than Owen himself. Miles Byrne ran to the scene of commotion and with the greatest difficulty got the men of fury to leave Owen alone for the time being. Several times Miles Byrne had to intervene to save Owen being savaged, for to north Wexford insurgents who had suffered under him, a clean musket shot offered him too easy a repose.[13]

Anthony Perry came forward to examine the prisoners and as if clutching at a long-lost comrade or enemy believed dead he laid his hands on two particular yeomen.[14] He yanked them forward. Both were active and violent men from his own area and from Perry's instant reaction they must have been implicated in his own betrayal, arrest and torture. One was Rogan of the Arklow Yeoman Corps, the other a man who had never disguised his zeal for terrorism before defenceless people, irrespective of sex or age. He was James Wheatley of the Castletown Yeoman Corps.

Perry stared at Wheatley when he dragged him out. He then said, 'I am giving you five minutes to prepare yourself for death'. Roger Owen cried out to Perry whether there was any appeal. 'I will hear no pleas in his favour', Perry replied.[15] A long time was taken to kill Wheatley. Perry fired three shots into his body. He was not killed and remained conscious. He asked for water. Then he told the executioners around him that he had ammunition in his pocket and requested them to put him out of pain. He was next shot in the thigh and then eventually he was released by a fifth shot in the head.

Rogan was next attended to but he did not have to wait for death as long as Wheatley. Every one of the prisoners was certain to be given like treatment for no one dared interfere with Perry, not Fr. John, not Miles Byrne, no senior United man; Perry's own scars and constant suffering made retribution palatable and he was by no means finished inflicting it.

The executions were interrupted abruptly by the return of Edward Roche and his detachment from the gunpowder mission to Wexford.[16] They brought an order from the Commander-in-Chief, Bagenal Harvey, which put a halt to the executions. The prisoners were actually on their knees facing a firing squad and a line of pikemen as Roche read out the written order. Amongst its stipulations there were some of immediate relevance:

> At a meeting of the general and several officers of the united army of the county of Wexford, the following resolutions were agreed upon:
>
> It is ordered, that a guard shall be kept in the rear of the different armies, with orders to shoot all persons who shall shy or desert from any engagement; and that these orders shall be taken notice of by all officers commanding in such engagement. All men refusing to obey their superior officers, to be tried by a court-martial and punished according to their sentence.
>
> It is also ordered, that all men who shall attempt to leave their respective quarters when they have been halted by the commander in chief, shall suffer death, unless they shall have leave from their officers for so doing.
>
> It is also resolved, that any person or persons who shall take upon them to kill or murder any person or prisoner, burn any house, or commit any plunder, without special written orders from the commander in chief, shall suffer death.
>
> By order of
> B.B. Harvey, Commander in Chief
> Francis Breen, Sec. and adj.
> Head Quarters, Carrickbyrne camp
> June 6, 1798

The resolutions were read out to a chorus of angry roars. Why should the monsters be spared? Men who had treated defenceless people like vermin? They had flogged honest men to death and now they were to be protected? The prisoners who so narrowly escaped execution were prodded back down into Gorey town and lodged under heavy guard in the Market House. Despite reprieve, Owen was a constant goad to revenge by his very presence. An idea gained ground, a substitute for total satisfaction. Why not give Owen and the other yeomen prisoners a dose of their own medicine? Why not pitchcap them and let them take their chance to live or die, just like the wretched croppies they pitchcapped themselves and then released, hand-bound, to run mad in their agony? The idea found favour during the night. Next morning the dreadful punishment was carried out. Owen and the other yeomen with him had their heads sheared and were pitchcapped.[17]

Edward Roche had been busy in Wexford and so had Harvey's printing press. Roche decided that a statement of intent and proper motive must be issued. He accordingly composed and published a proclamation.

TO THE PEOPLE OF IRELAND
Countrymen and fellow-soldiers!

Your patriotic exertions in the cause of your country have hitherto exceeded your most sanguine expectations, and in a short time must ultimately be crowned with success. Liberty has raised her drooping head: thousands daily flock to her standard: the voice of her children everywhere prevails. Let us then, in the moment of triumph, return thanks to the almighty ruler of the universe, that a total stop has been put to those sanguinary measures which of late were but too often resorted to by the creatures of government, to keep the people in slavery.

Nothing now, my countrymen, appears necessary to secure the conquests you have already won, but an implicit obedience to the commands of your chiefs; for through a want of proper subordination and discipline, all may be endangered.

At this eventful period, all Europe must admire, and posterity will read with astonishment, the heroic acts achieved by people strangers to military tactics, and having few professional commanders: but what power can resist men fighting for liberty!

In the moment of triumph, my countrymen, let not your victories be tarnished with any wanton act of cruelty: many of those unfortunate men now in prison were not your enemies from principle; most of them, compelled by necessity, were obliged to oppose you: neither let a difference in religious sentiments cause a difference among the people.

Recur to the debates in the Irish House of Lords on the 19th of February last; you will there see a patriotic and enlightened protestant bishop with manly eloquence pleading for catholic emancipation and parliamentary reform, in opposition to the haughty arguments of the lord chancellor, and the powerful opposition of his fellow courtiers.

To promote a union of brotherhood and affection among our countrymen of all religious persuasions, has been our principal object: we have sworn in the most solemn manner – have associated for this laudable purpose, and no power on earth shall shake our resolution.

> To my protestant soldiers, I feel much indebted for their gallant behaviour in the field, where they exhibited signal proofs of bravery in the cause.
>
> Wexford, June 7, 1798
> EDWARD ROCHE

Roche brought Fr. Murphy and the other leaders news of all that had transpired elsewhere during the week.[18] It was very bad news. Harvey's division had captured New Ross, rested, and lost it again. Several hundreds had been killed and wounded; many hundreds more were missing after a long days' battle. John Kelly of Killanne was badly wounded. While the battle was at its height, a mob of camp followers had burned to death a barn full of loyalist prisoners back at Scullabogue without mercy. The horror of a hundred defenceless prisoners given slow and awful death by wretches far from the peril of combat had sickened and depressed all the fighting men but Bagenal Harvey's morale was crippled. In addition, he was bitterly blamed for the defeat at New Ross. The man who was elected clear and unrivalled Commander-in-Chief at Wexford one week previously resigned his command. He had issued his last general order on 6 June with the ghastly murders of Scullabogue and the defeat at Ross overwhelming him. It was with astonishment that Fr. John Murphy heard that Harvey was succeeded in the command by a man whose stature in the society of the United Irishmen had been inadequately appreciated, the priest estimated by his bishop as an obnoxious agitator, Fr. Philip Roche. The survivors of the debacle at Ross were now camped well outside the town at Carrickbyrne, hoping for a favourable opportunity to launch another attack.

The only spark of favourable news brought back by Edward Roche was the capture of a ship off the Wexford coast by insurgent sloops. On board the ship were several officers, amongst whom was the most important establishment and enemy figure to fall into their hands, the Earl of Kingsborough, Commander of the North Cork Militia. He was identified and then taken under heavy guard to be imprisoned and kept alive in the cellar of a famous Wexford tavern, the *Cape of Good Hope* in the Bullring.

The defeat and heavy losses at New Ross were hard to absorb. The news might have quenched the spirit to carry on the revolt but instead it had the opposite effect. It steeled the determination of the leaders to advance north. Miles Byrne, after a distinguished career in the French army, recalled his reasons for optimism. That the division was not in want of chiefs to lead them to victory was his consolation for they 'had still Fr. John Murphy and Fr. Michael Murphy, both enjoying immense influence amongst the fighting men'. He was pleased with the presence of Perry and Esmond Kyan but mentioned not one of the other chiefs by name.

Fr. John Murphy himself had, however, to reckon with the fact that there were times when he had no control at all, nor did he possess any more than an equal voice at times of decision in a leadership group which had grown by two, Perry and Kyan, in recent days. In the situation obtaining, it could not be otherwise but the restless energy which moved Fr. John Murphy all his life was now in danger of consuming him as time was frittered away. Furthermore, his embrace of revolt contrary to his previous and recent discipline was exhausting him mentally. His own calling, what his Dominican superiors in Seville defined as his 'sacred mission,' was not easily discarded. He had to reflect on the terrible changes in fourteen days as he celebrated Mass for his men that Sunday morning on the open hillside outside Gorey. By that morning John Murphy had reached the end of his energy.

Delays which rarely blighted a regular force plagued an insurgent army.[19] Even as the sun rose high there were fighting men returning to the camp, men who had actually gone home the previous evening to see if their houses and families were safe. Edward Roche distributed the meagre supply of gunpowder he had been allowed at Wexford. When every preparation had been finalised, the only satisfactory weaponry was the artillery captured at Tubberneering. These guns, under the command of Esmond Kyan helped by Dick Monaghan, were tolerably well supplied with ammunition and were still being attended under threat by the redcoat gunners captured along with them.

There were less than 2,000 guns, some of which had become damaged in inexperienced hands and there were no gunsmiths in the camp. Neither were there blacksmiths present to repair pikes since the yeomen and militia had swept north Wexford clean of those vital and valuable men, now shot, transported or in prison. There were between three to four thousand pikes and the remainder of the rebels preparing to march were armed with farm implements, slash hooks, scythes, pitchforks and bill-hooks. The estimate of the numbers of effective fighting rebels fit for battle was much less than the 20,000 crowd reckoned by Miles Byrne to be camped around Gorey Hill.[20]

It was ten o'clock in the morning before the orders to march were shouted across Gorey Hill. The formed columns, the green banners, the artillery, the musket carriers, the pikemen in long lines, all were under way in memorable procession bearing down on Gorey's Main Street. Fr. John Murphy rode his mare in the midst of men blithely facing a lightly estimated task. As he rode down the Main Street, his eyes focussed on an awesome spectacle. Pushed and held by rebel guards halfway out of the top storey windows of the Market House for all to see was the pitchcapped Roger Owen. Stuck fast to his head was the pitch-holding cone cap. At the other windows, the yeomen who had been pitchcapped with him that morning were similarly displayed. The salute of the cheering and shouting throng was taken by this macabre tableau. As they marched underneath the insurgents raised their banners and caps, their pikes and muskets as high in the air as they could reach in unanimous approval of a job well done.[21]

At this time despite two major reverses, the United Irishmen controlled all of Wexford, its major port and landing beaches, the only exceptions being New Ross, Bunclody and Duncannon fort. They also controlled south-west Wicklow from Arklow to Carnew and for all practical purposes the adjacent Wicklow Mountains. From the Crown's point of view, things had gone very wrong. The 'peasant' revolt had taken place but far from being eliminated it had taken wings, a frightening echo of the French Revolution. The Wexford countrymen had provided the great surprise. Untrained and badly armed, they could fight splendidly. They were well built, well fed, superbly fit, dominant in close fighting with the pike, fearless in front of cannon and, as proven at New Ross, could fight on their feet for twelve hours. Here was an enemy that could win the day. Ireland could be lost and the security of England greatly endangered. King George III was informed that his viceroy in Ireland, Lord Camden, could not answer for the consequences unless massive reinforcements were sent from England immediately. His Majesty agreed. Furthermore, 'He trusted that as the sword was drawn it be not returned to the sheath until the whole country had submitted without conditions. The making of any compromise would be perfect destruction'.[22]

A former viceroy, the Marquis of Buckingham, an expert on tides, gave a comprehensive evaluation of the tides on Wexford's east coast. 'The effect of a landing in force on the beach would be very decisive'.[23] Already, many members of Ireland's power-wielding ascendancy families had concluded that their society was about to be torn apart. Evacuation to England took place from all parts, north and south and from the capital, Dublin. The wives and families of Anglican bishops, military officers, government officials, earls and other assorted ascendancy grades turned the trickle of evacuees into a torrent. Amongst them were many whose flight gave an indication of the changes wrought. One lady who abandoned Ireland in the greatest secrecy was Lady Camden, wife of the viceroy. The family of General Nugent fled. The brothers and sisters of one of the most influential men on the Viceroy's staff, Lord Castlereagh, also fled. The proximate ports in England and Wales had a refugee crisis, food and shelter problems, unprecedented in their history. In Milford Haven 'the distress of refugees, mostly of the genteeler sort, was particularly acute'.[24]

The insurgents marched with unhurried gaiety to attack Arklow.[25] Miles Byrne recalled the day in terms which inadvertently emphasised the conditions which dismayed the chief to whom he was devoted, Fr. John Murphy. 'Never did I witness anything before like the joy that seemed to brighten every countenance ... it had more the appearance of a march to some great place of amusement than to a battle field'. There was no urgency and this added to the frustration that was corroding John Murphy's heart. They were on the wrong route, he was convinced, and they were strolling. There was no comparison between this day's movement and the eager, forceful, disciplined assault on Enniscorthy. As they ambled along he grew in bitterness, a mood intensified by mental and physical strain. 'You are going to be defeated', he was heard to say, 'for it is too late in the day'.[26]

There was much amiss with John Murphy. If this bustling man who had driven his men like work-horses in battle was permitting lethargy to paralyse the division, then something indeed was seriously astray. There have been many explanations. One (disproved by his own activity) suggested that he was reluctant to fight outside county Wexford; another that it was the antagonism with Fr. Murphy and Philip Hay over strategy and the disaster at Ballyminaun Hill; yet another maintained that the turbulent somersaults his life had absorbed over the last three weeks had exhausted him, a novice in a military campaign. Whatever it was, the march on Arklow was unmanageable when harsh authority was needed.

After strolling for five hours during which they fed themselves on oaten meal and vegetables,the insurgents had covered a mere nine miles and were still more than a mile from Arklow. They had stopped outside Anthony Perry's home at Inch, where they called for cheers in his honour. Perry, also saw the danger and implored them to move on, but it was no use. That the day was young was a repeated observation. Insubordination had taken over. The discipline of a professional army could not be imposed and several hours were spent dawdling while a crowd of insurgents drank the village of Coolgreaney dry. When eventually they were routed out and the main body had rested, the insurgent army again faced towards Arklow. It was three o'clock in the afternoon and it was about then that John Murphy, whatever the precise cause, reached a personal crisis. He withdrew with his mare from the column of men easing their way towards Arklow and remained behind at Castletown.[27] Battle by committee directive was about to be put to the grimmest of tests without him.

Fr. Murphy was within earshot of Arklow when the artillery fire started shortly before four o'clock.[28] The crashing din of battle echoed across the countryside in unabated fury for one hour; then a second hour, a third and fourth. At eight o'clock the firing eased. The artillery was silent. There was only musket fire and after that ceased, silence clothed the land. Fr. Murphy pulled himself together, saddled up his mare and turned her head for Arklow.

Slowly the first insurgents came to Fr. John in tatters and in sweat, bloody and dejected. Their ammunition was spent. They were pulling back. Fr. Michael Murphy was dead in the streets. Hundreds had been blown to pieces, hundreds severely injured, hundreds abandoned. The full magnitude of the day's desolation was hard enough to bear but another factor angrily complained of was that there was no overall commander at the battle.[29] The ineptitude of divided command on that day was an invitation to the disaster which befell the insurgents. There was a vague central plan of attack but when it failed there was only improvisation.

When the first of the chiefs came back to Fr. John, he was told that no one knew who was issuing the orders that came down the line. Miles Byrne could not even tell him who it was who had issued the order to withdraw, or, indeed, why it was issued. In Byrne's sector, the Government troops were already on the run. They could see the redcoats in retreat across the bridge and up the Dublin road. Byrne was overwhelmed by fury. Another town, there for the taking, had been won and lost. Although he never laid the charge at Fr. John's door, he bemoaned the lack of one enterprising chief who could have followed up victory at Arklow to march on the city of Dublin, 'where they should have mustered a hundred thousand men'. To cap it all, two prominent county Wexford Catholics in the Castletown Yeoman Cavalry were seen fighting against them, Sir Thomas Esmonde of Ballinastragh, Esmond Kyan's cousin, and Laurence Doyle.[30]

Scores of wounded, shocked insurgents of Fr. John's division came by, exhausted and spiritless men. Gone was the braggadocio of the morning. 'No one in command!' The phrase was being repeated. 'What we wanted', said Byrne, 'was a commander-in-chief who should have been chosen by all the other chiefs previous to the battle and whose orders alone should have been punctually executed, and no other that did not emanate from him'. In hindsight, Byrne, the war veteran, would still have had the untrained curate of Boolavogue as the general-in-chief of the insurgent army.[31]

Everyone had a reason for the debacle. Some castigated the drinking and insubordination at Coolgreaney. Esmond Kyan reported that the royal artillery prisoners servicing the guns under pike threat deliberately misdirected their fire until he and Dick Monk detected what they were doing. Miles Byrne now regretted the assault on Carnew, the time spent repairing themselves in Gorey and the fact that they used artillery at the start of the battle instead of running the pikemen in to kill the redcoats right away. Garrett Byrne of Wicklow had distinguished himself at Arklow. He was convinced that they quit the field on the point of victory, although his men had used their last round and had no more to fire.[32] Esmond Kyan fought with the colourful Dick Monk, captain of Wexford's John Street Corps at his side.[33] Seeing the havoc created by the enemy guns with insurgents being 'tumbled in twenties', 'Monk' shouted to Kyan to direct their own artillery onto that point.

Monk with men of his John Street Corps now served the guns for Kyan whose very first shot passed through the enemy's ammunition cart. '£100 for a soldier!' Kyan shouted. His next shot made a direct hit on one of the guns, breaking its carriage in bits and killing all thirteen of the artillery crew. Even in adversity, Kyan's wit sparkled. When his artificial limb was blown away by a cannon shot, he hesitated not a second. 'My loose timbers are flying, God bless the mark', he cried 'and now for the right arm of the British line!'

Fr. Michael Murphy fought hard to the end in Arklow.[34] Answering an insurgent's despairing cry, 'We have no one to lead us', he grabbed a fallen banner, green with a white cross and the new slogan of revolution, 'Liberty or Death', appended. He rallied men nearby, led the charge and was killed by cannon fire. Not so brave but more prudent was Captain Philip Hay, his supporter in planning. Hay was seen absconding when the issue became clear.[35]

As darkness fell, the insurgents remained on the ground outside Arklow. Miles Byrne wanted to have fires lit to indicate that they were encamped there for the night with the intention of resuming the attack on the town next morning. The fear of renewed attack alone, he felt, would have caused a loyalist flight to Dublin. But there was no new attack and the night screened only the business of rescuers. Working at speed, they carried away as many wounded rebels as possible. The dead could not be buried and the wounded who could not be reached had to be left behind. There were no fewer than 1,000 casualties, dead or wounded, at the most reliable count, and a total of nine cartloads of wounded were extracted from the ruins of Arklow and brought back to Gorey.[36]

The wounded who were abandoned behind the enemy lines met their inevitable fate. Sergeant Archibald McLaren of the Dumbartonshire Highlanders recorded:

> On the Monday after the battle a yeoman found an old servant of his wounded in a ditch and while he was bringing him to the General, had it not been for the intervention of an officer, the soldiers would have killed him. On the same afternoon two men were

found among straw in one of the fishermen's huts. Tuesday afternoon a courtmartial sat and in the afternoon the three were hanged upon three trees in the centre of the town. The yeoman's servant said he would die by the Green; and strange to say, yet true it is, that as he hung a small piece of a green branch fell into his bosom by way of a posie.[37]

Miles Byrne held that they should have won Arklow had they pressed home their advantage, but the town remained in the keeping of the King's troops, a fortress astride the road to Dublin which the rebels had failed to take. On the opposite side, McLaren accounted the battle as an episode of clinical military precision which contrasted with the hopeless inefficiency of the rebel leadership. General Needham had been solidly prepared for the battle, commanding a mixture of veteran soldiers, militia and yeoman regiments, with artillery in strong and well-prepared positions on the outskirts of the town. Five pieces of field artillery had decimated the attacking waves of rebels but still they had persisted in throwing themselves at the government lines.

Needham in his report stated that the insurgents' perseverance was surprising. 'Their efforts to take the guns on our right was most daring, advancing even to the muzzles where they fell in great numbers'.[38] Detachments of pikemen had fought and broken through the front line and fired the houses of the town. Sections of Needham's cavalry had pursued retreating pikemen only to find themselves surrounded and then piked. Some of the garrison, believing the town and their lives forfeit, had retreated northwards across the bridge.

The Viceroy Lord Camden on receipt of the report from Arklow was not considering a victory. Taking it in conjunction with the news from Ulster and the possible arrival of the French, he came to the grave conclusion that: 'It merely confirms the awful situation of the country. It would only need a small French force to make their immense peasant armies, inflamed with religious enthusiasm, almost invincible. Yet how would they tackle the rebels? If they attacked too soon they risked another defeat; if too late they risked losing the capital'.[39] His staffman, Lord Castlereagh, confirmed in writing on 13 June that the government calculations had gone wildly astray in county Wexford. 'The rebellion in Wexford', he wrote, 'has disappointed all my speculations. I had not a conception that insurgents could remain together and act in such numbers'.[40]

On 10 June, the day after the battle of Arklow, London appointed Lord Charles Cornwallis to be the new political and military commander in Ireland.[41] He was to be Viceroy and also Commander-in-Chief. His immediate brief was to win the war. Camden was recalled to London.

On the day of Cornwallis's appointment, the military situation in Ireland had deteriorated for the Crown. In Ulster the counties of Antrim and Down were in open revolt.[42]

The Bible and Rosary beads belonging to Fr. Michael Murphy (now in the possession of his collateral descendant, Michael Murphy. *(Photograph courtesy of M. Murphy).*

Chapter 12

Revolt goes on

The defeat at Arklow, the heavy losses and the news that Fr. Michael Murpy had been killed affected Fr. John Murphy deeply, all the more so because of their heated opposition over the plan of campaign for the division. The news was doubly distressing for its gruesome details and the participation in hostilities for the first time of the most significant landlord in John Murphy's life, Lord Mountnorris. He was at Arklow with his Camolin Yeoman Cavalry. The once affable earl was venomous with mortification at what he regarded as betrayal on his own estates by priests and congregations. He ordered a butcher to cut off Fr. Michael's head along with his left arm and then had them both thrown into a burning house.[1] 'Let his body go where his soul is', was the noble lord's reported valedictory salute to a brave foe.[2] The ferocious 'Ancient Britons' were said to have cut his heart out, roasted the body and oiled their boots with the grease, an outlandish rumour, but true or false the news primed hatred to a fierce intensity.[3]

John Murphy might well have buckled under the weight of defeat and horror and a sense of personal guilt for the disaster at Arklow. For him there was no consolation in the belief held by surviving chiefs that the swing of battle had hinged on tactics, or in Miles Byrne's assertion that they would have gained the day had they pressed home their advantage. He now knew the weakness of the division, of the entire insurgent army of untrained, badly armed volunteer troops without sufficiently experienced military leadership at any level and apt to follow their own inclinations. He knew he should have led them in the battle for the town or else have ridden to the first sound of the guns. Instead he had remained at Castletown blocked in a cul-de-sac of the mind. Some of the men were asking questions he could not answer. Where were the French? How much more was expected of them before the French came or the Government sent an army to annihilate them?

118

Whatever about the answers, Fr. John knew the fight had to go on. They did not have a choice.

After the battle for Arklow, Fr. John's battered division returned to Gorey Hill and remained there for two days. Esmond Kyan was, however, compelled to leave them for Wexford in order to recover from his injuries. Battle experiences were exchanged by the weary men. Despite the disastrous defeat, it was held by the majority that, face-to-face in field combat, out in the open spaces, they were more than a match for the enemy. It had been seen that the King's troops had avoided the pikemen at Arklow, and the leaders of the division agreed that another attempt should be made to take the town. As a first stage, they planned to draw Needham's forces into the open fields by moving camp and marching and counter-marching temptingly close to the enemy lines.[4] But caution prevailed in Arklow and there was no offensive sortie by loyalist troops. Instead there was a preference for the slaughter of defenceless non-combatants. Units of the 'Ancient Britons' accompanied by yeoman cavalry sallied into safe areas and butchered without discrimination as they 'glutted their ferocious appetites in most monstrous deeds'.[5] The fury of total war spread and there were few who were not seared as affrays of revenge and counter-revenge mounted. Rebels left the camp to inspect their homes after the battle of Arklow; some never came back.

A proclamation issued from the United Irishmen's headquarters in Wexford was distributed to the leaders in Gorey. It took the form of a 'wanted criminal' notice in which four of the most notorious magistrates were named:

> *Proclamation of the people of the County of Wexford*
> Whereas it stands manifestly notorious, that James Boyd, Hawtry White, Hunter Gowan, and Archibald Hamilton Jacob, late magistrates of this county, have committed the most horrid acts of cruelty, violence, and oppression against our peaceable and well affected countrymen. Now we, the people, associated and united for the purpose of procuring our just rights, and being determined to protect the persons and properties of those of all religious persuasions, who have not oppressed us, and are willing with heart and hand to join our glorious cause, as well as to show our marked disapprobation and horror of the crimes of the above delinquents, do call on our countrymen at large to use every exertion in their power to apprehend the bodies of the aforesaid James Boyd, Hawtry White, Hunter Gowan and Archibald Hamilton Jacob, and to secure and convey them to the gaol of Wexford, to be brought before the tribunal of the people.

Done at Wexford, this 9th day of June, 1798.

God save the People[6]

Clearly, headquarters was not aware that Jacob and Boyd had fled to safe anchorage or that Gowan and White were not in the area held by their divisions. Roger Owen languished in the Market House in Gorey in daily danger of further retribution.[7] After the Arklow battle, men he had pitchcapped determined to pike him. Miles Byrne had to intervene again to save him. He pointed out Owen's own raw pitchcap scars, similiar to those the men themselves bore. Owen began to feign insanity. Having noted some young girls amongst those who came to the Market House to satisfy their curiosity, he offered his services to marry any of them who wished to be joined in wedlock with the boys of their choice. It happened that a boy and girl were near him at this point. He advanced, joined their hands and thereupon began the marriage service. The girl let out a shriek and ran from the Market House.

Demented or not, Owen was compelled to show his pitchcapped head from the upper windows of the Market House whenever a body of insurgents marched through the street. Miles Byrne recorded how fortunate it was for him that the windows were very high from the ground. The pikes could not reach him. A strong guard was constantly on duty at the Market House, for nothing less could protect the prisoners, some of whom were obnoxious beyond definition and among these Reverend Roger Owen had an unchallenged lead. Patrick Redmond, a captain in the Coolgreaney United Irishmen, organised a field court before which the prisoners in the Market House were brought to trial. Those found guilty, Owen included, were ordered to be marched to Wexford under a safe escort. Such escort duties were restricted to men like those in Dick Monk's John Street Corps who had not suffered the torments of the rural areas and consequently were less likely to seek summary revenge.

Owen requested that he might be allowed to see Fr. Francis Kavanagh, parish priest of Camolin. Kavanagh was quickly contacted and informed. He agreed to go to the Market House in Gorey and there he was confronted by the shocking spectacle of Owen. Horrified he procured refreshments for him and promised that he would gain his release from custody. Owen's wits sharpened as he realised that Owen released was Owen lynched. He firmly refused Kavanagh's offer and insisted on being brought a prisoner under guard to Wexford jail. Still wearing the cone pitchcap, he was led on foot down the long hot road to Wexford under escort.[8]

On Wednesday 12 June, a new proposal to take the action to the enemy was given the backing of the chiefs.[9] A garrison was left on the

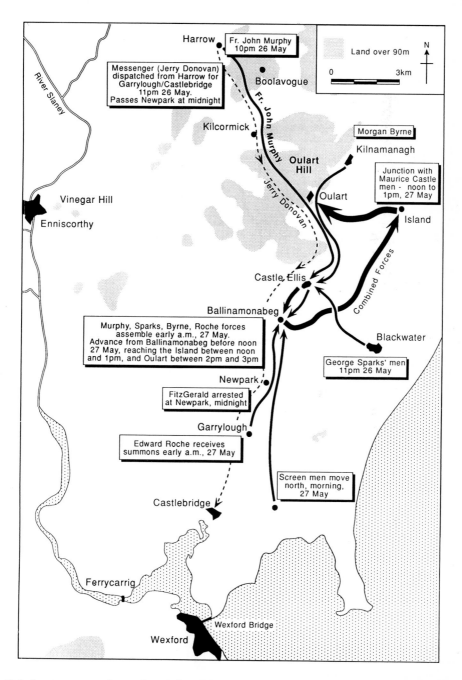

Rebel movements from the night of the outbreak of rebellion, 25 May, until Whit Sunday, 26 May. *(Based partly on the work of L. M. Cullen). (Map: Mathew Stout).*

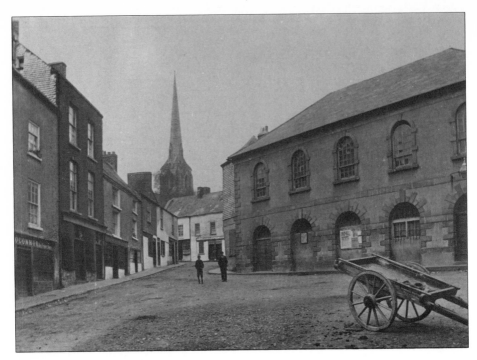

The Cornmarket, Wexford town, c.1900. With the exception of the church spire, this was the late eighteenth-century view of the principal shopping area of the town. The triumphant rebels entered the Cornmarket through the nearby St. John's Gate on 30 May, 1798. The whitewashed shops at the top of the Cornmarket were in Back Street, where the local clergy lodged. *(William Lawrence).*

Oliver Sheppard's superb sculpture *The Wexford Pikeman,* shortly after its erection in the Bullring, Wexford, in 1905. *(William Lawrence).*

Johnstown Castle, county Wexford. The ivy-draped tower at the left of the nineteenth-century entrance was the residence of Cornelius Grogan.

General Edward Roche of Garrylough. *(From a contemporary miniature).*

Esmond Kyan of Mount Howard. *(The '98 Centenary Album).*

The Battle of The Three Rocks. *(From a photograph by J. Hayes of a painting by Fr. E. Foran 1898).*

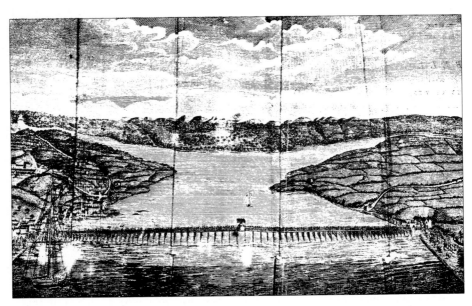

A view of Wexford Bridge, 1798. *(Taylor's **History of the Rebellion**).*

The Market House in Gorey. *(G. Leacy).*

The Main Street of Bunclody, seen from the elevation on the Carlow side. From this vantage point, the Main Street and Square were raked by gunfire inflicting considerable casualties on the occupying insurgents. *(J. B. Curtis).*

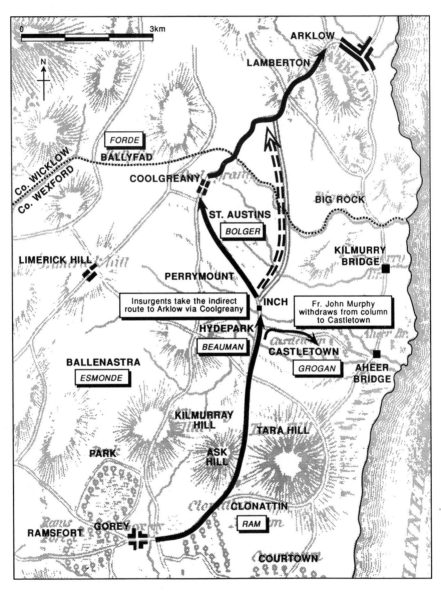

The insurgent's approach to Arklow. *(Mathew Stout).*

Map labels:
0 3km
N
ARKLOW
LAMBERTON
FORDE
BALLYFAD
Co. WICKLOW
Co. WEXFORD
COOLGREANY
BIG ROCK
ST. AUSTINS
BOLGER
KILMURRY BRIDGE
LIMERICK HILL
PERRYMOUNT
Insurgents take the indirect route to Arklow via Coolgreany
INCH
Fr. John Murphy withdraws from column to Castletown
HYDEPARK
BEAUMAN
CASTLETOWN
GROGAN
AHEER BRIDGE
BALLENASTRA
ESMONDE
KILMURRAY HILL
TARA HILL
PARK
ASK HILL
CLONATTIN
RAM
RAMSFORT
GOREY
COURTOWN

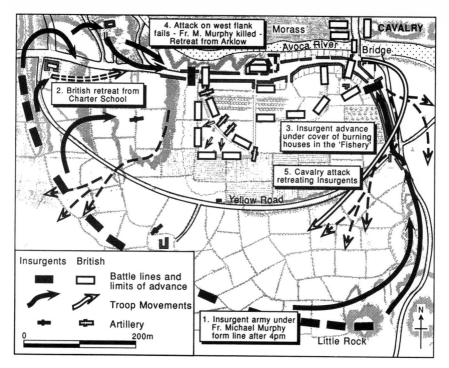

The Battle of Arklow. *(Redrawn by Mathew Stout from Musgrave's **Memoirs**).*

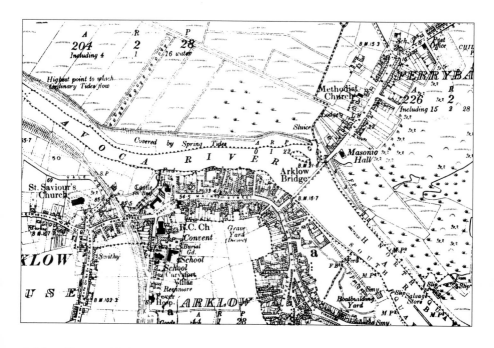

Arklow Town c.1900.

1 Light Infantry with Howitzer.
2 Gen. Lake where his Horse was killed.
3 Gen. Wilford's Brigade.
4 & 5 Gen. Dundas's Brigade.
6 Gen. Loftus's Brigade.
7 Gen. Sr. Js. Duff's Brigade.
8 Rebels Fort of Vinegar Hill.
9 Rebel Lines & forest of Pikes.
10 Ennisworthy side of the Slaney.

Contemporary view of the Battle of Vinegar Hill from the north-east side. (*Musgrave's* **Memoirs**).

hill of Gorey and the main body, rested and in fair order, moved forward to a dominant hill four miles north of Gorey, five miles outside Arklow and five miles from another loyalist enclave, the town of Tinahely. This was Limerick Hill, on whose summit roads converged from north, south, east and west. The move failed to lure either regular detachments or yeoman cavalry to battle and by next day the only enemy activity was the indiscriminate killing of people in their homes.

A phase of revenge developed, intensifying the retaliatory killings.[10] Neither Fr. John nor Miles Byrne could control time-wasting forays from Limerick Hill. Two days went by as atrocity answered atrocity. Insurgents searched for the two Tompkin brothers attached to Hunter Gowan's yeomanry corps, who had instigated several brutal murders. The brothers escaped but their father, John, was piked to death in their stead.[11]

Although enemy reinforcements were daily arriving at Arklow and other points encircling north Wexford, all efforts to entice out General Needham and the Arklow garrison ended in failure. There was no sign of the French, nor was there any news of the expected extension of the revolt in Ulster. The Wexford insurgents were not aware that the Northern United Irishmen had suffered crushing defeat at the battle of Antrim on 7 June, and again at Ballinahinch on 13 June and that all organised resistance in the northern counties had been brought to an end.

Of even greater and more far-reaching consequence than defeat in the field, however, were the accounts of the insurrection in Wexford which were now filling the Belfast papers.[12] These incited the most bitter Protestant reaction, for they reported the revolt in Wexford as a holy war of extermination of Protestants and the Protestant religion by Catholics. The role of John Murphy, Michael Murphy and a few other Catholic priests lent credence. Before any unsavoury episodes had occurred, the news from Wexford already featured accounts of 'killing [of Protestants] and looting by the peasant mobs; of priests leading them to war in a religious frenzy, and of Protestants being forcibly baptised to avoid death'.[13] The success of anti-Catholic propaganda and the ferocity with which the revolt in the North was quelled dampened Presbyterian radicalism.

On Saturday 15 June, reports at last arrived at the camp on Limerick Hill of enemy forces moving against them.[14] The insurgents learned that General Loftus at the head of a column had left the town of Tullow and was marching in the direction of Tinahely, about seven miles away from the camp by road. General Dundas with another column had arrived from Baltinglass at Hacketstown to link up in an offensive with Loftus. It was decided to meet this force in the open country and give battle.

Miles Byrne, now established as one of the most reliable and intuitive of the insurgent leaders, although a mere eighteen years of age, was once more committed to probing forward towards the enemy units. As he pushed ahead with his Monaseed men towards Tinahely, contact was made with the enemy cavalry who were also on reconnoitre. This was to Byrne's liking. In a series of skirmishes he captured a number of prisoners and drove the redcoats before him. He also took a great number of cattle from them. That evening the main body of insurgents under Fr. John Murphy marched through the valley known as the Wicklow Gap and next day, Sunday 16 June, they camped at Mountpleasant within musket shot of Tinahely.[15] Another confrontation, a chance to make some amends for Arklow, was anticipated. Preparations were made and instructions issued.

On Monday 17 June, the two columns of redcoats advanced against the camp at Mountpleasant in expectation of a brief engagement, followed by the rout and decimation of the insurgent's northern division.[16] The columns comprised regular military and yeoman units, infantry and cavalry; that led by General Dundas had two pieces of field artillery. As they drew near the rebel camp, they saw a line so formidably drawn up to receive them that they halted. The pikemen were ordered into action and charged instantly. The redcoat infantry stood still, seemingly in disbelief as the pikemen raced towards them. Then without further hesitation they turned and ran. They abandoned stores and provisions as well as units cut off by the charge despite the presence of cavalry corps covering their rear. The entire enemy force retreated precipitately until they had gained the safety of a distant hill where they regrouped and considered falling back on Tullow and Hacketstown. Miles Byrne deplored the lack of military experience and skill which again at Mountpleasant prevented the insurgents from following up their success and achieving a decisive victory. They had, he recalled, 'numbers and courage enough to overthrow any force that was sent against them, if they had been skillfully commanded'. The insurgents were left with a number of prisoners who had to be fed and protected. Fortunately, the enemy provided ample food and drink for friend and foe alike. In addition to the abandoned stores, they left a huge herd of cattle which they had optimistically moved up to the forward position of their troops.[17]

Tinahely was entered by the insurgents without opposition. A search for stores uncovered a quantity of gunpowder but little else of use; some firearms in bad condition were unearthed. The houses of known enemies were burned to the ground. Loyalists were rounded up and those amongst them accused of murder were put to death. Others were taken to the camp to answer charges of inflicting terror on the population in the vicinity of Tinahely. The lives of many would have been forfeit were it not for pleas on their behalf by Billy Byrne of Ballymanus. An appeal for mercy was also heard from a relative of the Ballymanus Byrnes, Mrs. Meagher of Coolalaugh, who came to the camp to urge upon the insurgents the futility of vengeance. Billy Byrne was badly repaid for his intervention. He was hanged after the rising on evidence of his influence in the insurgent ranks. His influence was implicit in the testimony of a grateful farmer and grazier, Thomas Dowse, one of the loyalists he had saved.[18]

Unknown to John Murphy or any of the chiefs in the two major insurgent divisions, a powerful army with eight general officers was being assembled for a campaign against them.[19] The operation was being planned by the commander-in-chief of the King's forces in Ireland, General Lake and his staff. Lake, who had overall command, established his first south-eastern field headquarters amidst the ruins of Carnew.[20] Meanwhile Lord Roden with a force mainly of cavalry appeared before Tinahely. Finding the insurgents well arranged and full of 'offensive spirit', he beat a retreat toward Hacketstown where he conferred with General Dundas.[21] The insurgents contemplated a swift swoop on Hacketstown but abandoned the idea following the arrival of three United Irish fugitives with news from Dublin.[22] The credentials of all three were vouched for by Daniel Kirwan, a leader of the county Wicklow United men. Most of the news presented to Fr. John was doleful. The movement in Dublin was broken, they reported, and the leaders arrested or in flight overseas. The Kildare insurgents had suffered heavy losses and were dispersed. The good news from Dublin was in the newspapers of the month of May. It was to the effect that Napoleon Bonaparte had been named Commander of the French army for the invasion of England and Ireland and it sent a wave of exultation through the camp. Gloom was swept aside. The insurgents would fight for many a day yet.

The insurgent leaders met to consider. Surprisingly the news of Napoleon's imminent campaign led to sharp conflict on the strategy to be employed. Some were in favour of rest and caution. 'It would be better', they believed, 'and a wiser policy to wait for the landing of the French in Ireland and not risk a general battle before a junction to co-operate with them could be effected'. On the other hand, the majority were convinced that to remain on the defensive would be attended with the worst consequences. The majority prevailed and carried a resolution to meet the enemy in the open and a decision was taken to choose positions where the pikemen could be brought speedily into action.[23]

Very early on the morning of Tuesday 18 June, General Dundas marched with his troops on Tinahely. Military wisdom on the insurgent side now dictated that they would not engage them at that point.

123

Instead the insurgents moved three miles to the south and had occupied strong positions on Kilcavan Hill by eight o'clock in the morning. There they drew up in line of battle, 'the most formidable one I had yet seen', wrote Miles Byrne, 'since the commencement of the war'.

Every insurgent at Kilcavan Hill was at his post ready for action. The musket men were placed and the artillery was drawn up. It was expected that General Dundas and General Loftus would commit their troops to action. However, as the morning wore on, it was evident from the distance they kept that it was they who hoped that the insurgents would be induced to come down from their strong positions.

Ultimately the insurgents took the decision to advance and give battle. Their intention was to bring the crown forces into action by advancing in the direction of Carnew. When within range, the insurgents opened musket fire. It was half past two in the afternoon. The redcoat lines returned fire and the preliminary skirmish was joined. Next, the little insurgent artillery rumbled forward and roared defiance. Then the line of pikemen, moving forward like a wall, was committed to battle. It remained a peripheral engagement for General Lake had ordered that his officers were not to become involved in general action.[24] His concern was to avoid dislocation of the overall strategy of encirclement.

Already the danger to the government forces had been observed for:

> their advancing column had only just swung into line when the insurgents opened fire and had not the troops changed formation a moment before, the first shot would have raked the column from the front to the rear, and did actually plough up the ground which had not been a minute receded from by the troops.[25]

The King's troops retreated before the pikemen and were quickly pursued, but the battle for the entire evening consisted of skirmishes and withdrawals, musket duels and cannon fire without the insurgents sinking their teeth into the enemy. That was the situation Lake desired. The engagement, one of the longest in the whole campaign, lasted until nightfall. Then the insurgents withdrew to their strongpoint on Kilcavan Hill, frustrated if undefeated, convinced they were more than a match for any regular units the King's officers could throw up against them.

As John Murphy made his way to the summit of Kilcavan Hill, an insurgent from the New Ross division brought him urgent dispatches from Fr. Philip Roche who had replaced Bagenal Harvey as field commander.[26] The news from Philip Roche was grim. Ross was irretrievably lost and he could not hold his position there. He was compelled to fall back to cover the port of Wexford, the presumed location for the French landing. He urged the necessity of concentrating all insurgent forces at Vinegar Hill so that an assault could be mounted to overwhelm the enemy in one great decisive battle.[27]

The leaders assembled for a crucial decision. Miles Byrne was absent in the countryside, still seeking out the enemy with his Monaseed contingent. John Murphy studied the Vinegar Hill proposal, the merit of which hinged on the expected arrival of the French off Wexford. The landing of the troops must be covered. A beachhead was a prerequisite. Without the French all would be lost, for the insurgents could not hold out indefinitely against the might of His Majesty's forces. Fr. John found the prospect an agreeable option but Anthony Perry opposed it and was supported in his opposition by Garret Byrne and the Wicklow insurgent chiefs. They put forward an alternative plan. They would march northwards to Rathdrum town with the intention of cutting General Lake's lines of communication with Dublin and keeping them cut. If this plan was rejected, they had another which they argued vehemently. They would manoeuvre and fight the enemy on their own terms in the open country which they now occupied and where they were still in control. They argued that neither regular English troops nor yeomen had ventured to come in close contact with the pikemen.[28] These contrary held opinions were hotly debated.

Both of Perry's plans were almost accepted when the intervention of a leader whose voice and influence had been subdued for a fortnight emphatically swayed the decision in favour of Vinegar Hill. Edward Fitzgerald of Newpark, the man whose rank in the United Irishmen and popularity amongst all the people had recently been conspicuous, insisted on the Vinegar Hill plan with a persistence that was long remembered.[29] He was supported by Edward Roche of Garrylough, and it was their combined persuasion which finally decided the issue. If, as Perry contended, choice of mobile warfare was based on the superiority of the pikemen, then, they insisted, the same claim must be made for a massive pike assault on a chosen battlefield like Vinegar Hill with its network of lanes, hedges and fields. Vinegar Hill could determine the issue for the entire summer, if not for all time. This concept won John Murphy's support and following vigorous sponsorship by Fitzgerald it was adopted by a majority of the insurgent leaders. Vinegar Hill it was. Once the decision was taken, Perry and Garret Byrne accepted the majority viewpoint. While skirmishing in the lowland fields still continued, the main body of the insurgents started to leave Kilcavan Hill. Through the evening, John Murphy's division set out for Enniscorthy. They met no opposition: near Camolin, their large straggling column halted to rest and the hungry men were given food and drink by the people on the roadside.

Next morning the movement towards Vinegar Hill was resumed. It was deliberately slow to enable stragglers and rearguard men like Miles Byrne to catch up, and unavoidably slow because the roads were cluttered with refugees, vast numbers of women and children carrying everything they could take with them, all making for the area under secure rebel control.

On the afternoon of 19 June 1798, John Murphy once more ascended the summit of Vinegar Hill overlooking the devastated town of Enniscorthy. The thought upon which his mind concentrated was whether it was to be the site of thorough victory or disaster. The rebel plan was to entice the crown forces to low-lying fields underneath. It was the insurgents' chosen battlefield, and so the outcome hung on the issue of who in fact were about to fall into a trap, John Murphy and the rebels, or General Lake, his staff and army.

Two typical Wexford pikeheads from 1798. These were discovered in the roof of an outhouse at Frenches of Newbay, close to the insurgent camp at the Three Rocks. *(J. B. Curtis).*

Chapter 13

The Battle of Vinegar Hill

General Lake was an uncomplicated man. Political considerations did not cloud his mind. The only spectre on his horizon was a French armada. His aim was a military victory with the annihilation of the rebels. This he proposed to achieve by driving them towards Wexford port where they would be trapped on all sides and then eliminated. He was not concerned with the presence of many loyalist inhabitants in the rebel-held areas. His orders to the general officers under his command issued on 16 June were:

> General Dundas will be directed to move on the seventeenth to Hacketstown, and to issue his orders to General Loftus at Tullow, to unite his force with him on the eighteenth at Carnew.
>
> General Needham, to move at three o'clock, a.m. on the nineteenth to Gorey; General Dundas having sent a strong patrol under General Loftus from Carnew, at six o'clock in the same morning to Grovesbridge, four or five miles on the road to Gorey, to support General Needham, in case he should meet with resistance at Limerick Hill or at Gorey, and to communicate to General Dundas General Needham's situation.
>
> General Johnson, on the nineteenth, at four o'clock a.m. to move to Old Ross, and unite with General Moore in driving the rebels from Carrickbyrne Hill. He will take up his position that day near Old Ross, and send a strong patrol to scour the country towards the Blackstair mountains, in junction with Sir James Duff. This movement will require a very particularly concerted arrangement between General Johnson and Sir James Duff. The patrols to return to their respective corps on the same day.
>
> Sir Charles Asgill, on the eighteenth, will occupy Goresbridge, Borris and Graiguenamanagh, and will remain in those positions

until the twentieth, three p.m. when he will return, unless he shall receive orders to the contrary.

Lieutenant-General Dundas, on the twentieth, will march to Ballycarney-bridge, keeping the east side of the Slaney to Scarawalsh-bridge, to arrive there at twelve noon.

Sir James Duff will also move on the twentieth, by the road on the west-side of the Slaney to Scarawalsh-bridge, where he will arrive at twelve o'clock.

General Needham on the twentieth, will move from Gorey to Oulart to be there at twelve o'clock.

General Loftus. The corps from Grovesbridge, will move on the twentieth, through Camolin and Ferns, and unite with General Dundas at Scarawalsh-bridge, at twelve o'clock.

General Moore, to land on the eighteenth at Ballyhack-ferry, and on the nineteenth, he will move at three o'clock, a.m. to Foulkes-mill, and unite with General Johnson in driving the rebels from Carrickbyrne-hill. He will take up his position that night at Foulkes's-mill, securing the escape of the rebels between that and Clonmines.

General Johnson on the twentieth, will move with his column to Ballymacus[Ballymackessy]-bridge, either to unite in the attack on Enniscorthy, if necessary, or to prevent their escape in that direction.

Should the rebels have evacuated Enniscorthy and Vinegar-Hill, the columns under General Dundas and Sir James Duff will take up their position that day in front of Enniscorthy; and General Johnson will at the same time receive orders to take a position on the great road from Enniscorthy to Taghmon.

General Moore, in this case, on the twentieth, will move from Foulkes's-mill, and take post at Taghmon, still securing the country between Taghmon and Clonmines.

But should the enemy maintain their position at Enniscorthy, the attack will be made on the twenty-first at day-light, by the columns under General Dundas and Sir James Duff, and General Needham moving from Oulart.

The general forward movement and investment of Wexford will take place on the twenty-first, when the several columns will be so united as to receive directions as circumstances may point out.

Gun-boats. Orders are to be sent to the naval commanders to station their gun-boats and armed vessels in Wexford harbour early on the morning of the twenty-first, to co-operate in such manner as may be necessary for the attack of the town, with the gun-boats from Waterford, which will be directed to support General Moore and the corps at Clonmines on the nineteenth.[1]

By 18 June, Brigadier General John Moore, later Sir John, was in Old Ross. He commanded the Light Infantry, militia and two German mercenary units, the Hompesch Cavalry and the 60th Jagers, commonly called 'The Hessians'. He was joined there by General Johnson. General Dundas had reached the Slaney at Ballycarney near Fr. John Murphy's birthplace by noon on the 20th. General Johnson and General Eustace moved on the 20th, through Clonroche, to the western approaches of Enniscorthy. General Needham pushed south from Arklow to Oulart on the 20th. General Lake moved with the force he had assembled at Scarawalsh bridge, and during the afternoon of the 20th reached Solsborough where they camped within sight of Vinegar Hill. His columns now included General Dundas and his contingents.

The well-equipped army which surrounded Enniscorthy on the 20th was estimated at 20,000. Whatever about the exact strength, it was estimated that the fighting men on both sides numbered about the same. There resemblance abruptly ended. The rebels had from three to four thousand with firearms and a very poor provision of powder and ball. The King's army and its eight general officers had a formidable train of artillery, 400 requisitioned coaches packed with ammunitions and military stores of every kind, including a large supply of newly developed explosive shells.[2]

Miles Byrne was one of the last to break off the engagement around Kilcavan. He was outraged to find that Vinegar Hill had been chosen, and he spent time castigating those responsible. He placed the blame for a bad decision on Edward Fitzgerald, although not without puzzlement, for he was well aware of the leadership stature which Fitzgerald 'deservedly' maintained amongst the county Wexford men and, in addition, the county Wicklow men. He lashed Edward Roche as well, but he never once attached a shred of blame to John Murphy, a man who in Miles Byrne's eyes could do little wrong.

Byrne covered the rearguard of the slow trek all the way to Vinegar Hill, hopelessly frustrated at the thought of the defenceless women and wounded men now abandoned. Many years later he would ask himself 'Why had not his country, witnessing the perpetration of monstrous crimes, the courage to rise en masse and rather be sacrificed to the last man than to lie prostrate at their tyrants' feet while they were committing outrage?' He was convinced that they could have turned the tables on the Government troops during the withdrawal from Kilcavan Hill. 'We might', he wrote, 'at any time on that night have turned about with ten thousand resolute pikemen and have attacked the English troops following us, commanded by Generals Dundas and Loftus, with a certainty of defeating them and of being avenged for the cruelties they had committed'.

When John Murphy rode up the slopes of Vinegar Hill, he met a situation which caused him alarm. Nothing had been done to make it formidable against the enemy.[3] This jolt was followed by another. There was no sign of the New Ross division under Fr. Philip Roche who had demanded the rendezvous in the first place; combined with the exchanges at Kilcavan on the choice of battlefield, this had the effect of smartening John Murphy and his chiefs. They ordered mobilisation.[4] If there was going to be a decisive open battle, all available hands must be there with pikes and a hunger for war. Three leaders were chosen to round up reinforcements. Edward Roche, Dick Monk and Garret Byrne with their men and most of the Shelmalier marksmen were sent to Wexford town to collect or press every available unmarried man fit to bear arms.[5] They set out immediately on this urgent enterprise. The insurgent enclave had, however, been reduced by now. North of Enniscorthy the county had been abandoned. Into the insurgent-held area flowed the flotsam and jetsam of war, the terrified, the injured, the women and children.[6]

The insurgent call to arms became general in south Wexford. Although there had been disagreement about the choice of Vinegar Hill as a battlefield, there was no despondency in the ranks. They were determined to fight for their land, freedom from coercion and tyranny; they cared little for the forces they were inviting to attack them. They regarded the yeomen as cowards when the odds were even, and pondered on personal experience to confirm conviction. It is a fact that the insurgents at Enniscorthy on 20 June had what one of their prisoners, Alexander Hatterick of the Dumbartonshire Highland Regiment, reported as 'the impudence to entertain some hopes of victory'.

The battlefield had two obvious sectors, Vinegar Hill with its underlying fields, and Enniscorthy town. William Barker was put in command in Enniscorthy with Fr. Mogue Kearns as his second-in-command.[7] John Murphy had already decided that he would fight on Vinegar Hill but his concern was growing as 20 June wore on. Why was there no preparation to facilitate offence or defence made around the huge camp despite three weeks of insurgent occupation? To that fear was added the absence of Edward Roche and his contingent of the Shelmalier marksmen and the reinforcements. With no sign of Roche as evening approached, an express message was sent to him in Wexford town demanding the reinforcements and expressing surprise that he had not returned as expected with the fresh men from his neighbourhood.[8]

Fr. John Murphy, Edward Fitzgerald and Anthony Perry now directed events on Vinegar Hill. The strategy to be used in the event of retreat was considered. Whatever happened, even if they lost the day, their army had to be kept intact. The insurgent plans remained conditioned by the probability of substantial French help and the necessity of holding out until it arrived.

John Murphy had much to occupy his mind that night of Wednesday, 20 June. What would happen, if they lost, to the wounded packed in their hospital? Or to any of them, if their retreat was cut off? It was apparent from the reports and the shallow graves that the non-fighting garrison on the hill had been settling scores in the execution of loyalists over the previous three weeks. There would be no mercy for any rebel. Mercy and generosity to foes were casualties long before the outbreak on 26 May. John Murphy knew that if he himself were captured he could not expect a soldier's treatment or a soldier's death.

On that Wednesday night as dusk descended, the leaders again argued the most urgent step to take. Miles Byrne, covering the rearguard on the Gorey to Enniscorthy road, had not yet arrived. Edward Roche, Dick Monk and Garret Byrne had not returned from Wexford. The news came that Fr. Philip Roche in command of the New Ross division was now falling back to the defence of Wexford. It appeared that he had been gaining the day against General Moore at Foulksmills when the scales tipped against him and his men. No help could be expected from him on the morrow. Then why wait for the morrow? Why not go down from the hill in a wave that night and attack the Government soldiers where they lay around their fires? The idea was put forward, urged, debated.[9] None of the leaders – Murphy, Perry, Fitzgerald – had the nerve to take that risk. They fell back on the fact that their supply of gunpowder was so very low they could not afford to shoot at targets until they could see them in daylight. A dawn battle was accepted.

As insurgents were deployed and points fortified, the big sprawling camp around Vinegar Hill lit the sky as the leaping flames of fires warmed fighting men, women and children. Down below across the lowlands and ringed around Enniscorthy to the west, hundreds of camp fires of the King's army burned brightly in a broad, scimitar-shaped perimeter.

Green flags were hoisted at every vantage point on Vinegar Hill and in Enniscorthy town. Castle and church steeple were adorned, while the mill ruin at the camp summit bore the emblem common in that year of liberty, the green-leaved bough.[10] Late on the night of the 20th, after all the dispositions had been agreed upon, Miles Byrne arrived. His men were exhausted and he was still raging over the choice of Vinegar Hill, annoyed by the absence of Roche, Monk and Byrne and horrified by the news of the defeat at Foulksmills. He and his fatigued men fell down to sleep but at two in the morning he was awakened by thunderous cannon roars. He leaped for action, but soon realised that they were shots to signal that each enemy division was present, drawn up and prepared. The cannon shots ringed Enniscorthy town and Vinegar Hill totally. The insurgents were surrounded on all sides.[11]

It was daylight on the longest day of the year 1798. Skirmishes at the outposts started early. The first of these commenced in Barker's sector when his outposts at Bloomfield House on the New Ross road and Cherry Orchard on the Killanne road, west of Enniscorthy, were attacked by General Johnson.[12] Although his men succeeded in knocking out one of Johnson's artillery pieces, they were eventually driven back to the streets through the Duffry gate. At seven o'clock, the decisive battle of the insurrection commenced simultaneously on all sides around Enniscorthy and Vinegar Hill.[13] The signal guns roared again from the ring of artillery around Enniscorthy but, as time went on, the insurgents noted a factor which was to save many of their lives. One sector remained silent, the sector south of Vinegar Hill on the east bank of the Slaney.

The battle became general, but the planned attack by pikemen was diverted by a new and totally unexpected ingredient in the enemy's fire power.[14] Lake's artillery moved forward from Solsborough and raked the slopes and summit of Vinegar Hill with anti-personnel shells. These did not explode at once but fizzed as the hissing fuse burned down to the explosives.

At first the insurgents, not realising that they were bomb shells, did not even attempt to seek cover from them. Fifty men of one group were blown to pieces as the deafening blast devoured them. These bomb shells, dropped with accuracy from all sides, struck terror into the insurgents. 'They spit fire at us', was a cry remembered from Vinegar Hill that day. 'I can stand anything only those guns that fire twice', was the bewildered reaction of a veteran.

The little artillery that the insurgents had on the hill was brought into action to offer challenge; in attempting to compete, the gunners quickly ran through the stocks of ammunition. The Crown forces, covered by a storm of cannon and musket fire, advanced towards the slopes from the east and north. Again the insurgent musket men expended their ammunition in challenge. The redcoats advanced from field to field pushing their cannons under cover of the hedges and ditches. As footholds were gained, gaps were torn in the ditches to allow heavy guns to fire. In spite of exposure to artillery and musket fire, the pikemen, under Dan Kirwan of Kilpipe, were committed to battle and their desperate charges were punished. Kirwan was killed and with him fell many of the best and longest-serving of the fighting insurgents.

In the bursting shell and shot, John Murphy saw his brother Pat who had followed him fall and die on the hill.[15] Nonetheless, he carried on, urging, fighting, shouting orders and in ghastly circumstances for the rebels distinguished himself. Amongst the other insurgent chiefs who were long remembered as fighting with heart and hand were Edward Fitzgerald, whose insistence led them there, Anthony Perry and the Wicklow leader, Billy Byrne.[16]

The women were not content to leave the fighting to their men. They mingled with them, encouraging them and fought with fury themselves. Several were found slain among the fighting men, where they had fallen in crowds, felled by the delayed bursting of the bomb shells. Their fortitude amazed eye witnesses:

> The peasantry, uncovered, stood the tremendous fire opened upon four sides of their position; a stream of shells and grape was poured on the multitude; the leaders encouraged them by exhortations, the women by their cries, and every shell that broke amongst the crowd was followed by shouts of defiance. General Lake's horse was shot, army officers were wounded, some killed and a few gentlemen became invisible during the heat of the battle. The troops advanced gradually but steadily up the hill; the peasantry kept up their fire and maintained their ground; their cannons were nearly useless, their powder deficient, but they died fighting at their post.[17]

Battle raged simultaneously around Enniscorthy town.[18] William Barker withdrew and counter-attacked General Johnson with the tenacity of a badger. He held his own despite the rain of shells upon his ranks and turned his years of service in the French army to excellent effect. He kept a strong guard in reserve at the town bridge and with a four-pounder cannon mounted on a cart as a morale stiffener he took the fight to the enemy. Ground gained by redcoats to the west of Enniscorthy was paid for in casualties, but ultimately Barker and his men were forced back into the town where the pikemen continued to dispute every position.

The insurgent musket men kept fire on the advancing soldiers from the windows of the houses as the bitterest hand-to-hand fighting of the campaign developed. General Johnson's artillery was advanced down hill into the town's Market Square. A six-pounder artillery piece was readied for action when desperate rebels counter-attacked, captured it and killed all its crew. The streets were now being raked with grape shot, and the rebels were inched ever closer to their last line of defence, the bridge over the river Slaney.

After one hour of bombardment, it was plain to all on Vinegar Hill that with the enemy's advantage in artillery a last stand there meant annihilation. Amidst the relentless shelling, John Murphy and Fitzgerald considered a concentrated attack on Lake's left flank to overturn it and march the way they had come, back to the security of Wicklow.[19] As this would have meant abandoning Barker and his men below them in the town, it was dropped. Another half hour of shelling was absorbed in which the inexhaustible Miles Byrne observed rebel chiefs displaying 'the greatest coolness and courage, charging at the head of their men under the tremendous fire of the enemy's batteries which were sending cannon ball, grape shot and musket ball as thickly as a shower of hailstones'. The infantry assault on the summit came from the east and gradually the outposts were driven in from that direction. Packed closer together in ever tightening space the insurgents were many times more vulnerable. Desperate pike charges failed in the face of cannon fire combined with intensive small-arms fire. As the insurgent artillery was long silent for want of ammunition, Lake's guns were easily moved forward and the mixed multitude on the hill was shattered with grape and cannister.

The insurgents in Enniscorthy fell back fighting. Barker held his position defending the bridge 'with a valour beyond description'. Then disaster overtook the man who was the inspiration of the insurgent defence. Barker's arm was blown off and the badly wounded chief was carried to shelter. Mogue Kearns took over command and soon after he too was badly wounded. The King's troops were pouring down the steep streets into the town and a rain of shot and shell dismissed the best that pikemen could do. There was no longer any doubt that the day was lost.

On Vinegar Hill the decision to abandon the killing fields was taken and a retreat started towards the one sector from which there was no artillery fire and where no troops were visible. That was the Drumgoold-Templeshannon sector south of the hill next the east bank of the Slaney. It was hoped in desperation that Edward Roche would be there keeping that route to Wexford intact. If he was not there, the likelihood of ambush was certain, but it was the only available option. The retreat from the hill became general as the insurgents made for the Wexford road past Beale's barn and Darby's Gap. The retreat from Enniscorthy town was the next and inevitable outcome. Barker had to be left behind but Kearns was carried as the surviving insurgents and followers made for the same avenue of escape east of the river.

The Light Brigade under Colonel Cambell was the first to reach the summit.[20] As the insurgent retreat became apparent, fighting men and camp followers were raked with grape shot from the field pieces attached to the Dumbartonshire Highland Regiment. Still the 'croppies' fought a rearguard action, some 'having the impudence when they got

134

on the inside of a ditch to turn about and fire on their pursuer'. Fr. Thomas Clinch, fighting conspicuously on a white horse, was singled out by Lord Roden, possibly in the belief that he was the now infamous Fr. Murphy. His Lordship pursued him for a mile, succeeding in wounding him. Clinch returned fire, wounded Roden and was preparing to finish him when he was shot down by an officer of Roden's regiment. He died on the roadside between Darby's Gap and Mye Cross.[21]

There was no sign of Miles Byrne in the retreat and as John Murphy rode amidst the pandemonium he must have judged that the end had come, that all the war and suffering, sacrifice and upheaval since The Harrow was now to terminate in massacre. Behind him, gaining ground rapidly, came Lake's redcoated avengers. Before him on the road to Wexford lay ambush and annihilation, or a safe haven. Was there no hope? Were these the last minutes of his life and the lives of his men? No, by Heavens! There beyond Darby's Gap was Edward Roche and Dick Monk with their men, moving forward to form the rearguard and protect the retreat.[22] Roche opened attack on the pursuers at once. Lake's troops were halted and the insurgents streamed through the gap left unattended by General Needham.

Roche's covering of the retreat kept down casualties amongst the fighting insurgents during that long, hot afternoon. The Crown forces, making approximate but reasonably accurate estimates, reckoned their dead at about 100 and the number of insurgents killed at not more than 500.[23] A remarkable aspect of the battle was that so many leaders who had fought hard with their men left the field uninjured. The exceptions were Barker, Kearns, Clinch and Kirwan. Two divisions of insurgents lived to fight another day.

It was General Lake's finest hour. Here at Enniscorthy was the opportunity for him to teach a lesson to the disaffected. He took no prisoners. He sought and killed every wounded man in field, street, roadway and ditch. His troops killed everything that resembled 'a countryman' in their follow-up operations.[24] The courthouse which had been turned into a temporary hospital filled with eighty wounded insurgents, was burned to the ground and its inmates burned along with it. Their corpses still hissed in the embers the following day.[25]

Chapter 14

The Unwanted

John Murphy stumbled through scenes of desolation which as Thomas Cloney recalled filled the mind with horror:

> The dead and dying were scattered promiscuously in fields, in dykes, on the roads or wherever chance had directed their last steps. In one place some men with arms and some with legs off, and others cruelly mutilated in various ways; horses with their necks broken and their carts with women and children under them, either dead or dying in the road and ditches where in their precipitate flight they had been upset.[1]

In anguish over the carnage, John Murphy now carried the memory of the death of his own brother, killed before his eyes. He had a messenger sent back with the news to the family in Tincurry so that some attempt might be made to give him decent burial.[2]

The insurgents limped towards Wexford town, the dusty road choked with men bearing pikes, grimy, sweaty, tattered men, disconsolate women and crying children. They struggled on, thinking of the haven of Wexford and the welcome they enjoyed four short weeks before.

John Murphy was riding with the Boolavogue men in the middle of the column when half way to Wexford there was a commotion up front.[3] There were angry shouts and the column halted. Fitzgerald, who was at its head, waved two men towards him. One was a redcoat officer bearing a white flag. The other was Thomas Cloney, the popular hero of the Three Rocks engagement. His news provoked an instant mixture of rage and despair. He was an emissary chosen by Captain Matthew Keugh, Wexford town governor, and the townspeople, to seek terms from General Lake. His escort was Captain O'Hea of the North Cork Militia. The situation was black, even worse than John Murphy could have thought, for the Wexford town government had obviously taken the decision to sue for peace hours before the outcome at Vinegar Hill could have been known. John Murphy read Cloney's dispatches. They were written by Lord Kingsborough to every military commander, informing them that:

> the town of Wexford had surrendered to him and in consequence of the behaviour of those in the town during the rebellion, they should all be protected in person and property, murderers excepted, and those who had instigated others to commit murder, hoping these terms might be ratified as he had pledged his honour in the most solemn manner to have these terms fulfilled on the town being surrendered to him, the Wexford men not being concerned in the massacre, which was perpetrated by country people in their absence.

Massacre! What massacre? Cloney and his redcoat escort were in no situation to discuss details, surrounded as they were by men raw with fury. One thing was plain as a pikestaff. If such a man as Thomas Cloney considered it necessary to parley with Lake, then the situation was hopeless. John Murphy gazed intently at his comrade-in-arms, now an emissary with an escorting redcoat officer. Then he allowed them to pass and carry on their mission.

As the battered army of insurgents drew near to Wexford and Ferrycarrig bridge, John Murphy assessed the day's developments and then took a decision on his own initiative. He would not follow Edward Fitzgerald again. As Fitzgerald and Perry with their contingents made into Wexford town, John Murphy and his Boolavogue men veered right after crossing the Slaney at Ferrycarrig and headed for the Three Rocks camp nearby.[4] He was followed by old, faithful veterans, the wounded and the women but the greater number of the insurgents parted company with him in order to experience again the hospitality of the town. At the Three Rocks camp, he discovered Fr. Philip Roche resting with some of his New Ross division.[5] Roche, a disillusioned man, spilled out a sorry tale. The people of Wexford who last month had thrown their arms around them now treated them like lepers, he said. They couldn't get rid of them out of the town fast enough. Organised groups of 'respectable' townspeople went around begging them to leave.[6] Even Bishop Caulfield had put in an appearance, bleating for their evacuation.[7] The town and hinterland were lost. General Moore was at that moment ready to walk into Wexford.

Philip Roche had not finished yet. He told John Murphy about the New Ross campaign, the Scullabogue barn burning, the loss at Foulksmills, the inferiority of Harvey as a commander. He told him of the revenge missions from his own ranks, of loyalist lives he had been compelled to save from his own men. Lastly, he gave him what details he had heard of the executions of prisoners on Wexford bridge by Captain Thomas Dixon of Castlebridge, his wife and a crowd of followers who believed punishment was not being issued fast enough. Roche's story confirmed to John Murphy that while he and his men were bursting their hearts in combat, others were dispensing death without hindrance far from the battlefields. And there was no doubt whatever but that those in authority in the revolt would be held responsible.[8]

As the afternoon of 21 June wore on, uncertainty, dark rumour and fear escalated. Of Miles Byrne and his men there was no sign or account. The only cheering presence at the Three Rocks was the irrepressible Dick Monk and the survivors of his John Street Corps.[9] More discouraging news followed. The other leaders had decided that the position in Wexford was irretrievable. Without consulting or notifying John Murphy, Fitzgerald, Perry, Garret Byrne, Esmond Kyan and Edward Roche had marched across Wexford Bridge with the remnants of their army and taken the road hugging the coast north to Gorey *en route* to the Wicklow mountains.[10] John Murphy was isolated before the enemy. It should have occurred to him that the end of the road had been reached.

It was then, however, at that moment of utter dejection that John Murphy's courage and willpower reached its pinnacle. Despite the apparent hopelessness of his position, he determined that he would not accept defeat.[11] He would fight on while there was a breath in his body with two thousand men, two hundred men, twenty, or if necessary, alone. But by some means as yet unrecorded he had information which gave him a gleam of hope.[12] At the other side of the Blackstairs Mountain range in the county Laois, far from Wexford, was a district teeming with coal miners who had revolted even before he himself had called his people to arms. They were Irish colliers working the northern end of the large Castlecomer coalfield around the village of Doonane, some seventy miles distant. These men were employed by the Royal Canal Company. At the southern end of the field at Castlecomer, owned by the Wandesford family, many of the miners were of Welsh and Yorkshire extraction and decidedly loyal to London.[13]

The Doonane miners had opened hostilities as early as 23 May by attacking the military barracks in their village.[14] Their object had been to coalesce with the United Irishmen planning to attack Carlow but they were dispersed with heavy losses and had gone into hiding in the wooded and hilly district near their homes. There they still remained, poorly armed, desperate and with receding hopes. John Murphy's fresh endeavour was aroused by the belief that they would revitalise and

138

reinforce him and whatever men would follow him.

He gathered around him the remnants of the insurgent army the women and wounded included, and told them that he was going to fight on. He would not wait to be caught in any trap as he intended to break out of the ring encircling Wexford. There were, he said, brave men in Laois, Carlow and Kilkenny who were yet to be rallied. There would be no surrender. Give in after what they had been through? Never! He would carry on and he intended to start a march to the Blackstairs Mountains there and then, and the sooner the better. He was waiting for no one. In fact, if they did not leave immediately, the next arrival would be General John Moore.

All who listened to Fr. John were aroused from despair and they agreed to follow him no matter what the consequences. That evening he led them down from the Three Rocks. He had studied the countryside from the summit, seen the enemy positions and decided on the route to cut through them. He made for the road south-east of the Three Rocks which passed through the burnt-out village of Murrintown, and kept going until he and his followers reached the woods of Sleedagh. There he decided that they had sufficient security to spend the night, nurse the wounded and search for provisions. Fr. Mogue Kearns was with them, a heavy encumbrance. He was weak from loss of blood and carried a shattered arm. Another wounded man laboriously carried alongside Kearns was Miles Byrne's brother, Hugh.

As the insurgents settled down in the great wood, the alarm was raised. It was a large body of pikemen approaching and the cheers and celebration when they were identified resounded through the trees of Sleedagh.[15] It was Miles Byrne with his Monaseed contingent. Byrne was unhurt, overwhelmed with delight to see his chief alive and well, for John Murphy had been reported to him as amongst the dead on Vinegar Hill. Byrne and his men had just quit Wexford town where the greatest tumult and disorder reigned. Searching for the other leaders, they had come upon Bishop Caulfield's house in High Street, from the upper windows of which His Lordship harangued them. He beseeched them to quit the town, declaring that their generals were already out at their camp. Byrne set out for the Three Rocks. When he reached the almost deserted camp, he was told that John Murphy had left with his followers, determined to continue the struggle. Miles Byrne set off in search of him and his insurgent army.

When the welcomes to the Monaseed men subsided, a meeting of the leaders present in Sleedagh was called by Fr. Philip Roche.[16] He bluntly demanded a realistic appraisal of a situation that he deemed lost. Fr. John on the contrary had grown in fresh resolve. He told the gathering of his plan to revitalise in revolt the miners of the Castlecomer region and with them the whole of the Midlands. He emphasised that they must resume their march to the Blackstairs Mountains at dawn the next morning on a route of anything upwards of forty miles. To Philip Roche this was madness. He resolutely opposed John Murphy's plan or for that matter a march one inch beyond Sleedagh. He was confident of obtaining a cessation of arms, he told the meeting, and added that he was certain to get 'good terms from the English general in chief, Lake'.[17]

It is difficult to envisage what passed through John Murphy's mind following Philip Roche's flat rejection of his plan in favour of an approach to Lake for terms. Was it conceivable that Philip Roche allotted to Lake a scintilla of humanity? Whatever the reason, Roche persisted in the belief that good terms could be had from the Crown's Commander-in-Chief. Byrne and the men gathered around waited for Fr. John's view of the proposal. When he did speak he was brief and to the point. 'For my part', he responded, 'I can have no reliance on such negotiations. I will never advise anyone to surrender and give up their arms'.[18] An outburst of cheering greeted his statement. Byrne, Dick Monk and all the men declared that they were prepared to follow him through thick and thin. Philip Roche saw that his proposal had no support. Yet he remained adamant. He resolved to turn around and go back to Wexford to the English army headquarters there and then.

Roche mounted his horse but before setting off he turned once more to Murphy. He wanted to know from him how he was to find him in the event of obtaining the terms he expected. 'You will have no difficulty to learn the direction our army will take', was the reply. 'Everywhere we pass we will burn the isolated slate houses which might serve as a refuge to the enemy'. These were the last words they exchanged. Philip Roche, the man who had succeeded Harvey as United Irish Commander-in-Chief, spurred his horse and galloped back alone into Wexford. He trotted into the town so little apprehensive of danger that he had advanced within the army's lines before he was recognised.[19] He was, without question or challenge, dragged down from his horse, kicked, punched and hauled around by the hair of the head. He was beaten the length of the town up to the Windmill Hill camp and back down again to the jail at the Stonebridge. By then he was scarcely recognisable as Philip Roche. Arraigned before a hastily convened courtmartial, he was condemned and hanged on Wexford Bridge along with Captain Matthew Keugh. His head was severed and his body, stripped naked as was Keugh's, was treated with indecent brutality and thrown over the bridge.

In the early dawn of Friday 22 June, John Murphy's force set out for its destination in Laois.[20] They took their wounded. They marched hard, too hard for many of the exhausted and injured, far too hard for the women. Many drifted away, were lodged in safe houses, or sympathetically swallowed up amidst an understanding country people. For a while the march was over the exact ground traversed by the retreating Wexford garrison the previous month. Later the battlefield at Foulksmills littered with the debris of war was crossed by the insurgents. Broken carts and wagons and the unburied dead were scattered all over the field of battle and on the adjacent roads. The sight did not halt the marchers. They forged ahead as the hot June sun rose in the sky. From Foulksmills they struck rapidly for the hill of Carrigbyrne and Old Ross, their lives and future dependent on their breaking out of Lake's web. No enemy units were sighted and as the day wore on it looked as if they had not been detected. On towards the beckoning mountains of the Blackstairs they marched, their every step sharpening the definition of outline features and slope homesteads. Soon they were underneath Grange, with the grey towering background of the mountains ranged like a mighty fortress. They passed the thirty-mile mark, then up to Killanne, the home and birthplace of John Kelly and there, for the first time that day, they sighted an enemy patrol but it made a rapid retreat without offering opposition.

Finally, towards the north beyond Killanne, the insurgents turned left for the gateway to their escape, the wild and beautiful Scullogue Gap. They went through unmolested into county Carlow after a march of forty miles. John Murphy took care to have Mogue Kearns carried past his homeplace in Kiltealy until he had him deposited in a safe house, the home of their kinsmen, Murphys of the Bawnogue, Rathgeeran, on the county Carlow side, where both priests had often lodged when hunting game in peacetime.[21]

Two villages straddled the road inside the Scullogue Gap. The first was Rahanna in a setting of mountain, grey rocks, furze and fern, its Catholic chapel uncharacteristically prominent on a hillside next to the village street. The second village, two miles further on, contained a military barracks. It was Killedmond which at this time of upheaval housed a garrison of yeoman cavalry and infantry guarding the pass between Wexford and Carlow.[22] John Murphy ordered that this threat to their security be eliminated before nightfall, even if his men were on their last legs. As he led the main body of insurgents through a bog at the back of Rahanna, a route taken in caution, a member of a patrol he had sent ahead came with a request that he give the last rites to a dying villager, shot by the redcoats that day.[23] Though he was very anxious to keep going, the old vocation held its grip. He galloped away from his column, attended the dying man and then returned immediately to his role as commander of fighting men.

Allowing no further halt or hesitation, John Murphy ordered the advance on Killedmond. The village garrison of cavalry and infantry had received reinforcements. Miles Byrne did not identify them but reported that they seemed to be there 'in great force'. The insurgents were expected. Before any hostilities opened, the garrison set all the thatched houses in the village on fire. Fr. John wasted no time, but sent his men into battle at speed. The pikemen charged like fresh men into the street and came to grips with redcoats mounted and on foot. The attackers held the initiative, for their lives depended on it. The redcoats wilted, hesitated, fell back and finally fled. John Murphy ordered that the slated barracks be burned to the ground. That accomplished, the exhausted little army, famished for food and drink, bivouacked outside the burnt-out village, fifty miles beyond Lake's forces.[24]

The field where they camped in the townland of Tomduff is still called the Camp Field. The Wexford insurgents were a source of wonder to the local people and they crowded around to look at them, anxious to see if there were any of their own neighbours with them. Protestant and Catholic villagers mingled freely. One of the insurgents named Tom Doran became attracted to a local girl named Mary Little. She was a Protestant but before nightfall the son of the Catholic Doran family and Mary Little discovered a mutual attraction. Her father was present at the camp and the enterprising Doran requested from him the favour of his daughter Mary's hand in marriage, provided he returned safe from the campaign. Little agreed, probably convinced that Doran would not survive the week. Tom Doran marched off next day. He fought in several battles and survived the entire campaign. He returned to Mary Little when the dust had firmly settled, and with or without parental blessing they were married. Mary lived to be ninety-four, and the direct descendants of the couple, bearing their name, live near Tomduff to this day, and so do the descendants of the Little family.[25]

Next morning, 23 June, scouts reported that a force of cavalry and infantry was in occupation of the small town of Goresbridge, seven miles away in Kilkenny.[26] Goresbridge defended a convenient passage across the river Barrow and John Murphy at once decided to attack it. He and his men, rested and out of the confines of Wexford, were in good spirits. He sent foraging parties well ahead and they crossed the river a little above the town. The main body advanced by the old road over Knockmanus Hill. The garrison consisted of the Fourth Dragoon Guards and the Wexford Militia.[27] John Murphy did not give them time to compose themselves. The pikemen were sent into attack at violent speed. The conflict which followed was brisk, with sustained fire and hand-to-hand combat until eventually the pikemen overcame the cavalry. Then the day's exchanges were brought abruptly to a halt with one of the most flagrant desertions of the long hot summer. The officer in command at Goresbridge, himself unhorsed, was seen to leap on another horse behind a dragoon and gallop from the action.[28] Resistance collapsed as the militia men in the street signified that they had no intention of continuing hostilities in the face of the advancing pikemen.

The prisoners now in insurgent hands were mainly Wexford Militia, the unit of Captain James Boyd, remembered as the one which ambushed a crowd of Wexford protesters in 1793 causing heavy casualties. The unit contained Catholics as well as Protestants and the first noises some of them made to Fr. John Murphy as he looked them over were predictable. The Catholic militiamen professed their willingness to fight under him but they indicated dire hostility towards their Protestant and loyalist comrades-in-arms.[29] He did not know at first what to do with any of them. FInally the Protestants were declared prisoners of war and the Catholics were given the task of guarding them, with his strict orders that the prisoners were not to be molested.[30]

Goresbridge was ransacked for provisions.[31] It was stocked-out with food and drink but especially flour. The forge was taken over and every man who could do the work of a blacksmith was made busy. In the repair of weapons and shoeing. John Murphy's eyes were, however, fixed upon the coal-mining area of Doonane. He intended to carry on without much delay and his men responded to every demand he made upon them. After rest, recuperation and repairs, they left Goresbridge, heading for the very long hill known as the Ridge of Leinster which lay twelve miles further on. Any cattle they found on the way to the Ridge they brought along, for there were more than three thousand mouths to be fed. That night as they set up camp on the Ridge in the commons of Baunreagh, they were seventy miles from Wexford town.[32]

The camp was 1,000 feet above sea level, with a commanding view of the Leinster midlands. Fires were lit in shelter and the women who succeeded in keeping up with their men baked bread and slim cakes. Meat was available and everyone of the three thousand managed to have a full meal. The wounded were assembled, amongst them Jacob Byrne of Ballyellis, seriously injured in Goresbridge.[33] A musket ball had entered under his hip and passed right through to the other side. No hope was entertained for him when a young insurgent presented himself to Miles Byrne and declared himself to be a medical student. He insisted that he could operate successfully on the stricken rebel. Byrne allowed that he had nothing to lose and told the student to carry on the agonising task. To the utter bewilderment of everyone, the young 'surgeon' operated with assurance and dexterity. Jacob Byrne was a fit and active man going about his business one year later in Dublin.

It was at this stage that a new anxiety began to chill John Murphy. He found that the atmosphere in the area where he now campaigned was different from that in county Wexford. In Goresbridge, no volunteer had come forward to clutch a pike. Men sent out scouting for information found that they could glean no intelligence whatsoever from the local people about the enemy's movements, numbers or dispositions.[34] John Murphy had to send out more scouts in all directions to gather visual intelligence and probe the lie of the land. Some of these returned with what appeared to be confirmation of his high expectations. They had made contact with armed men ahead of them in the Doonane coal-mining area. This could be the stimulus which spurred Fr. John, the certainty of fresh and armed recruits in great numbers. He allowed but a short respite on the Ridge. He told all that they were to be fit and ready to march at two o'clock the following morning. It was during this phase of action that concern for their commander made the insurgents assign bodyguards to him.[35] It is not known whether they were self-appointed or chosen. What is certain is that two insurgents watched over their charge with vigilance at all times and took care of his every need. Of the two the more tireless was James Gallagher of Tomahurra, a near neighbour of John Murphy's mother's family in Tomgarrow.

At 2 o'clock the following morning, Sunday 24 June, the camp on the Ridge bustled with activity as the insurgents made ready to march. In the midst of that urgency Dick Monk rushed to John Murphy to report that Boyd's Wexford militiamen had turned on one another during the night. Seven of the prisoners had been killed at a smaller camp sited at Kellymount, four miles to the south-east of the main insurgent base.[36] Monk brought with him a militia man, Sergeant Tuttle, whom he had saved from death with the greatest difficulty. John Murphy demanded the facts. It transpired that some of the Catholic militiamen captured at Goresbridge had changed their red coats for insurgent civilian clothes and so, 'confirmed in authority', they piked and shot five Protestant militiamen for whose safety they had been made responsible. The Fourth Dragoons, Fowkes and Hawkins, were piked as well.

The prime instigator of the murders was a Catholic militia man named Bruton. Despite the surge of urgency in the camp, Bruton was hauled before the leaders. He did not deny that he was guilty but protested that he had been cruelly punished and flogged on evidence sworn against him by the five dead militiamen that he, Bruton, was a United Irishman. He protested that all five were sworn Orangemen who did everything in their power to have him and his fellow Catholic militia-men put to death. There was no time for protracted examination in the small hours of the morning, and despite the recorded revulsion no action was taken against the killers.

The insurgents left the Ridge of Leinster as early as 2.30 that morning. On their way they commandeered a good horse from an eighteen-year-old local, Michael Cantwell of Coolnacuttia.[37] As they passed through Cruttenclough a woman named Dooley lay dying. Fr. John Murphy was once more called upon and at once left the column to give her the last rites. While he was at her bedside, there was a heavy explosion in the direction of Castlecomer. He blessed the dying woman. 'I must be going', he said then, 'I hear roaring Bess at work in 'Comer'.[38] That was the name he had heard given to the biggest artillery piece the enemy possessed.

John Murphy rejoined the march. Confidence was high. One insurgent with food on his mind piked a goose and carried it along on his shoulder. On passing a cottage with a friendly face in the doorway, Mrs. Lyng's of Cruttenclough, he threw the goose over the half-door, telling her to 'be sure and have it cooked for them when they were coming back'.[39] It was there too that horses in need of shoeing or nails were given attention in Joe Poole's forge. By five o'clock on that Sunday morning of dense mist, the insurgents were before Doonane, the first village in the coal miners' country. It was towards that country that John Murphy had lashed his column forward. The least he expected to find there were fresh men, eager soldiers whose hunger for revenge would be harnessed in the campaign he now intended to pursue.

The turbulent mining area around Castlecomer was well garrisoned. Even in a village like Doonane there was a barracks and a garrison. Doonane was garrisoned by between 300 and 400 of the Waterford Militia. There was no hope of taking them by surprise or overwhelming them, for they had been forewarned of a rebel force marching on the village and had time to prepare while the insurgents heard Mass celebrated by their commander on the way to Doonane. Not long after dawn the garrison was standing by, equipped in full readiness, but at the first sight of the approaching insurgent column they abandoned Doonane and retreated to the defences of Castlecomer.[40]

John Murphy was now riding at the head of the column with Miles Byrne at his side.[41] He watched the bloodless rout without emotion for his great concern lay ahead. In that area and upon that day lay his hope, perhaps ultimately his only hope. Then, as he rode slowly down the street, colliers seemed to come from everywhere, from every house, lane and field they came, cheering their welcome in the early morning. Their numbers seemed vast and, his own veterans apart, they appeared the most determined-looking fighting men that either he or Miles Byrne had laid eyes on for days. The colliers were ready to join them. They were prepared to go anywhere, fight anywhere, although they were badly armed. They had old rusty swords and pistols but they intended to make the best use of them. At the first available opportunity they would exchange them for better weapons.

The scene exhilarated John Murphy and his men. Here were fresh, good-hearted men, thronging around. The village rang with shouts of exultation. Now the scene seemed set fair for an open, nationwide revolt once more, all the better if the French were about their business. John Murphy was riding the crest of the wave again.

The town of Castlecomer c. 1960. A: Ruins of Wandesford mansion house; B: Bridge; C: Bridge (or High) Street; D: Clohogue Street. *(St. Joseph aerial collection, Cambridge University).*

Chapter 15

The Last Campaign

John Murphy grew in energy and resolve. All his instincts of leadership and military cunning surfaced, renewed and, what was more, he alone was in command. His words with the colliers were few because a rapid consideration of the fleeing redcoats and the colliers' needs forced urgency upon his mind. Weapons, ammunition, gunpowder! All thoughts of rest were blotted from him. In response to terse enquiries, the colliers gave him comprehensive information. Enemy dispositions, units, leadership personalities, weapon strengths were known to them. John Murphy devised a two-pronged plan of attack within seconds, a plan to trap the Waterford Militia and take Castlecomer, its garrison and supplies as well. He launched Miles Byrne and his Monaseed men in pursuit of the Waterfords right behind their heels. He elected himself to attack Castlecomer from the opposite side to the approach taken by Byrne.[1] In this strategy the local knowledge of the Doonane miners was of fundamental importance.

Castlecomer was an elegant town on the junction of the Clohogue and Deen rivers, built by the English Wandesford, coal mining dynasty on land taken from the O'Brennans in the previous century.[2] It was a planned town and an admired example of ascendancy power. The houses generally were of sturdy stone, there was a wide main street and a spacious market place. The medieval parish church had been taken down by Sir Christopher Wandesford who replaced it with a very handsome edifice for the Established Church, endowing it with O'Brennan lands. In the mid-seventeen-hundreds, the Wandesfords permitted a small Catholic chapel of ease to be built in the town and their prestige was further consolidated when Anne Wandesford married the Butler Earl of Ormonde. Her younger son, Captain James Butler, was now the officer in command in Castlecomer and her town house close to Castlecomer's big bridge was military headquarters. Lady Anne Butler herself and the Wandesford family 'had retired from the country at that season of alarm'.

In response to words of caution from the colliers, John Murphy dispatched one of their leaders, Ned Bergin of Kilgory, to instruct friends on their route to hang green boughs from their windows.[3] This was essential because a great many houses in that area belonged to the Wandesford colliers who were decidedly unfriendly and whose hostility was expected. The whole area anticipated the imminence of eruption and from early morning fleeing loyalists choked the main road to Castlecomer and well beyond it. Guided by the colliers, John Murphy and his men crossed the river Deen at Massford, north of Castlecomer, and marched smartly down along the western bank via Loon and Clohogue bridge.[4] At the outskirts of the town, the position was briefly considered. The garrison, mostly cavalry, consisted of a company of the Downshire Regiment, the Waterford and Cullinagh Yeoman Infantry and Cavalry and two troops of dragoons, 300 well-armed men.

John Murphy decided on a ploy to avoid battle.[5] He elected to send an emissary with a white flag forward to the garrison offering terms of surrender. It was shortly before ten in the morning when the chosen collier captain rode forward with the terms. Unconcerned and resplendent in newly borne green sash, he trotted out of a by-road and succeeded in reaching Captain James Butler in person at the head of his corps.[6] With 'uncommon audacity' he requested the safe passage of his insurgent comrades through the town. They had no desire, he declared, to cause damage or injury and if permitted to proceed on their route through the town, Captain Butler, his men and Castlecomer would not be harmed. Butler recovered from the shock of this delivery by a local man and replied by drawing his pistol and opening fire on him. He missed. The astonished collier wheeled about and returned the fire. He too missed and galloped back towards the insurgent ranks. He was pursued by a cavalry yeoman, overtaken and the enterprising bearer of the flag of truce was shot dead from his horse in full view of his comrades.

The raw fury of the insurgents doomed Castlecomer. John Murphy led them into the assault with a fever and drive which belied five continuous weeks of battle and march. Miles Byrne had not yet arrived from the east when the attack from the west began in an abandon of fury. John Murphy lashed his men into action, sometimes two astride the one horse to bring them to the point of combat with greater speed.[7] They swept all opposition before them and the leading attackers had penetrated to the bridge of Castlecomer almost as soon as the retreating Waterford Militia gained it. John Murphy's entry by the unexpected route had been a complete success. He and his men now menaced the garrison headquarters close by the bridge. The Waterford Militia Cavalry, retreating at full gallop before Miles Byrne, stampeded across the bridge in sure expectation of security, only to find that they were in the front line of battle.[8] They created utter confusion amongst their own desperately defending infantry. They now found themselves surrounded by the men immediately under John Murphy's command. Some burst their way to the stable yards behind the strongly built headquarters, under covering fire from soldiers and loyalists in occupation of the adjacent stone houses. Another contingent flogged their horses through to Kilkenny to implore reinforcements.

Lady Butler's town house on the western side of Castlecomer bridge was a large three-storey stone mansion with a courtyard and stoutly built stables to the rear. It was a strong defensive position for the survivors of the overwhelmed garrison, since the insurgents had no artillery. The troops whom John Murphy had beaten from their positions in the town's high ground settled themselves for a siege situation and kept up a devastating fire from every window at all levels. Byrne and his men, newly arrived from the river's east side, had to fight their way across the bridge to link up with John Murphy. In the fierce fighting which followed in that sector alone, the insurgents lost one hundred men.[9] Miles Byrne had loads of hay and straw pushed across the bridge by his men using them as cover but it failed as a protection as the military were able to shoot through the angles of the loads. Miles Byrne's own horse was killed under him in the action, a sorry but bearable loss.

Fr. Murphy's column, having taken the military barracks in the west of the town, concentrated their attack on Castlecomer's military headquarters from the rear. Another contingent took Castlecomer House, the family seat, with its sheltering woods. It was, however, around Lady Butler's house in the square and the three other strong slated houses nearby that the action developed. John Murphy now controlled the entire town with the exception of these houses and he proposed to eliminate those last obstacles by burning the armed occupants out of them. He had loads of straw, hay and anything else that would burn trundled over through the gardens to the rear of the Butler house, rammed against the wall below the window and set on fire. Negotiations for surrender commenced at once. Miles Byrne effected the negotiations from one side of the river Deen as John Murphy conducted military operations from the opposite side.

From amongst the prisoners they held under guard, Byrne chose an emissary to treat with the military, a man who could not be other than a neutral in a war beyond his comprehension. He was Wandesford's black African servant in livery. Carrying a white flag, he brought simple conditions to the military; surrender or be burned to death. The door of Lady Butler's house opened and he was admitted. In five minutes he was out again. The answer he brought from the besieged was that while they knew their strong point was on fire and they wished to surrender, they required written protection, signed by Reverend John Murphy, whom they understood to be the insurgent commander-in-chief, otherwise they could not venture. Their fear was explained by the fact that one of the Waterford militiamen had earlier been piked by Byrne's men who did not realise that a parley was taking place at the time.

Miles Byrne set off to confer with his chief. He proceeded with his African along the east bank of the Deen. John Murphy was called and met him in the gardens on the western side at the narrowest part of the river. Murphy may not have carried on a conversation with an African since his student days in Seville but he was able to communicate clear instructions. He approved of the threats that Byrne had made to the besieged. He told the African to return with Byrne, to enter the besieged house and inform the military that immediately he procured pen and ink he would send them the written protection they required. He would then,he said, give orders to stop adding more fuel to the house now in flames and he expressed the hope that they would not hesitate in getting out of it before it was too late, adding that he himself would be at the bridge along with Byrne to receive and protect them. Byrne emphasised the stipulation that the moment they came out and handed over their arms and ammunition they would be put at liberty to go where they pleased.

Before noon, John Murphy took a respite in the blazing town. The Protestant church was taken over by colliers who sought out known enemies with vigour. They used the church as both court and prison.[10] There too John Murphy organised his headquarters and arranged for the burial of his dead in the surrounding St. Mary's churchyard. At least two men were brought before the insurgents' tribunal. One, an Orangeman named Arthur Williams, a tradesman, was found guilty as charged and hanged. A prosperous landlord's agent named Kane was tried but after intercession on his behalf by a Castlecomer colliery woman he was found not guilty and released. John Murphy received before him two of the several 'country gentlemen' who had fallen into their hands. They were not imprisoned or molested. What they may have discussed is not recorded except a later observation made in safety that 'General Murphy was dressed in black, affected the appearance of a stupid enthusiast and showed some bullets which he said had been fired at him but had rebounded from his invulnerable body'.[11]

Early in the afternoon, John Murphy learned that in the Queen's county [Laois] and in the surrounding areas, the town of Athy in county Kildare included, thousands of men awaited his arrival to come flocking to his standard.[12] If the reports were correct, the men in those areas were sufficiently numerous to overthrow the King's forces. He intended to enlist their strength. Despite the gruelling march and actions of the morning he resolved to move on Athy that very evening. Before further arrangements could be put in train, however, a message arrived from Miles Byrne that the negotiations with the garrison in Lady Butler's residence had broken down. From the upper windows, some of the trapped soldiers had seen the approach of reinforcements. The offer of surrender was withdrawn. Musket fire and the whistle of shells through the trees signalled the arrival of the reinforcements outside the town. That, however, was the extent of activity by the fresh troops. They remained outside the town without even attempting to reconnoitre, still less to rescue their comrades. Their commander was General Sir Charles Asgill.

Fr. John sent out his entire force to battle. They had some time to rest, eat and drink, for they had been in effective occupation of Castlecomer since eleven o'clock. It was now two o'clock on a hot afternoon as all the insurgents, colliers included, marched out to take battle stations. They could see Asgill's troops drawn up in formation little more than a musket shot away. To their astonishment, Asgill allowed them to march out with all the ease in the world and take up their positions on the rising ground opposite the military's own ranks. Not a volley was fired by the King's troops; no attempt to outflank the insurgents was made, even where they were vulnerable while marching to their stations.

As this prelude to engagement was being enacted, a sensational incident took place. Suddenly a redcoat soldier from the middle of Asgill's front line took off from his position and started to run toward the insurgents. He carried his arms and equipment. It was a front line desertion and the instant Asgill's officers realised what was afoot they ordered their men to fire on the deserter but running and swerving he gained the insurgent lines unscathed. The rebel jeers and cheers resounded around the hills. The militia deserter told John Murphy and Miles Byrne that they could count on many of his comrades following his example. This confirmed what Byrne had consistently argued, that in the event of a few insurgent victories thousands of militiamen would desert to them.

With the insurgents exuding confidence, Asgill and his well-equipped force unexpectedly abandoned the field and withdrew towards Kilkenny city. John Murphy was left at liberty to return to Castlecomer, or advance in whatever direction he might choose. Asgill was nevertheless not lacking in imagination. 'Having cleared the town with guns', he reported to Lord Castlereagh, 'I attacked them on all sides. About four hundred were killed and the remainder fled. They were commanded by a priest called Murphy and their numbers are said to amount to 5,000. Our loss was inconsiderable'.[13]

John Murphy suspected that Asgill was attempting to entice him into a trap on the road to Kilkenny. He had no intention of accommodating him. Nothing but the certainty that the entire population would rise against their masters would justify an assault on Kilkenny with its arsenals.

John Murphy decided to adhere rigidly to his new plan. Regardless of the exhausted state of his men following the all-night march and the battle for Castlecomer in which he lost over one hundred killed that morning, he ordered the column to prepare for the march to Athy. Any further indulgence of fatigue was dispelled when he found a group of his men drinking to their hearts' content outside Purcell's brewery at Cloneen bridge.[14] Seizing a sledge, he smashed a barrel of ale to pieces and then drove the men back into the ranks, his rage banishing both thirst and fatigue from their bodies. Once more he sent picked men forward towards Athy with orders for friendly houses to show green boughs. He also instructed them that wherever the expected groups of new recruits rallied on hill tops in the country ahead of them, they were to signify their presence and the sympathy of their area by lighting a fire on the hill of their choice.[15] No more time was lost. His tough orders were not disputed and his men marched, on heading north with the sun still shimmering in the sky.

Castlecomer was left behind, like Lady Butler's rapidly evacuated town house, emptied of redcoats, but in smoking ruins.[16] John Murphy, inexhaustible, carried on, still convinced that all they had to do was show their pikes and standards and every man worth his salt would join them in the piecemeal destruction of the King's troops.

Driven remorselessly, the jaded insurgents took the route through Moneenroe.[17] Before Clonbrock they crossed the river Deen into the Queen's County, many of them fighting hard to stay awake. They struggled on through Clonbrock and then Fairy Mount but it had become evident that the limit of human endurance was reached. Men were dropping with fatigue and falling asleep on the roadside. The column, with the exception of the colliers, was on its last legs. Athy must await the next day. It was decided to make camp and the worn-out men and the few women who followed them fell flat with weariness on Keeffe's Hill in the townland of Slatt.[18] All but the colliers had marched eighty miles from Wexford in three days.

John Murphy' morrow of hope and glory never dawned. Instead of recruits flocking to his standard, there were no welcoming cheers, nothing but a blanket of silence. The insurgents were on their own, with a middle-aged-priest as their general, and a youth scarcely out of his teens as their second-in-command. Not alone were there no volunteers to their ranks but there seemed to be a determined bar against helping them in any way. They were not wanted in an area where from Miles Byrne's own certain knowledge and United Irish records, they should have obtained mighty reinforcements. The colliers were the first to read the signs. A number of them left the camp and vanished into the night.[19]

The government troops were active in the area. A large force of yeomen and militia from Maryborough [Portlaoise] had advanced towards the camp during that night of 24 June. They came probing as close as Aughadreen near Timahoe where they were within sight of the insurgents, but they did not attack, moving more like hunters stalking a wounded lion.[20] It was hinted in the camp next morning that the missing colliers had deserted to these troops. This was a terrifying thought, for if only one of them had joined the redcoats the whole strategy, equipment and morale of the insurgents was known to the enemy.

The camp was on an elevation in a countryside of low hills, distant valleys, and far-off mountains. To the south-east the hazy outline of Mount Leinster's peak could be seen against the horizon. The whole beautiful prospect was silent and lonely as the grave that morning, 25 June. There was not a friend in sight. For the first time since he had taken up arms, John Murphy showed despair. 'We have lost', he said, 'we will go home to Wexford to meet our fate'.[21] He conferred with all who could be described as senior insurgents, the leaders of the colliers included. Their thoughts turned to the larger division of the insurgent army which, under Edward Roche, Edward Fitzgerald, Anthony Perry and Garret Byrne, had vacated Wexford town on 21 June and headed for the vast natural fortress of Wicklow's mountains. They decided that they would leave the broken Midlands and link up with their comrades.

The decision taken, another long march of nearly thirty miles began, back as close as possible to the Blackstairs Mountain range. It was a bleak hour of undisguised disillusionment. The men had little ammunition and they grew in apprehension about their isolation in a countryside where they found they were regarded as intruders. John Murphy gave simple orders which were vital in the circumstances. He directed all who had any quantity of gunpowder to divide it with comrades who had none and all whose firearms were out of repair to provide themselves with pikes or some weapons or implements such as pitchforks or slash-hooks which would do the same work. With everyone armed in that way and marching in close order they felt that they had nothing to fear from cavalry or infantry. They were certain that they could force their way through the passes but they would avoid risking battle against superior forces. When they left Keeffe's Hill in Slatt Lower, Queen's County, there was no one near to bid them stay, bid them good luck or farewell. It was one calendar month to the day since John Murphy had emerged from clerical and rustic obscurity.

Chapter 16

Lost

The road was long and the day was hot. The insurgents trudged wearily where previously they had marched with bursting hope. Every step of the way was more fatiguing. One month of hard fighting and marching with little rest, indifferent food in variable quantities, living in the open under constant strain — all were a drain on energy. The column was now exhausted. The colliers who remained with the Wexford men may well have become disenchanted with the cause and the remorseless leader who drove them until they dropped.

The insurgents marched back to Gorteen in county Kilkenny, through Cruttenclough, to the top of Old Leighlin Hill where they turned south and continued until they reached the cool bog of Baunreagh.[1] John Murphy at last called a halt. Sentinels were placed. The coalmining areas around Castlecomer had been avoided but the colliers had marched on in the column leaving their families and homes behind and knowing nothing of what lay before them. The rest at Baunreagh was of necessity prolonged. Redcoat patrols from a large well-equipped force under the command of General Asgill had the camp under observation soon after midday, but from a safe distance. Although he had seasoned regular troops, including horse, foot and artillery, as well as the yeomanry of counties Kilkenny, Carlow and Kildare, he still feared battle with the weary insurgents.

Fr. John had the camp roused at 4 o'clock that afternoon. The column marched off to Kellymount through the bogs of Annagar and from there by Boherboy and Duninga to Goresbridge. Some of the women and fighting men were missing; dead or asleep in wayside meadows. Still, the harsh pace of the march was maintained. Near Paulstown even Fr. John's mare gave up.[2] He was loaned a fresh and valuable black horse by a tenant farmer named Kehoe. The strange animal agreed with him at once and he pressed on. That night, he chose another camp site. It

154

was on the hill of Kilcumney which squatted like a giant watchdog, guarding a majestic sweep of country on all sides from the Ridge of Leinster beneath to the adjacent Blackstairs Mountain range. No enemy could approach undetected. The wounded were brought to the centre of the camp with the women and the colliers, comparatively fresh men, offered to man the watch and keep guard while the utterly exhausted Wexford insurgents rested and had a night's sleep. Their offer was accepted with gratitude. Miles Byrne posted a few of his men on guard at one end of the long hill also. Soon all was quiet.

The dawn awakening of the camp was brutal. The trust of the exhausted Wexford insurgents had been betrayed during the night by the colliers 'on whose great exertions and assistance', Miles Byrne recalled, 'we counted so much and which was the principal cause that induced Fr. John to come into that country'. They had deserted, every man of them, and taken every gun and pike with all the gunpowder they could carry away with them from the camp. What gunpowder they could not take with them they pissed on.[3] Cries of helpless fury were raised on all sides, for the treachery was general, the theft and destruction comprehensive.[4] John Murphy was awakened and the ghastly news blurted into his ears. Byrne came forward. The guns had been wrenched from the arms of his own men as the last colliers ran from the camp.

The chasm of despair created in the insurgents was real and wounding, but its impact on their Commander-in-Chief was immeasurable. Were these scoundrels the men upon whom he placed so much reliance? He thought of the groups of them who had skulked away from the camp near Athy on the previous night. Miles Byrne was in an awful rage. To the extensive farmer's son, the collier deserters 'were only like the fellows fighting at fairs and patterns who are never seen first in any battle'. According to Byrne, the only dependence was to be placed on farmer's sons ... 'brave, modest, young fellows who would regard it a dishonour to be in a fair day fight ... always first in danger; in the lead to victory'.

The chorus of helpless protests subsided when scouts brought reports that they had heard the King's troops moving to surround the camp. Dense fog covered the redcoat movement and masked their strength.[5] For all the insurgents knew they could be out there in thousands. In fact, Major-General Sir Charles Asgill was there from Kilkenny with 1,200 men and Major Matthews from Maryborough with a force of 500, mainly Downshire Militia.

Fr. John gave his orders to Miles Byrne at once.[6] He resolved that they should break camp immediately and march to attack whatever enemy forces were blocking the way through the Scullogue Gap, even though their ammunition was low and the colliers had robbed them of the best

155

of their firearms. The insurgents collected their wounded and the women and began to withdraw towards the Blackstairs and the Gap, leaving nothing on the hill that could be of use to the enemy. They receded, one by one, group by group, into the fog, as actors from a well-lit stage are swallowed up in the gloom of the exit wings. Boolavogue men, Ferns men, Ballaghkeen men, Faythe men, Dick Monk and his John Street Corps, the Monaseed men, Miles Byrne, all walked out of Fr. John Murphy's life. Soon there was not a sound about him, save for the man who watched over him, his bodyguard, James Gallagher.[7] It was a lonesome spot and no place to remain. All was lost. The insurrection was quenched and with it the spirit of the people. This had been staring him in the face for an entire week and he had refused to look.

By the time John Murphy tried to follow his men through the fog, it was too late to overtake them. He was now an outlaw on the run with James Gallagher at his side in an isolated region. If caught and recognised by the enemy, he was doomed to a dreadful end and so was Gallagher; even as strangers unable to account for their presence, the best they could hope for was a quick death. The fog lifted and it was not long before the two fugitives were spotted by two recently recruited yeomen, John McNabb and Joseph Smith of Tullow.[8] These were in no hurry to pounce. The insurgents had an established reputation in hand-to-hand combat. The yeos could bide their time and they decided to do that.

Avoiding the roads, John Murphy guided Gallagher and the horses through briars and bushes, across fields and bogs on the way to a friendly house well known to him in the foothills of Mount Leinster. The first home that he knew nearest the mountains was O'Connells of Killoughternane and he reached it on the evening of 26 June.[9] The spectacle he presented on arrival there must have greatly distressed the family, for he was more like a scarecrow than the decently turned-out priest they knew. The twelve-year-old daughter of the house made herself busy repairing his worn and torn clothes. The O'Connells told him that a body of hungry insurgents were with them that morning and that they had given them every available scrap of food. It was good news, for it assured Fr. John that these men had used an escape route that he knew well through the mountains. They had gone through the Cromwell Gap into Wexford instead of through the Scullogue Gap which the enemy were thought to be holding in force.[10]

The O'Connells could have sheltered the fugitives but John Murphy was on edge, so anxious to be on his way that he would not allow the young girl time to finish the repairs to his clothes. As soon as they had refreshments, both men rode off into the night, cautiously making for the place where the wounded Mogue Kearns had been lodged the previous week. It was the home of family connections of his own, the Murphys of the Bawnogue, Rathgeeran.[11] He had frequently stayed there when out hunting or fowling. When they reached the shelter of this house, they found that Kearns, having recovered his strength, had crossed back to north Wexford to rejoin the other fighting division. But John Murphy was drained. Amidst the balm of close friends he was overwhelmed by total exhaustion at last.

Fr. John and his bodyguard remained concealed in Murphy's for three days and nights, resting in peace for the first time in five weeks.[12] News of a battle in the Scullogue Gap was brought to him. There were few insurgent losses and he knew that his men were safe and on their way to Wicklow at the other side of the mountain range. This, however, was not the end of the story. Instead of pursuing the fighting men through the Scullogue Gap, the King's troops turned on the defenceless non-combatant people of the area and slaughtered more than one hundred in their houses by the roadside. General Asgill reported the butchery as a famous victory, with the additional news that the rebel general, Murphy, was amongst the slain.[13]

'Eleven hundred rebels were left dead on a field of action', *Finn's Leinster Journal* reported, 'amongst whom was the invulnerable Commander, Murphy'. Fr. Murphy was officially declared dead and this explains why there was not a hue and cry for him. The *Journal* issue with the dramatic news had been published in Kilkenny under military censorship.

After three days of rest, refreshment and repair, the fugitives bade farewell to Fr. John's old friends and resumed their hazardous journey on the morning of 29 June. The Murphys gave him a fresh horse in exchange for Kehoe's black mount. They understood from him that he and Gallagher would head for the Wicklow Mountains, travelling across county Carlow and taking care to avoid all towns and villages.

John Murphy became a man of the shadows, but one who left a memory everywhere he called. His first stop after leaving the Bawnogue was at the home of Welsh immigrants named Griffiths, who lived at Rossdillig not far from Killedmond. Their sympathy was well known to him. They had saved rebel lives and given decent burial in Kiltennel to his men killed in action. In what was now a lost cause, their continued friendship might have been in doubt but instead they welcomed the fugitives. In a long-remembered outburst of emotion at their house, Fr. John Murphy struck the table with his clenched fist and prayed that as long as grass grew and water ran there would be Griffiths at Rossdillig.

The two fugitives returned to Killoughternane and at the forge of reliable blacksmiths named Tuite they had their horses shod with the shoes back to front, one of the oldest schemes for sending pursuers in the opposite direction to that taken by the pursued.[14] This done, they visited the O'Connells again and remained until the early hours of the 30th. At Killoughternane, the Blackstairs Mountain range points north to the Wicklow Mountains. The two men cautiously skirted the slopes, pausing, peering and listening until they arrived at Jordans of Coolnasneachta in the parish of Myshall later that morning. It was there that Fr. John celebrated his last Mass and the incongruous sight of the shabby outlaw going through the time-honoured sacred rubric made a long lasting impression on the Jordans.[15]

The priest and his faithful guard and comrade remained with the Jordans until the early hours of the following morning. They then set out on another hazardous stage of their journey, more perilous even than heretofore, following, or being compelled in caution to follow, a course that took them away from the ridge of the Blackstairs and over north-west in the general direction of Bagenalstown and Ballon. Their next place of refuge was at Jacob Nolan's of Kilmaglen near Kilconnor. During the sojourn in Nolan's, Fr. John plotted the next stage in their journey. All going well, his idea was to cross the Slaney river above Tullow at the ford of Slaney Quarter.[16] When it was thought safe, they left Jacob Nolan's and set off furtively once more. However, there were evening patrols in the vicinity of Ballon and these had finally the effect of driving the fugitives to a despairing decision. They were compelled to seek refuge at a homestead they did not know. It was a two-storey house. They entered the backyard and the stable, taking the chance of resting themselves and the horses in safety. The place was Ballyveale House, the home of Protestant farmers, George and Anne Keppel and their family.[17]

The Keppels became aware that they had strangers on their premises, unexpected and unannounced. In the summer of 1798, an intrusion of this kind could mean anything for people living in an isolated rural homestead, plunder and slaughter not excluded. It must have been with feelings of acute fear that the family watched George Keppel go out into the farmyard to investigate. He opened the stable door and saw within a strange pair of horses and a couple of ragged men lying down. It is not known what preliminary words were exchanged, but something in the middle-aged trespasser's bearing and that of his companion moved George Keppel, for he invited them into his home.

No ordinary measure of Christian charity and courage was required by those who would shelter rebels in 1798 and strangers of unexplained presence could be no other. The penalty for giving aid and comfort to the King's Irish enemies was certain death, not infrequently a prolonged and agonising process. Brushing aside their reluctance to place his house in mortal danger, George Keppel insisted that they accompany him inside for rest and refreshment. The two trespassers entered the Keppel home, were seated, talked at some length and became better acquainted. It soon became evident to the Keppels that at least one of their guests was no ordinary fugitive. He told them who he was: John Murphy, an outlaw, a Roman Catholic priest on the run. It made no difference. The Keppels wished them to remain until they had fully recovered from the hardship they had endured. This they had to refuse, for if they were discovered about the place their host and his family would be severely punished.

When it was safe to move, probably approaching dusk on 1 July, the two men headed north towards Tullow, once more over a heavily patrolled area across the main Carlow to Wexford road. Tullow was the field headquarters of General Sir James Duff and his staff. Regular army, yeomen and militia constantly patrolled, for the insurrection spurted briskly in Wexford on the other side of the mountains. The shorter way to the Wicklow Mountains would have been directly east from Ballon, but in the conditions obtaining it must be assumed that the fugitives' route was determined by the necessity to avoid enemy patrols.

Fr. John knew Tullow and district well. His sister's sister-in-law, Mrs. Dawson, lived on the outskirts of Tullow, but it is unlikely that this had any bearing on the way he selected to go.[18] There is a persistent tradition that he wished to meet Bishop Delaney of Kildare and Leighlin in order to explain his role in the rebellion and become reconciled to the Church he had served so steadfastly. The bishop lived in Tullow. The tradition has it that Fr. Murphy did have a meeting with him, probably in his home in the early hours of 2 July but so deadly was the danger in which the bishop was placed by the rebel curate's presence in his house that any record of it is deeply shrouded.[19]

A little to the south-west of Tullow town near the crossroads of Castlemore lived the O'Tooles, a small-acreage Catholic tenant farm family. Into their yard John Murphy and James Gallagher led their horses at break of day when it had become apparent that it was not safe for them to journey further in the open.[20] They must have ridden hard, for the horses were sweating heavily and they were themselves fatigued. They entered O'Toole's house and asked for refreshment and a place to rest. The O'Tooles, who were getting ready for the day's work, gave them food and allowed them to put their horses in the stable. Later the rebel chief and his bodyguard lay down in the hayloft over their horses.

The task of saving the hay for the next winter's feed was in full swing and the O'Tooles were out early with their own team of horses. It was a vital day, a day perhaps of hay rick-making with neighbours' help. They were seen by a party of yeomen from Tullow who happened to pass by, amongst them John McNabb and Joseph Smith who claimed to have spotted two fugitives on the run after the flight from Kilcumney Hill on 26 June.[21] The yeomen, comprising some farmers from the Tullow area, decided to confiscate the two horses already in harness and at work. They needed them for the army, they said. The O'Tooles became incensed by this robbery-under-arms, which would ruin them. In an outburst, O'Toole's wife shouted that if they looked around they would find better horses, so why should they unyoke? The yeos entered the farmyard and found the two horses in the stable and remarkably both had their shoes nailed on back to front.[22]

John Murphy, unshaven, in torn clothes, woke up and found himself confronted by the group of excited yeomen. Gallagher, in similar plight, was also wide awake and in shock within seconds. The Tullow yeomen exulted. Two ragged and armed strangers, both possessing good horses, and asleep when other men were at work? Who could they be? What was their business? Whoever the two strangers were, it was clear to the yeomen that they could be nothing else but stragglers from the rebel hordes. The thing to do was to bring them into army headquarters in Tullow.

The two tattered scarecrows were shoved into General Duff's headquarters.[23] It was a hot day, an uneventful day for the military. The major tasks of containing the rebellion had been accomplished. Certainly the lower elements were still disaffected, but sufficient examples had been made to induce them to return to their allegiance. Here, however, was some diversion. Two scruffy country fellows, armed, with horses, and hiding.

In that headquarters a hasty court of enquiry was assembled.[24] It consisted of a distinguished group of officers. They were General Sir James Duff and his aide-de-camp, Colonel Foster; Colonel Piggot, the Earl of Roden, Captain McClintock, an officer named Robert Crawford (later Major-General Crawford), Colonel Eden, Major Hall and others; in all, about twenty officers. The two prisoners, who would not account for their movements or arms, were quickly brought into the officers' presence. They had nothing to say. They were ordered to be searched. The search on Gallagher provided nothing, but on John Murphy's person they found his stole, then a pyx, a small crucifix and the small vial he carried containing the oils for the last rites.[25] This was revealing. A priest, a popish priest on the run. It greatly intrigued one officer, Major Hall, who assumed the role of interrogator.[26]

The priest was subjected to selective jibes at his profession and religious persuasion. He was scoffed at and insulted by Hall. The Major desired him to work miracles. In a mocking gesture he grabbed Fr. John by the crotch.[27] For the first time John Murphy lost control. He doubled his fist and launched Major Hall fully down on the floor with a violent blow.[28] When order was restored, more questions were urged on him.[29] Was he one of the priests on Vinegar Hill? Was he one of the priests present on Vinegar Hill when loyalists were collected and murdered? Was he one of the council of priests that ordered these murders on Vinegar Hill? On and on the interrogation went, but it became a tedious exercise, for no information could be elicited from either the priest or his companion. The matter was cut short when, without any possible defence, they were found guilty of being rebels. They were both sentenced to death there and then, but if it were possible to get any information out of the two rogues, it should be tried. They were handed over to the yeomen.[30]

The Market Square of Tullow is more like a long triangle than a square and it tilts down an incline toward the river Slaney. It was a roasting July day and the square was filled with soldiers of all sorts, lounging about in a relaxed situation with imminent peril no longer a threat. The ordinary work of a provincial town was carried on, and the people of Tullow prospered from the influx of military while their town enjoyed the trappings of a major military base.

The yeomen pushed the two rebel captives through the passing people into the square, where punishment was no novelty that summer. Of the two, they picked on James Gallagher first. He was stripped and tied to the whipping post. It was a common sight, one which had been witnessed so often that yeomen looked on the convulsions of a flogged man with as little interest as they would regard a horse bolting under the whip. They stood the priest to one side. Then they commenced flogging James Gallagher. They kept questioning him alternately between lashes, but Gallagher said nothing. They were getting very little satisfaction out of the afternoon, so they tried another method of extracting information. It was known as half hanging. Gallagher was hanged by the neck and, just before the approach of death, taken down, revived and interrogated. As no satisfactory replies were forthcoming from the prisoner, the process was repeated. Still James Gallagher refused to talk or betray John Murphy, so they tired of him and left him there dangling on the gallows until the life choked out of him.

John Murphy was then made fast. His rags were ripped off him. Some of the yeomen had proposed that he be burned alive, but most of them were content that he be flogged in the hope that he might yet have information of value to offer. Soon the swish cracks of the whip rained on his bare back.[31] It is strange to report, but it was well noted that John Murphy never cried out. The yeomen might as well have been flogging a corpse. They took it in turns to flog him, but it made no difference. John Murphy had nothing to say. Then they did him a great mercy. They

161

hanged him until the life left his body.

As John Murphy's last spasms wrenched convulsively in the Market Square of Tullow, the unsatisfactory entertainment of the day was taken into account. Two captured rebels had been flogged and hanged, one of them a popish priest. It had been a trifle tedious and what, the yeomen thought, would be all that wrong with a bit of entertainment? One of the houses overlooking the square was occupied by a prosperous Catholic family named Callaghan. The Callaghans were terrified and from time to time their frightened faces had flitted across the window panes. The yeomen got a barrel of pitch and manoeuvred it to Callaghan's front door. Then they took John Murphy down and cut his head from his body. They heaved his torso into the barrel of pitch and then demanded Callaghan's presence before them. They informed him and his fearful family that they were about to be entertained with a holy fricassee, as 'there could be no objection to the incense of a priest'. The barrel of pitch containing the body was set on fire. There was more fun to be extracted from the Callaghans, so yeomen went into the house and forced all the windows open to admit the 'holy smoke' which, they promised, would redeem the Callaghans from sin.

At length the fire burnt itself out. There was nothing left but the bones, the ashes and the smell. The yeomen scrabbled the bones into the clay and dust in front of Callaghan's hall door.[32] That evening's sport was completed with a procession of the yeomen bearing the head of John Murphy to the Sessions House.[33] There they impaled it on a spike. It was a well-chosen site because the popish congregation could see it clearly on entering or leaving the nearby chapel. Romanists were greeted in hearty jest during the days when John Murphy's head remained blistering high above them. Yeomen pointing to the head advised them to apply for forgiveness of sins to their priest.[34]

What remained of the body was collected from the front of Callaghan's door by two masons. They were brothers named Manzor and they had watched the whole business, the punishments, the executions and the aftermath.[35] They put the remains in their aprons and carried the bones with the ashes to the old Mullawn graveyard which is girded by the fast-flowing Slaney river. The actual location of Fr. John Murphy's last place of rest is no longer known. His severed head remained spiked at the Sessions House until finally an influential Protestant lady objected. She persisted in her objection until she obtained permission from the authorities to have it removed. Then, in a final furtive rubric, the decaying head of Fr. John Murphy, Roman Catholic curate of Boolavogue and insurgent commander, joined his ashes in The Mullawn.[36]

Fr. John Murphy, the most wanted, the most notorious insurrection leader, the man likened by Sir Richard Musgrave to Attilla, Gengis Khan and Tamerlane, went to his death in the Market Square of Tullow without being recognised or identified by the enemies in whose hands he was captive.[37]

The premises in the Market Square, Tullow, owned by the Callaghan family in 1798, in front of which John Murphy's body was burned in a tar barrel.

(J. B. Curtis).

Epilogue

Fr. John Murphy's division had crossed over the Blackstairs Mountains through Cromwell's Gap into county Wexford on the morning of 25 June 1798.[1] They were appalled to discover that their commander was missing. They divided forces. A smaller portion left to hold out in Killoughram woods where they joined many militia deserters. The larger group under Miles Byrne fought with considerable success from the Scullogue Gap to the Wicklow Mountains. The division under Fitzgerald, Roche and Perry met with Miles Byrne's division at the Whiteheaps mountain near Croghan Kinsella.[2] Having enjoyed advantages in the field they had at last reached the haven of the Wicklow Mountains. Here another clash of minds took place. Anthony Perry, Fitzgerald and Garret Byrne adopted the strategy used by John Murphy the previous month. They elected to leave the Wicklow Mountains and to strike north into the flat open country of the midlands in the belief that thousands would rally to their standard.

They reached the river Boyne in county Meath before being reduced to a tattered remnant.[3] Miles Byrne remained battling on in the Wicklow Mountains convinced of imminent French aid. As autumn deepened Lord Lieutenant Cornwallis, the man who co-ordinated the government campaign initiated a policy of amelioration.[4] He invited all those who had taken part in the war, except the chiefs, to return to their homes where they would received his formal protection. A stop was put to the careers of the hard-line magistrates.

In the east and midlands of Ireland significant rebel hostilities ended by the middle of July 1798. Steps were then taken by the military authorities to oppose the expected French landings with regular British army troops. The French landed over one thousand men in Killala bay on 24 August 1798, the advance guard, they claimed of a force of thirty thousand.[5] After initial successes they were contained and the nationwide rebellion of 1798 was over. The surviving rebels from county Wexford returned to their homes or sheltered with hospitable families in counties Meath, Kildare, Kilkenny and Carlow, depending on where they fought last. The majority resumed work with renewed vigour.[6] Silence about their movements was strictly enforced within their families, leading to what became known as 'the horrible blank in the folk memory'.[7] Discussion of 1798 was silenced down to this century, especially in families related to either participants or observers of the terrible events.

Many weapons were surrendered; many were brought home and hidden in the roof thatch. The total of all surrendered or captured rebel weapons given by Lord Cromwallis's headquarters in August 1798, amounted to 129,583. It consisted of 79,630 pikes; 48,109 guns, 4,463 pistols, 4,183 swords, 1,756 bayonets, 248 blunderbusses, 119 musket barrels, 106 sword blades and 22 pieces of artillery.[8]

Edward Roche of Garrylough surrendered to General Hunter on terms of transportation towards the end of August 1798.[9] He was sent to Newgate prison in Dublin, but before the vessel was ready to convey him and other convicts abroad, he died abruptly. It is believed that he was poisoned. His collateral descendants still farm at Garrylough and Screen, county Wexford. Anthony Perry of Inch and Fr. Mogue Kearns were captured at Clonbullogue, county Offaly, and both men were hanged at Edenderry on 12 July 1798.[10]

Edward Fitzgerald of Newpark fought on with the scattered remnants of Wexford rebels in county Meath.[11] He surrendered conditionally to General Dundas on 12 July 1798, accepting exile and settled in Hamburg where he died at a comparatively early age in 1807. Garret Byrne of Ballymanus, who obtained similar terms from General John Moore, also settled in Hamburg.[12]

Beauchamp Bagenal Harvey with his friend, Dr. John Colclough and their wives, while awaiting passage to France, found refuge in a large cave on the southern side of the Great Saltee island off the coast of Wexford.[13] Their presence there was betrayed by Richard Waddy. Bagenal Harvey and John Colclough were arrested, taken by boat to Wexford, court-martialled and hanged on Wexford Bridge. Their heads were cut off and spiked on the courthouse opposite the bridge on 28 June, 1798. Cornelius Grogan of Johnstown Castle, aged seventy and suffering from gout, a former High Sheriff of the county and M.P. for Enniscorthy, was court-martialled, sentenced and hanged on the same day.[14] His body was treated in like manner.

Esmond Kyan, though severely wounded, marched north with the contingent heading for the Wicklow mountains on 21 June 1798. Seriously injured during the rebellion and therefore unable for the rigours of guerilla warfare, he returned to the outskirts of Wexford.[15] He was identified, tried and hanged within twenty-four hours. John Kelly of Killanne, severely wounded, was taken from his bed in his sister's Wexford town residence, rapidly tried by court-martial and hanged following the entry into Wexford by General Lake.[16] Richard Monaghan (Dick Monk) of John Street, Wexford, fought with John Murphy until the return of that division to Wexford. The wounded Monaghan was discovered in the vicinity of Bunclody by a party of yeomen who shot him dead.

Captain Matthew Keugh was Military Governor of Wexford during the insurgent occupation. When General Lake entered Wexford, Keugh was arrested, tried and hanged.[17] His head, with those of Harvey, Colclough and Grogan, was displayed on the spikes over the courthouse opposite Wexford Bridge. John Hay of Ballinkeele and Newcastle left Wexford with the Roche-Fitzgerald division on 21 June 1798, but later, displaying an amazing lack of discretion, returned with a servant to his home. He was betrayed to a patrol of General Dundas. Orders from Anthony Perry were found on him and he was arrested. He was tried, sentenced and hanged on Wexford Bridge.[18]

Thomas Cloney of Moneyhore survived vengeance with remarkable good fortune to reach old age.[19] At the age of sixty he wrote an account of his life and the 1798 period. It is a most valuable work, but it is not surprising that it concealed much compromising detail. General Cloney, as he was invariably known, died in Graiguenamanagh on 20 February 1850, aged 76. He was held in honour as the senior surviving insurgent officer of 1798 in Ireland. Edward Hay of Ballinkeele also survived many brushes with mortal peril.[20] His account of the 1790s, *History of the Insurrection of the County of Wexford,* was published in 1803. This was a reply to Sir Richard Musgrave's bitter and partisan account and was the first treatment of the rebellion from a sympathetic stance. Hay continued his active involvement in national politics, becoming secretary of the Dublin based Catholic Committee. His disagreements with Daniel O'Connell, the dominant force in that movement, resulted in Hay being effectively edged out of political power and he died in poverty in Dublin on 13 October 1826.

The young Miles Byrne was able to hide among relatives and sympathisers in Dublin city in the aftermath of hostilities.[21] He was deeply implicated in Robert Emmet's ill-fated rebellion. Byrne trained as a bookeeper and worked in that capacity until he was sent to France by Emmet to brief the French Government and to urge them to render immediate assistance. He was never to return to Ireland again. This remarkable young man, conscious that the cause of Irish independence was lost at least for his generation, embarked on a distinguished career in the French army. His memoirs, compiled with the support of his devoted wife, Fanny, were written in his Parisian home between 1854 and the year of his death, 1862, in his eighty-second year. They were published in 1863. The first volume deals specifically with the events in Wexford and Dublin up to the year 1803. His account of the 1798 period, written in a clear, honest style, is accurate and detailed, considering that it was compiled over half a century later. Byrne's *Memoirs* are today regarded by historians as the most reliable account written by a partisan on the rebel side. Miles and Fanny Byrne are buried in Montmartre, Paris, where their resting place is distinguished by a prominent Celtic Cross.

William Barker, experienced veteran of Walsh's Regiment in the

French army, was arguably the best strategist in the rebel ranks.[22] After the loss of the summer war in Wexford he defended himself by every subterfuge he could devise. In a memorandum to the Lord Lieutenant he protested his loyalty. He was acquitted of all charges at his court-martial in January 1799. His actual movements are unclear at this period but he was suffering intensely from the after effects of an arm amputation. He finally left county Wexford with his wife and family and resided in Hamburg. He and Miles Byrne met in the Irish Legion at Marlaix in 1803, both hoping in vain for another French expedition to Ireland.

The Catholic bishop, James Caulfield, though of frail constitution, was possessed of an iron determination. He continued his commanding role, insisting on the rectitude of his position before, during and after the rebellion. Thirty-three of his chapels were burned down but he allotted blame to sources other than the yeomen and orangemen who actually did the deeds, instead focussing on the Catholic priests involved on the rebel side.[23] Though almost all were either hanged or shot, he denounced them as 'renegade, abandoned, reprobate priests'. He introduced himself to General Lake and described Lake's attention to him as 'polite and kind'. He dined with army generals and officers. 'But for the regular English military', he wrote, 'they [the Catholic clergy] would all be killed by the yeomen'. He expressed his gratitude to the Midlothian Regiment for saving him when his house was under attack.[24]

On 13 September 1798, Caufield issued a pastoral letter, to be clearly proclaimed from every altar in the diocese.[25] In it he denounced the rebellion's 'diabolical conspiracy' and claimed that 'this accumulation of misfortunes [was] brought on the country by the machinations of crazy, ambitious, revolutionary adventurers, through the credulity of the incautious and ignorant multitude'. Caulfield's frail health worsened in 1803 and he was granted a co-adjutor bishop but 'he lingered on' until his death – eleven years later on 12 January 1814.[26]

On a careful examination of Caulfield's words and position, his knowledge of what French revolutionary activists did to the Pope and the Catholic Church on mainland Europe, it must be allowed that deep concern for his flock and Church along with the urgency of his 'sacred mission' were the prime factors uppermost in his mind throughout his career. In 1801, Sir Richard Musgrave compiled his history of the rebellion, with the object of proving that the insurrection was a carefully prepared Popish plot, in which the Catholic clergy were the sinister conspirators.[27] Musgrave emphasised the role of one particular villain. This villain is depicted as a conniving, fawning, blood-thirsty satyr, a man who amidst the shrieks of piked Protestants could drink wine with the utmost composure; a man who invoked the blessing of God upon the savage pikemen and their work as they proceeded to the massacre of Protestants on Wexford Bridge. Musgrave's villain is presented as a man who directed the revolt, and the annihilation of Protestants in conspiracy with his priests at their secret Enniscorthy rendezvous. The name of the villain of Musgrave's widely read work was James Caulfield, Catholic bishop of Ferns.

No side in county Wexford escaped hardship after the Rebellion. Protestants were compelled to beg in the streets for a morsel to stay alive or a coin to purchase food. In 1799 the distressed Protestant poor became so numerous in Gorey that the Select Vestry ordered that 'such poor [Protestants] only shall be allowed to beg in the parish as are authorised by a magistrate and signed by the minister and church wardens'.[28] Jane Barber recorded:

> One evil not generally known rose from the rebellion, the ill effects of which may be said still to continue. The yeomanry was composed mostly of fine boys, the sons of farmers, some of whom had scarcely attained the age of sixteen. These, removed from the eyes of their parents with weapons placed in their hands, raised to the rank of men before they had discretion to behave as such and exposed to all the temptations of idleness, intoxication and bad companions, when peaceful times returned were totally unable to settle to their farms, often by their fathers' death left to them alone, but continued the same careless, disorderly life till they became quite unable to pay their rents. They then were ejected and emigrated to America and on the very grounds which thirty years ago were in the possession of old Protestant families there now live the descendants of these very rebels who may be said to have been the origin of all this evil.[29]

Brigadier General John Moore (later Sir John Moore of Corunna fame) is the only British officer of the 1798 hostilities to be recalled kindly in the folk memory of county Wexford. The four most notorious magistrates slipped quietly back into the county in the aftermath of the rebellion. James Boyd spent his remaining years prominent in the social and farming life of Wexford. The other three all fell foul of Cornwallis's administration which was determined to run the country on impeccably fair lines. Archibald Jacob faced charges of illegally arresting people in the post-rebellion purges. Hunter Gowan was treated by the military as a lying scaremonger and was charged with robbery. Hawtrey White was arrested on charges of 'spreading rumours calculated to cause disturbance and loss of confidence in the intentions of government'.[30] Their excesses offended the conciliatory Cornwallis administration but they contrived to escape punishment and were still regarded as heroes by the triumphant loyalists of county Wexford.

As for Fr. John Murphy, it was some time after the insurrection before word percolated from those who had sheltered him in county Carlow that he had been executed in Tullow on 2 July 1798. Bishop Caulfield gave complete details of his Boolavogue curate's death in his letter to Archbishop Troy of 2 September 1798.[31] A great many people did not realise or want to believe that Fr. John was dead. There were those, especially the survivors of his division like Miles Byrne, who did not know that John Murphy was no more. They believed that he was well and in hiding. One unscrupulous Dublin entrepreneur exploited this longing for the departed chief. He initiated a collection to get 'Fr. John Murphy' away to America almost a year afer he was hanged in Tullow.

Martin Byrne, a woollen draper of Francis Street, Dublin and a committee of patriots worked to organise 'Fr. John's' escape. They had interviewed the 'priest' who claimed to be Fr. John Murphy. No one in Dublin, not even Miles Byrne, would credit the report that the man who so distinguished himself in 1798 had been executed in Tullow. They argued that had he been executed the Government papers of the day would have only been too glad to publish and publicise the event. The Government did not publicise it because they did not find out who it was they had captured and hanged. Nonetheless the collection was organised and in full spate when Byrne, hiding in Dublin, was contacted. None of the Dublin committee knew what Fr. John looked like and they asked Byrne to identify the priest. Delighted at the marvellous news, Miles was taken to meet him. He was brought into the room where 'Fr. John' was kept. There he was severely shocked to find not his chief but 'a black looking impostor'. It is not known what became of that man but the swindling of patriotic funds was halted. Even after that confrontation Miles and his friends remained convinced that Fr. John Murphy was still alive.

There was a further legacy of John Murphy which is unique – he was spoken of down to this decade as if he had lived recently. People spoke about him in a way which indicated that they personally knew him very well, especially in the Boolavogue area. This matter of fact intimacy is frequently met in descriptions of his physical appearance and manner. A recent visitor to the Boolavogue district made an enquiry without expecting positive enlightenment. He asked an inhabitant what sort Fr. John Murphy of 1798 was. He was startled when the elderly man threw back his head and in a hearty voice replied, 'Ah, by God, he was the right sort of a man'.[32]

For a great many years county Wexford did not recover from the holocaust of 1798. After a while books began to be published about the upheaval. In the folk memory and tradition there are character pictures and recollections of the events and the most memorable leaders. The memories were as interesting and varied as the '98 leaders themselves

Harvey, Perry, Cloney, Edward Roche, Philip Roche, Kelly, Monk, Kearns, Kyan, Michael Murphy, Boxwell, Grogan, Colclough, Barker, Keugh, Byrne and Fitzgerald. Their weaknesses and their flaws were remembered. One man, however, emerged and remained as beyond reproach in the insurgents' memory. That man was John Murphy, the curate of Boolavogue.

Sources

Abbreviations

Anal. Hib.	*Analecta Hibernica*
Archiv. Hib.	*Archivium Hibernicum*
Collect. Hib.	*Collectanea Hibernica*
Cork Hist. Arch. Soc. Jn.	*Cork Historical and Archeological Society Journal*
D.D.A.	Dublin Diocesan Archive
Et seq.	et sequitur
Ibid.	The same
I.F.C.	Irish Folklore Commission
I.H.S.	*Irish Historical Studies*
Jn. Old Wex. Soc.	*Journal of Old Wexford Society*
Loc. Cit.	*Locus Citatus*
Mic.	Microfilm
N.L.I.	National Library of Ireland
Op. Cit.	*Opus Citatus*
R.D.	Registry of Deeds
S.P.O.R.P.	State Paper Office, Rebellion Papers
Studia Hib.	*Studia Hibernica*
T.C.D.	Trinity College Dublin
Wex. Hist. Soc. Jn.	*Wexford Historical Society Journal*

Manuscripts

Aquilar y Ribon, Don Franscisco, Biographical Notes 'Informaciones de legitimided y Limpieza desde el ano 1754 a 1756', Book 701, pp 407-22; Books 632, 633, 634 (higher degrees), Book 777, pp 495-9. List of Professors in Philosophy and Theology, file 609, Cloister Books 945 and 946, Library of the University of Seville.

Barber, Jane, 'Recollections of the summer of 1978' (Typescript copy) in Wexford County Library, Wexford.

Letters of James Caulfield, R.C. Bishop of Ferns, to Archbishop Troy, Dublin, in the Dublin Diocesan Archives, Holy Cross College, Clonliffe, Dublin.

Report of Bishop Sweetman, 1785, Ferns Diocesan Archives, Bishop's House, Summerhill, Wexford

Luke Cullen, Manuscript, N.L.I., Ms. 9, 760; T.C.D., Ms. S.5.19.

Letters of Charles Erskine, papal envoy in London, to Archbishop Troy, Dublin Diocesan Archives.

Elmes family letters, 1790-1810, in possession of King Milne, Ballymorgan, Ferns, county Wexford.

Thomas Handcock, Narrative of the Battle of Enniscorthy and events preceding and during the Rebellion, N.L.I., mic. 1,044.

Letters and other papers relating to Irish affairs 1788-1801, N.L.I., mic. 5,407-5.

John Kavanagh, Life and Travel of the Rev. John Kavanagh of Annagh (Diocese of Ferns) 1790, Passionist Fathers Archives, Mount Argus, Dublin.

Diary of Charles Lett; Family history of the Letts of county Wexford, copy in possession of Mrs Cecil Miller, Shortalstown, Killinick, county Wexford.

Madden papers, T.C.D., Ms. 19-22.

Richard Musgrave papers, N.L.I., Ms. 4,156-7.

Aodh Ó Rathoilligh, Rathnure, School manuscript, Irish Folklore Commission, Ms. 890.

T.J. Powell, The Background to the Rebellion in County Wexford, 1790-8, unpublished M.A. thesis, 1970, U.C.D.

Margaret Reck, Family Recollections, Wexford County Library.

Diary of Elizabeth Richards, Rathaspeck, 1798, N.L.I., mic. 6,486.

Letters, reports and other papers relating to Irish affairs, 1788-1801, Archive of the Sacred Congregation for the Propagation of the Faith, Rome.

Charles Vallancey, The Defence of the Southern part of Ireland (1797), in Ferns Diocesan Archives, Bishop's House, Summerhill, Wexford.

Newspapers and Periodicals

Free Press, Wexford.

People Newspapers, Wexford (includes *New Ross Standard* and *Enniscorthy Guardian*).

Finn's Leinster Journal, Kilkenny.

Echo and Leinster Advertiser, Enniscorthy.

Irish Magazine and Monthly Asylum for Neglected Biography, Dublin

Published Works

Adams, Jane, 'Narrative' in T. Crofton Croker (ed.), *Researches in the South of Ireland* (London, 1824), pp 347-85.

Alexander, James, *A Succinct Narration of the Rebellion in the County of Wexford, especially in the vicinity of Ross* (Dublin, 1800).

Barrington, Jonah, *Personal Sketches and Recollections of his own Times* (Glasgow, 1827).

Ibid., Rise and Fall of the Irish Nation (Dublin, 1833).

Bevan, Brian, *King James the Third of England* (London, 1967).

de Bhál, S., 'An Ghaeilge i Loch Garman' in M. Berney (ed.), *Centenary Record* (Wexford, 1958), pp 114-9.

Browne, Kathleen, *Wexford; For Senior Pupils in National Schools* (Dublin, 1927).

Brownrigg, Mrs., 'Narrative' in A. Wheeler and A. Broadley, *The War in Wexford* (London, 1910), pp 162-99.

de Brún, Pádraig, 'A Lament in Irish for John Stafford' in *The Past*, viii (1970), pp 43-51.

Burke, Bernard, *Burke's Genealogical and Heraldic History of the Landed Gentry of Ireland* (London, 1912).

Byrne, Miles, *Memoirs of Miles Byrne*, 3 vols (Paris, 1863).

Carrigan, William, *History of the Diocese of Ossory*, 4 vols (Dublin, 1905).

[Castlereagh, Viscount], C. Vane (ed.), *Memoirs and Correspondence of Viscount Castlereagh*, 12 vols (London, 1850-53).

Catholic Encyclopaedia (New York, 1913).

Caulfield, James, *The reply of the Right Reverend Dr. Caulfield to Sir Richard Musgrave* (Dublin, 1801).

Chart, D. (ed.), *The Drennan Letters 1776-1819* (Belfast, 1931).

Cloney, Thomas, *A Personal Narrative of Those Transactions in the County Wexford, in which the Author was engaged, during the awful period of 1798* (Dublin, 1832).

Comerford, Michael, *Collections Relating to the Diocese of Kildare and Leighlin*, 3 vols (Dublin, 1883-1886).

Corish, P., 'Reformation and Counter Reformation 1500-1700' in Berney (ed.), *op. cit.,* pp 31-4.

Ibid., (ed.), 'Bishop Caulfield's Relatio Status 1796' in *Archiv. Hib.*, xxviii (1966), pp 103-13.

Ibid., 'The Diocese of Ferns and the Penal Days' in *The Past*, viii (1970), pp 5-17.

Ibid., 'Documents relating to the appointment of Bishop John Stafford 1772' in *The Past,* ix (1972), pp 73-9.

Cornwallis, Charles, *Correspondence* (London, 1859).

Cullen, L.M., *The Emergence of Modern Ireland 1600-1900* (London, 1981).

Ibid., 'The 1798 Rebellion in its eighteenth century context' in P. Corish (ed.), *Radicals, Rebels and Establishments* (Belfast, 1985), pp 91-113.

Ibid., 'The 1798 Rebellion in Wexford' in K. Whelan (ed.), *Wexford: History and Society* (Dublin, 1987), pp 248-95.

Ibid., 'Late eighteenth-century politicisation in Ireland: problems in its study and its French links', in L. Cullen and P. Bergeron (ed.), *The Proceedings of the Fourth Franco - Irish Historical Conference* (Paris, 1991), pp 137-58.

[Cullen, Luke], *Personal Recollections of Wexford and Wicklow Insurgents of 1798* (Enniscorthy, 1959).

Dickson, Charles, *The Wexford Rising in 1798* (Tralee, n.d. [circa 1950]).

Ibid., *Revolt in the North* (Dublin, 1960).

Ibid., 'The Battle of Vinegar Hill 1798' in *Irish Sword,* i (1949), pp 293-5.

Ibid., 'Reign of Terror blurred '98 Tradition', Inaugural paper read to New Ross Historical and Archaeological Society, (reported, *People,* Wexford, 24 Nov. 1956).

Doblado, Leucadio, *Letter from Spain* (London, 1822).

Dolan, T. and Ó Muirithe, D. (ed.), 'Poole's Glossary with some pieces of Verse of the old dialect of the English Colony in the baronies of Forth and Bargy' in *The Past,* viii (1979), pp 5-71.

Dowling, Patrick, *The Hedge Schools of Ireland* (Cork, 1968).

Farrow, John, *Pageant of the Popes* (St. Paul, 1955).

Fenning, Hugh, 'Some Problems of the Irish Mission, 1733-1774' in *Collect. Hib.,* viii (1965), pp 58-109.

Fitzgerald-Uniacke, R., 'The Uniackes of Youghal' in *Cork Hist. Arch. Soc. Jn.,* No. xxxii (1894), vol. iii pp 113-6, 146-52, 183-91, 210-21, 232-41, 245-55.

Flood, W. Grattan, *History of the Diocese of Ferns* (Waterford, 1916).

Fraser, Robert, *Statistical Survey of the County of Wexford* (Dublin, 1807).

Furlong, Nicholas, 'A History of Land Reclamation in Wexford Harbour' in *Jn. Old Wex. Soc,* ii (1969), pp 53-77.

Ibid., 'Life in Wexford Port, 1600-1800' in Whelan, *Wexford,* pp 150-72.

Gardiner, M. and Ryan, P. *Soils of County Wexford* (Dublin, 1964).

Gibbons, Margaret, *Glimpses of Catholic Ireland in the Eighteenth Century* (Dublin, 1932).

Giblin, Cathaldus, 'Letters from Sydney of a '98 deportee' in *The Past,* vi (1950), pp 45-103.

Goodall, David, 'Dixon of Castlebridge' in *Irish Genealogist,* vi (1984), pp 629-41.

Gordon, James, *A History of Ireland* (Dublin, 1805).

Ibid., *History of the Rebellion in 1798* (Dublin, 1801).

Gough, Clement, 'Some notes on Arthur Young's Tour in County Wexford' in *The Past,* i (1920), pp 107-17.

Grattan, Henry Jr., *Life of Henry Grattan,* 5 vols. (London, 1839-1846).

Ibid., *Speeches of Henry Grattan,* 4 vols (London, 1844).

Hay, Edward, *History of the Insurrection of the County of Wexford* A.D., 1798 (Dublin, 1803).

Hayes, Richard, *Ireland and Irishmen in the French Revolution* (Dublin, 1932).

Herr, Richard, *The Eighteenth Century Revolution in Spain* (Princeton, 1958).

Hore, Philip H., *History of the Town and County of Wexford,* 6 vols (London, 1900-1911).

Jacob, William, *Travels in the South of Spain* (London, 1811).

Johnson, E.M., *Ireland in the Eighteenth Century* (Dublin, 1974).

Joyce, John, *General Thomas Cloney* (Dublin, 1988).

Kavanagh, Patrick, *A Popular History of the Insurrection of 1798* (Dublin, 1918).

Kerrigan, Paul, 'Defences of Ireland 1793-1815' in *An Cosantóir* (April, 1974).

Killen, W., *The Ecclesiastical History of Ireland,* 2 vols (London, 1875).

Lecky, William, *A History of Ireland in the Eighteenth Century,* 5 vols (London, 1902).

Leslie, J.B., *Ferns Clergy and Parishes* (Dublin, 1936).

List of Yeomanry Corps (Dublin, 1797).

Lyng, Thomas, *Castlecomer Connections* (Castlecomer, 1984).

Madden, R.R., *The United Irishmen,* 4 vols (Dublin, 1857-60).

Maurice, J. (ed.), *The Diary of Sir. John Moore* (London, 1904).

Maxwell, William, *History of the Irish Rebellion in 1798* (London, 1845).

McAnally, Henry, *The Irish Militia 1793-1816* (Dublin, 1949).

McCracken, J.L., *The Irish Parliament in the Eighteenth Century* (Dundalk, 1971).

Mac Dermot, Frank, *Theobald Wolfe Tone* (London, 1939).

McDowell, R.B., 'The Personnel of the Dublin Society of United Irishmen, 1791-4' in *I.H.S.,* ii (1940), pp 12-53.

Ibid., 'Proceedings of the Dublin Society of United Irishmen' in *Anal. Hib.,* xvii (1949), pp 1-143.

MacLysaght, Edward, *Irish Families* (Dublin, 1972).

Moody, T.W. and Martin, F.X. (ed.), *The Course of Irish History* (Cork, 1967).

Musgrave, Richard, *Memoirs of the Rebellion in Ireland,* 2 vols (Dublin, 3rd ed., 1802).

Nolan, Timothy J., 'Wexford Parish in the eighteenteenth and early nineteenth centuries' in Berney (ed.), *op. cit.,* pp 61-8.

Nolan, William, 'Fr. John's Last Journey, 1798' in *Carloviana,* i, no. 18 (1969), pp 23-5.

O'Brien, George, *The Economic History of Ireland in the Eighteenth Century* (Dublin, 1918).

O'Byrne, E. (ed.), *The Convert Rolls* (Dublin, 1981).

Ogle, T. Acres, *The Irish Militia Officer* (Dublin, 1873).

Ohlmeyer, Jane, '"The Dunkirk of Ireland", Wexford Privateers during the 1640s' in *Jn. Wex. Hist. Soc.* xii (1989), pp 23-49.

Ó Snodaigh, Pádraig, 'Notes on the Volunteers, Militia, Yeomanry and Orangemen of County Wexford' in *The Past,* xiv (1983), pp 5-48.

Ó Súilleabháin, Pádraig, 'Documents relating to Wexford Friary and Parish 1733-1798' in *Collect. Hib.,* viii (1965), pp 46-62.

Ó Tuathaigh, Gearóid, *Ireland Before the Famine* (Dublin, 1973).

Paine, Thomas, *The Rights of Man, Being an answer to Mr. Burke's attack on the French Revolution* (Dublin, 1791).

Pakenham, Thomas, *The Year of Liberty* (London, 1972).

Plowden, Francis, *The History of Ireland from its Invasion under Henry II to its Union with Great Britain,* 2 vols (London, 1812).

Powell, Thomas, 'An Economic Factor in the Wexford Rebellion of 1798', in *Studia Hib,.* xvi (1976), pp 144-70.

Prior-Wandesforde, R.C., 'Coalminng in the Castlecomer area' in *Carloviana* (December, 1975), pp 33-8.

Programme of Historical Exhibition of '98 Relics in the Athenaeum (Enniscorthy, 1938).

J. Ranson (ed.), 'A '98 diary by Mrs. Barbara Newton Lett' in *The Past,* v (1949), pp 117-49.

Renehan, Laurence, *Collections on Irish Church History,* 2 vols (Dublin, 1873).

Roche, Richard, *Here's to their Memory* (Wexford, 1966).

Sinnott, Peadar, 'Duncannon Fort' in *Jn. Old Wex. Soc., iii* (1970), pp 62-80.

Sinnott, Thomas, 'God grant you glory, brave Fr. Murphy' in *Shelbourne Journal* (Wexford, 1962), pp 141-60.

Ibid., 'Fr. John Murphy of Ninety Eight' in *The Redemptorist Record,* iii, (1938), pp 23-7.

Ibid., 'Fr. Michael Murphy' in *People,* Wexford, 11 Dec., 1948.

Ibid., 'The Battle of Foulksmills. An Eyewitness account' in *The Past,* vi (1950), pp 104-17.

Taylor, George, *An History of the Rise, Progress Cruelties and Suppression of the Rebellion in the County of Wexford in 1798* (Dublin, 1800).

Teeling, Charles, *History of the Irish Rebellion of 1798* (Glasgow, 1876).

Ibid., Sequel to the History of the Irish Rebellion of 1798 (Glasgow, 1876).

Thom, John (ed.), *The Life of Blanco White* (London, 1845).

Tobin, Andrew and O'Leary, Seamus, *The Bold Shelmaliers* (Wexford, 1988).

Tone, William Theobald Wolfe (ed.), *Life of Theobald Wolfe Tone, with Political writings and fragments of Diary,* 2 vols. (Washington, 1826).

Townsend, Joseph, *A Journey through Spain in the Years 1786 and 1787* (London, 1791).

Trotter, John, 'Walks through Ireland' in *The Past,* x (1974), pp 48-54.

G. O'Brien (ed.), *Catholic Ireland in the Eighteenth Century. Collected Essays of Maureen Wall* (Dublin, 1989).

'Veritas', *A Vindication of the Roman Catholic Clergy of the Town of Wexford in reply to 'Verax'* (Dublin, 1798).

Walsh, John, *Frederick Augustus Hervey 1730-1903, Fourth Earl of Bristol, Bishop of Derry* (Maynooth, 1972).

Whelan, Kevin, 'The Religious Factor in the 1798 Rebellion in County Wexford' in P. O'Flanagan, P. Ferguson and K. Whelan (ed.), *Rural Ireland 1600-1900* (Cork, 1987), pp 62-85.

Ibid., 'The role of the Catholic Priest in the 1798 Rebellion in county Wexford' in Whelan, *Wexford,* pp 296-315.

Ibid., (ed.), *A History of Newbawn* (Enniscorthy, 1986).

Ibid., 'Catholic Mobilisation, 1750-1850' in Cullen and Bergeron, *op. cit.,* pp 235-58.

Ibid., 'Politicisation in County Wexford and the origins of the 1798 Rebellion' in H. Gough and D. Dickson (ed.), *The French Revolution and Ireland* (Dublin, 1990), pp 156-78.

Ibid., 'Catholics, politicisation and the 1798 Rebellion' in R. O Muirí (ed.), *Irish Church History Today* (Armagh, 1991), pp 96-116.

Ibid., (ed.), *Wexford: History and Society* (Dublin, 1987).

Young, Arthur, *A Tour in Ireland* (Dublin, 1776).

NOTES
(For full citation of commonly used references see under sources)

Chapter 1

1. *Free Press,* Letters: 'Grandson of Rebel', January 1898, cited in 'Fr. Murphy of '98, issue of 15 Apr. 1955; 'Grand-nephew of Fr. Murphy', James Murphy of The Harrow, 1 Feb 1898; Patrick Murphy, Knockaree, Strahart, 1 Mar. 1898 (Patrick Murphy adds that the Murphy homestead at Tincurry was eventually levelled); 'Grandson of Rebel', 14 Mar. 1898; Edmond Walsh, Arklow, 26 Mar. 1898; P. MacSuibhne, *'98 in*

Carlow, (Carlow, 1974), p. 12; T. Sinnott, 'Fr. John Murphy of '98' in *The Redemptorist Record* (Nov. 1938), p. 23; *Ibid.,* 'God Grant you Glory, Brave Fr. Murphy:' in *Shelbourne Journal* (1962), p. 142; Kavanagh, *A Popular History,* p. 304. There are inconsistencies in sources about Tincurry-Murphy family names and members. I believe this list to be the correct one. The consensus of tradition, oral and written, along with reasonable deduction, is that Fr. John Murphy was forty-five in 1798.

T.D. Sinnott, late County Manager of Wexford, was the foremost authority on the oral tradition of 1798 in Wexford. A descendant of the insurgent leader Thomas Sinnott, he was personally acquainted with Nicholas Keating of Ballinavarry (Davidstown), whose father had fought in the Rebellion with Fr. John Murphy. Nicholas Keating was over one hundred years old when he was killed in a fall from a horse in 1916. (His father may have escaped the vengeance of the Crown because of his marriage to a yeoman's daughter). The Keatings lived near the Tincurry Murphys, and through the Keatings were passed on exact details of family, events, contacts, disputes and engagements which would otherwise have been lost. T.D. Sinnott's published work on 1798 is meagre. The bulk of his information was passed on in lectures to various societies over four decades, and to the University College, Dublin, extramural diploma students, Wexford, 1950-1952, of whom this writer was one. His few published historical items indicate extemporaneous dictation to a secretary by a busy executive. He knew far more than his times would find palatable or that a public official could prudently disseminate. It is noteworthy that this reticence was shared by contemporary authorities on the period in county Wexford. (I am grateful to T.D. Sinnott's secretary, Ursula Kelly, for her assistance).

2. M. Gardiner and P. Ryan, *Soils of County Wexford* (Dublin, 1964); Hore, *Wexford,* v, p. 401.

3. E. MacLysaght, *Irish Families* (Dublin, 1972), p. 235; B. Burke, *Burke's Genealogical and Heraldic History of the Landed Gentry of Ireland* (London, 1912), pp 429, 462; T. Sinnott, 'Fr. Michael Murphy', *People,* 1 Dec. 1948; 'Ildana', *Ireland's Own,* p. 5, 24 Feb. 1909.

4. Whelan, 'The Catholic Priest', p. 307.

5. R.D., 65-248-593, 65-248-594; R.G. Fitzgerald - Uniacke, 'The Uniackes of Youghal' in *Cork. Hist. Arch. Soc. Jn.,* xxxii (Cork, 1894), pp 113-6, 146-52, 183-91, 210-21, 232-41, 245-55.

6. Sinnott (1938), *loc. cit.,* p. 23 and *Ibid.,* (1962), *loc. cit.,* p. 143; Musgrave, *Memoirs* i, p. 404; P. Kennedy, *The Banks of the Boro* (London, 1867), pp 255-6; P. Dowling, *The Hedge Schools of Ireland* (Cork, 1968).

7. Dickson, *The Wexford Rising,* pp 2-3; R. McDowell, 'The Protestant Nation' in T.W. Moody and F.X. Martin (ed.), *The course of Irish history* (Cork, 1967), p. 241; P. Corish, 'The Diocese of Ferns and the Penal Days' in *The Past,* viii (1970), p. 5; E. Johnston, *Ireland in the eighteenth century* (Dublin, 1974), pp 61, 172.

8. S. de Bhál, 'An Ghaeilge i Loch Garman' in M. Berney (ed.), *Centenary Record* (Wexford, 1958), p. 116; P. de Brún, 'A Lament in Irish for John Stafford, Coadjutor Bishop of Ferns' in *The Past,* viii (1970), p. 43 *et. seq.*; J. Trotter, 'A Walk through county Wexford in 1812' in *The Past,* x (1974), p. 49; [C. Gough], 'Some Notes on Arthur Young's Tour in County Wexford' in *The Past* (1920), p. 107; Whelan, *Newbawn,* p. 63.

9. W. Grattan Flood, *History of the Diocese of Ferns* (Waterford, 1916), p. 29.

10. Sinnott (1962), *loc. cit.,* pp 144-5.

11. *Free Press,* Wexford, Letter, Patrick Murphy, 2 Mar., 1898.

Chapter 2

1. N. Furlong, 'The Times and Life of Nicholas Sweetman, Bishop of Ferns' in *Jnl. Wex. Hist. Soc.,* ix (1984), p. 10; Whelan, *Newbawn,* pp 56-60; J. Mannion, 'A Transatlantic Merchant Fishery: Richard Welsh of New Ross and the Sweetmans of Newbawn in Newfoundland, 1734-1862' in Whelan, *Wexford,* pp 373-405.
2. Life and Travel of the Rev. John Kavanagh of Annagh, 1790.
3. Renehan, *Collections,* ii, p. 43.
4. N. Furlong, 'Life in Wexford Port' in Whelan, *Wexford,* p. 150.
5. Musgrave, *op. cit.,* app. xviii. Fr. John Murphy's diploma and testimonial were found during the raid on his lodgings at Tomnaboley following the outbreak and found their way to Musgrave through Lord Mountnorris, who was his brother-in-law. See also Musgrave, i, p. 406 and footnote on same page.
6. J. Townsend, *A Journey through Spain in the years 1786 and 1787* (London, 1791).
7. Musgrave, *op. cit.,* ii, app. xviii, Testimonium.
8. Aquilar y Ribon Mss., Library of the University of Seville; *Catholic Encyclopaedia* (New York, 1913), vol. xiii (Seville).
9. Townsend, *op. cit.;* L. Doblado, *Letters from Spain* (London, 1822); J. Thom (ed.), *The Life of Blanco White* (London, 1845).
10. Renehan, *op. cit.,* ii, p. 43.
11. Flood, *op. cit.,* pp. 370-8: Sinnott (1961), *loc. cit.,* p. 144.
12. This situation obtained as late as 1795 at Amen Cross, Killiane, in the modern Catholic parish of Piercestown. Flood, *op. cit.,* p. 172; G. Griffiths, *Chronicles of the County Wexford* (Enniscorthy, 1878), pp 245-6.
13. Flood, *op. cit.,* p. 38; James Caulfield to Archbishop Troy, 3 Nov. 1799, D.D.A.
14. Whelan, 'Religious factor', pp 62-5.
15. Leslie, *Ferns Clergy,* p. 176.
16. Oral testimony of Margaret Hall, James Hall and Benjamin Chapman of Boolavogue. Mrs Margaret Hall, nee Turner of Tomnaboley, was reared in the farmstead where Fr. John Murphy lodged, formerly Donohues. She married Walter Hall of Boolavogue and went to live in the farm house incorporating the former home of Thomas Donovan where Fr. Murphy ate his breakfast daily, close by his thatched chapel. Ben Chapman is a great, great, great grandson of John Donovan and resides with his family in the former homestead of John Donovan of Tobergal.
17. Sinnott (1962), *loc. cit.,* p. 144; Kavanagh *op. cit.,* footnote, p. 101; E. O'Byrne (ed.), *The Convert Rolls* (Dublin, 1981), p. 79.
18. Musgrave, *op. cit.,* ii, p. 90; Kavanagh, *op. cit.,* p. 296.
19. Sinnott (1938), *loc. cit.,* pp 23-4.
20. Flood, *op. cit.,* pp 29-30.
21. *Ibid.,* pp xix, 226; Renehan, *op.cit.,* pp 42-3; Furlong (1984), *loc. cit.,* pp 18-19.
22. Caulfield, *Reply,* p. 20.
23. Renehan, *op. cit.,* pp 46-7; T. Nolan, 'Wexford Parish in the eighteenth and early nineteenth centuries' in Berney, *op. cit.,* p. 63.

Chapter Three

1. Johnson, *op. cit.,* p. 164.
2. Kavanagh, *op.cit.,* p. 296; Sinnott (1962), *loc. cit.,* pp 144-5; *Ibid,* (1938), *loc. cit.,* p. 241. Oral testimony of Art Sinnott and James Hall, Boolavogue.
3. Sinnott (1962), *loc. cit.; Ibid* (1938), *loc. cit.*
4. Musgrave, *op. cit.,* ii, p. 90. It is possible that Musgrave was a guest in his brother-

in-law's, Lord Mountnorris' residence, at Camolin Park, on some occasions when Fr. John Murphy was present. His accurate description indicates close observation.

5. Sinnott (1962), *loc. cit.; Ibid* (1938), *loc. cit.*
6. L. Cullen, 'The 1798 Rebellion in its eighteenth century context' in P. Corish (ed.), *Radicals, Rebels and Establishments* (Belfast, 1985), pp 98-9; Whelan, 'Religious factor', pp 65-7.
7. Hay, *History,* p. xi. For the names of sympathetic Protestant liberals (1795), see p. 32 and app. vi, p. xviii.
8. Killen, *Ecclesiastical History,* ii, pp. 278, 280, 341; McDowell, *loc. cit.,* pp. 240-1.
9. Johnson, *op. cit.,* pp 46-7; F. MacDermot, *Theobald Wolfe Tone, A Biographical Study* (London, 1939), pp 69-72, 84-8, 96, 121-2, 147.
10. McDowell, 'The Personnel of the Dublin Society of United Irishmen, 1791-4', in *I.H.S.,* ii (1940), pp 12-53.
11. McDowell, 'Proceedings', p. 51. The list of early adherents is in harmony with Cullen, 'The 1798 Rebellion in Wexford', pp 269-74, 281, 290-4, and Whelan, 'Catholic Priest', p. 302. See also Whelan *Newbawn,* pp 45-6 and Whelan 'Religious factor', pp 66-7. It is now accepted that Edward Hay had a much more significant role in the United Irishmen than his *History* admits. His camouflage of James Kenny, a United Irish officer, on p. 138 is eloquent. My volume of Hay was formerly the property of his contemporary, Rev. James Symes, Protestant rector of Kilmallock and Castle Ellis (see Leslie, *op. cit.,* p. 133). The Hays acted as tithe proctors for Rev. Symes and were closely and critically observed by him. Rev. Symes annotated the copy. He castigates Edward Hay in colourful language, being in no doubt that Hay was himself a rebel, e.g., 'A scandalous misrepresentation of facts' (p. 247). In relation to Hay's description of Kenny on p. 138 as '... Mr. Kenny, a tanner and shopkeeper, confidently asserted to be a loyal man...', Symes writes on the page, 'Kenny was a leader of the rebels on that day and had just fled to Ballycanew when he was killed'. Symes was cited for non-residence and was deprived by the Protestant bishop of Ferns in 1802.
12. Leslie, *op. cit.,* p. 176.
13. Thomas Handcock, Rector of Kilcormuck, 'Narrative of the Battle of Enniscorthy and events preceeding and during the Rebellion', N.L.I., mic. 1,044, p. 21.
14. H. McAnally, *The Irish Militia, 1793-1816* (Dublin, 1949), p. 28 *et. seq.*
15. Hay, *op. cit.,* p. 21 *et. seq.;* Handcock, *op. cit.,* pp 7-9.
16. Dickson, *op. cit.,* p. 10; Oral testimony of T.D. Sinnott.
17. Hay, *op. cit.,* pp 30-4; Johnson, *op. cit.,* pp 181-4; McDowell, *loc. cit.,* (1967), p. 241; MacDermot, *op. cit.,* p. 147 *et seq.*
18. MacDermot, *op. cit.,* p. 133.
19. Caulfield, *op. cit.,* pp 20-1.
20. MacDermot, *op. cit.,* p. 189.
21. Rathnure I.F.C. Schools ms. 890, p. 83. This excellent volume completed under the supervision of the teacher, Aodh O'Rathoilligh, was regarded by T.D. Sinnott as one of the most important folk memory research projects successfully undertaken since that of Luke Cullen in the previous century.
22. Dickson, i, *op. cit.,* p. 11.
23. Byrne, *Memoirs,* i, p. 6.
24. Ó'Snodaigh, 'Notes', p. 30*; List of Yeomanry Corps* (Dublin, 1797).
25. Whelan, 'Catholic Priest', p. 308; Sinnott (1962), *loc. cit.,* p. 149.
26. Byrne, *op. cit.,* i, pp 8-10.
27. I am grateful to Dr. David Dickson, Department of History, T.C.D., for providing me with these figures.

Chapter 4

1. Tone, *op. cit.,* ii, p. 329 *et. seq;* H. Wheeler and A. Broadley, *The War in Wexford* (London, 1910), p. 26.
2. MacDermot, *op. cit.,* p. 207.
3. Byrne, *op. cit.,* i, p. 10.
4. MacDermot, *op. cit.,* pp 228-9.
5. Dickson, *op. cit.,* p. 194.
6. James Caulfield to Archbishop Troy, 2 Sept. 1798, cited in Whelan, 'Catholic Priest', p. 315; *Ibid.* to *Ibid.,* 21 May 1799, D.D.A.; Whelan, 'Religious Factor', pp 300, 302, 303, 305- 311, 315.
7. Handcock, *op. cit.,* p. 2; Cullen, '1798 Rebellion in Wexford', p. 275; Powell, Background to the Wexford Rebellion, pp 286-7.
8. Caulfield to Troy, 23 Sept. 1799, D.D.A.
9. Dickson, *op. cit.,* p. 46.
10. Caulfield, *op. cit.,* p. 54; Byrne, *op. cit.,* pp 12, 13.
11. Caulfield to Troy, 2 Sept. 1798, cited in Whelan, 'Catholic Priest', p. 315.
12. Hayes, *Ireland and Irishmen,* p. 198.
13. Whelan, 'Catholic Priest', p. 307. See also L. MacShane, *People,* 24 Dec. 1898.
14. S. MacDómhnaill, 'Notes on Fr. John Murphy in Counties Carlow and Kilkenny' in P. MacSuibhne, *'98 in Carlow* (Carlow, 1974), pp 66-70.
15. L. Cullen, 'The 1798 Rebellion in its eighteenth century context', p. 98, *et seq.;* Whelan, 'Religious Factor', pp 65-6.
16. Elmes family letters, 1797, by courtesy of King Milne; Handcock, *op. cit.,* pp 9-10; T. Powell, 'An economic factor in the Wexford Rebellion of 1798' in *Studia Hib.* xvi (1976), pp 144-70; T. Pakenham, *The Year of Liberty* (London, 1972) p. 158. The extent of this debacle can only be appreciated to the full by tillage farmers. My father, Patrick Furlong, Mulgannon, Wexford, recalled that the best price for barley that my family could obtain in Wexford in 1914 was twelve shillings per barrell, one hundred and eighteen years *after* a period when twenty six shillings per barrel obtained. The collapse in price from 26 shillings to 9 and even 5 shillings per barrel in 1797, in an intensively farmed region, was never given the significance it merited.
17. Byrne, *op. cit.,* i, pp 20, 27, 28; Lett Diaries, by courtesy of Mrs Cecil Miller; Plowden, *op. cit.,* ii, p. 401; Hay, *op. cit.,* pp 40, 56; Sinnott (1962), *loc. cit.,* p. 147; Cullen, 'The 1798 Rebellion in Wexford', pp 262-9.
18. Caulfield to Troy, 21 May 1799, D.D.A.; 'Veritas', *A vindication,* p. 47; Whelan, 'Catholic Priest', pp 305-8.
19. Caulfield to Troy, 2 Sept. 1798, cited, Whelan, 'Catholic Priest', p. 315.
20. Whelan, 'Catholic Priest', p. 304.
21. Caulfield, Pastoral letter, 13 Sept., 1798, in P. Moran (ed.), *Spicilegium Ossoriense* (Dublin, 1874), iii, p. 57. Caulfield was compelled to emphasise from every surviving altar in the diocese that he had not been in the pay of the Government. Sinnott (1962), *loc. cit.,* p. 147; Oral testimony of Rev. P. Murphy, P.P., Glynn and Rev. M. Berney, Monaseed.
22. Caulfield to Troy, 23 Sept 1799, D.D.A. The bishop's description of 'General Murphy' carried a palpable note of pathos – the 'poor, giddy mortal'.
23. *Idem.*
24. Handcock, *op. cit.,* pp 9, 10; Byrne, *op. cit.:* p. 31; Maxwell, *History,* p. 151.
25. *Castlereagh Correspondence,* i, pp 165-8; Pakenham, *op. cit.,* pp 36-7.
26. Musgrave, *op. cit.,* i, pp 394-5; Hay, *op. cit.,* p. 52.
27. Caulfield, Pastoral letter, undated, D.D.A.
28. Musgrave, *op. cit.,* ii, app. xviii.

29. *Ibid.*, app. xvii.
30. Taylor, *A History,* p. 22.
31. *Idem.*
32. Caulfield to Troy, 23 Sept. 1799, D.D.A. Caulfield, reporting to his archbishop after strenuous and lengthy questioning in correspondence, chooses his words carefully, '... often reproached, reprimanded and threatened'. The most effective immediate threat that Dr. Caulfield could wield was suspension. The circumstances in which it was used here is in harmony with the traditional belief in Boolavogue that (a) harrassment, eviction and then replacement on their own lands by loyalists was deliberate policy and (b) that Fr. John Murphy 'always stood up for them' (his parishioners).
33. Byrne, *op. cit.,* i, p. 31; Taylor, *op. cit.;* p. 24; Caulfield, *Reply,* p. 45.
34. Byrne, *op. cit.,* p. 31; Dickson, *op. cit.;* p. 36; Dr. Euseby Cleaver, Protestant Bishop of Ferns, cited in Pakenham, *op. cit.,* p. 159.
35. Byrne, *op. cit.,* i. pp 14, 44, 45; Dickson, *op. cit.,* p. 22.
36. Camden to Portland, 26 March 1798, with Sir John Camden's report, cited in Pakenham, *op. cit.,* p. 66.
37. Dickson, *op. cit.,* pp 12, 38; MacDermot, *op. cit.,* pp 277-9.
38. Caulfield, *Reply,* p. 22.
39. Sinnott (1962), *loc. cit.,* p. 145; *Ibid,* (1938), *loc. cit.,* p. 24, and oral testimony.
40. Caulfield to Troy, 23 Sept., 1799, D.D.A. See Sinnott (1962), *loc cit.,* p. 147.
41. Musgrave, *op. cit.,* ii, app. xvii.

Chapter 5
1. Cullen, 'The 1798 Rebellion in Wexford'; pp 286-7; Powell, Background to the Wexford Rebellion, pp 182-3. The *Journal of the Irish House of Commons, 1798,* appendix, lists the men charged.
2. Hay, *op. cit.,* p. 57; Plowden, *op. cit.,* ii, p. 453.
3. Lett Diary, by courtesy of Mrs Margaret Miller; Cullen, 'The 1798 Rebellion in Wexford', pp 265-7.
4. Hay, *op. cit.,* p. 57 *et. seq.;* Luke Cullen Mss., T.C.D. Ms. S.5.19; Cloney, *op. cit.,* p. 193; Sinnott (1962), *loc. cit.,* p. 148; Plowden, *op. cit.,* ii, p. 453; Dickson, *op. cit.,* p. 43; Letter, Thomas Canon Doyle, *People,* 21 May 1898. The memory of 'Tom the Devil' and the North Cork Militia was alive in Shelmalier in recent times. The All-Ireland Hurling Final between Wexford (represented by Castlebridge) and Cork (represented by Aughabullogue) in November of 1890 had to be abandoned. The Cork team left the pitch and was eventually awarded the championship. Lines from the contemporary ballad explain why:
    'Tom Murphy and Will Neville,
    Began to lay them level,
    When they thought of Tom the Devil,
    With his pitch cap and shears';
    See A. Tobin and S. O'Leary, *The Bold Shelmaliers* (Wexford, 1988), pp 41-52.
5. Oral testimony of T.J. Nolan, St. Peter's College, Wexford, and Michael Kehoe, N.T., Glynn. The last Catholic chapels where this spectacle was seen were in Kilmuckridge and Screen. It was still spoken of in the 1940s.
6. Hay, *op. cit.,* p. 59.
7. Byrne, *op. cit.,* pp 33-6; Cloney, *op. cit.,* p. 216 *et. seq.;* Hay, *op. cit.,* pp 64-7; Lecky, *History,* iv., p. 39; Morton to Lees, 22 May 1798, cited in Pakenham, *op. cit.,* p. 165.

8. Luke Cullen, Mss.

9. Byrne, *op. cit.*, p. 34; Hay, *op. cit.*, p. 75; Wheeler and Broadley, *op. cit.*, p. 81; Dickson, *op. cit.*, p. 38; Sinnott (1962), *loc. cit.*, p. 148.

10. Barrington, *Personal Sketches*, pp 143-4; Killen, *op. cit.*, ii, p. 387.

11. I.F.C. Schools Ms. 896, p. 19; Byrne, *op. cit.*, p. 46; Sinnott (1962), *loc. cit.*, p. 148.

12. Hay, *op. cit.*, pp 73-4.

13. Byrne, *op. cit.*, p. 33; Kavanagh, *op. cit.*, pp 191-2.

14. I.F.C. Schools Ms 890, pp 19-43; Byrne, *op. cit.*, p. 46; Sinnott (1962), *loc. cit.*, p. 148.

15. Gordon, *History*, p. 453; Dickson, *op. cit.*, pp 43-7.

16. Oral testimony of Margaret Hall, James Hall and Michael Gough of Boolavogue. See unsigned account in the *New Ross Standard*, 7 Jan. 1938. Clement Gough's direct descendant, Michael Gough, quoted above, acted the part of Fr. John Murphy on horseback at the 1938 commemorations in Boolavogue and was described in the *Enniscorthy Echo* newspaper report as 'most impressive'. See also E. O'Byrne (ed.), *The convert rolls*, p. 120.

17. Oral testimony of Margaret and James Hall. Letter, 'Ildána', *New Ross Standard*, 22 Oct., 1898. 'An Ildána' was the pen name of the journalist Clement Gough, a direct descendant of the slain Clement Gough. Luke Cullen, Mss; letter, 'Oulart Hill', *People*, 9 Apr. 1989.

18. I.F.C. schools Ms. 890, p. 88.

19. Luke Cullen, Mss. cited in Dickson, *op. cit.*, pp 53-6. The convergence of attention on the Boyne family home firstly by the Camolin Yeoman Cavalry (specifically, Lieutenant Bookey and John Donovan) in an area outside their allotted jurisdiction, and secondly by Fr. John Murphy's group (which included committed United Irishmen) leads me to but one conclusion. Repeated reports in the folk tradition of John Donovan's hatred for his servant 'boy', and a stated determination to kill him supplies us with adequate support for the 'boy's' identification as a Boyne.

20. Letter, 'Oulart Hill', *People*, 9 Apr. 1898; I.F.C. Schools Ms 890, p. 83; Sinnott (1962), *loc. cit.*, p. 148.

21. *Idem.*

22. MacSuibhne, *op. cit.*, p. 13.

23. Oral testimony of Margaret and James Hall, Boolavogue. For sometimes differing version see unsigned account, *New Ross Standard*, 7 Jan. 1938; I.F.C. Schools Ms 896, p.19, Ms 890, p. 87.

24. Byrne, *op. cit.*, p. 46; I.F.C. Schools Ms., 896, pp 13, 43; Musgrave, *op. cit.*, i, p. 400; Sinnott (1962), *loc. cit.*, p. 148. That Fr. John Murphy 'minded nothing but Church business up to the outbreak', is the persistent tradition in the Screen-Castlebridge area, a United Irish stronghold where the committed United Irishmen responded promptly to Jerry Donovan's mobilisation call during the night of May 25-6. Oral testimony of Mrs Maure Roche, Ballyhoobeg, Screen.

25. Luke Cullen Mss., cited Dickson, *op. cit.*, p. 51.

26. I.F.C. Schools Ms 896, p. 157.

27. Luke Cullen Mss., cited in Dickson, *op. cit.*, p. 52.

28. MacSuibhne, *op. cit.*, p. 12; I.F.C. Schools Ms. 896, p. 99; Oral testimony of Mrs Margaret Hall, Boolavogue.

29. Luke Cullen Mss., cited Dickson, *op. cit.*, pp 52-3; *Ibid.*, pp 12, 35, 126; Cullen '1798 Rebellion', pp 263-6.

30. Luke Cullen Mss., cited in Dickson, *op. cit.*, p. 52; Byrne, *op. cit.*, i, pp 35-6; Musgrave, *op. cit.*, i, pp 298-9; Sinnott (1962), p. 148.

31. Sinnott (1962), *loc. cit.*, p. 148; I.F.C. Schools Ms. 896, pp 19, 43; Musgrave, *op. cit.*, ii, p. 400; Letter, 'Oulart Hill', *People*, 9 Apr. 1898.

32. *Idem.* 'Oulart Hill' was the pen name used by Pierce Rowe of Ballinoulart, a grand-nephew of Fr. Michael Murphy. Hay, *op. cit.,* list of liberals in 1795, p. 32 and app. vi, p. xviii.

33. Kavanagh, *op. cit.,* p. 94. Kavanagh reflects a lingering puzzle. He states that the Boolavogue men, 'did not, *as they expected,* meet Cornock', there. I.F.C. Schools Ms, 896, p. 43; Unsigned account, *New Ross Standard,* 7 Jan. 1938; Sinnott (1962), *loc. cit.,* p. 148; oral testimony of John Sinnott, Ballintore.

34. Luke Cullen Mss., cited in Dickson, *op. cit.,* p. 53.

35. Letter signed 'Oulart Hill', *People,* 9 Apr. 1898.

36. Cullen, '1798 Rebellion', pp 287, 288, 293; Whelan, 'Catholic Priest', p. 308.

37. Luke Cullen Mss., cited in Dickson, *op. cit.,* pp 53-4.

38. Letters, 'Oulart Hill', *People,* 9 Apr. 1898, 30 Apr. 1898, 7 May 1898.

39. Letter, 'An Ildána', *People,* 22 Oct., 1989, has a variation; I.F.C. Schools Ms. 890, pp 88, 93.

40. Letter, 'Oulart Hill', *People,* 9 Apr. 1898.

41. Luke Cullen Mss., cited in Dickson, *op. cit.,* p. 53; Sinnott (1962), *loc. cit.,* p. 149 and footnote.

42. Letter, 'Oulart Hill', *People,* 9 Apr. 1898; I.F.C. Schools Ms. 890, p. 83; Wheeler and Broadley, *op. cit.,* p. 83. The oral testimony of James Hall and Ben Chapman of Boolavogue to the effect that Fr. John Murphy was involved in a 'situation which developed, rather than one which was developed', and again that he 'just happened to be in the 'right place at the right time', is itself informative. It suggests the wish being father to the thought. I have formed the impression from interviews in Boolavogue and surrounding district that Fr. John Murphy was regarded as 'a great capture' for the insurgent cause.

43. *Idem.* John Donovan's wife had her husband buried on the farm at Tobergal. Whatever interpretation may be put on it, he had taken a comparatively large sum of money with him that day. Seventy five guineas in gold, a guinea banknote and a gold watch were all found intact in his uniform when his body was taken home. 'It was not for his money that they killed him', his widow said. Oral testimony of Ben Chapman, Tobergal.

Chapter Six

1. Oral testimony, James and Margaret Hall, Boolavogue; Luke Cullen Mss., cited in Dickson, *op. cit.,* p. 54; Byrne, *op. cit.,* p. 46. Byrne was not present at The Harrow skirmish and some of his details are out of sequence.

2. Dickson, *op. cit.,* p. 57; Hay, *op. cit.,* p. 88; Musgrave, *op. cit.,* i, pp 404-7; Wheeler and Broadley, *op. cit.,* p. 85.

3. Byrne, *op. cit.,* i, pp 48, 95; Taylor, *op. cit.,* p. 36; Wheeler and Broadley, *op. cit.,* pp 84-5.

4. Musgrave, *op. cit.,* i, pp 407-8; Taylor, *op. cit.,* pp 36-7; *The Irish Magazine and Monthly Asylum for neglected Biography* records (June, 1811) that it was at Rockspring, Bookey's mansion, that Fr. John Murphy first 'unsheathed his sword'. This is in accord with the local tradition.

5. Letters, 'Oulart Hill', *People,* 7 May 1898, 'An Ildána', *People,* 22 Oct. 1898; Sinnott (1962), *loc. cit.,* pp 149-50. T.D. Sinnott, knowing the significant role of Jerry Donovan, always referred to him as the 'Paul Revere of the Insurrection'. My home parish priest of Piercestown (1956-66), Fr. Denis Doyle, was a great grandson of the same Jeremiah Donovan. I used source books from his library in my research. He never once mentioned the relationship.

6. Luke Cullen Mss., cited in Dickson, *op. cit.,* p. 39.
7. Oral testimony of T.D. Sinnott, extra mural diploma lectures, Wexford, 1951. Sinnott stressed that the outbreak and its immediate aftermath grew around Fr. John Murphy but that the United Irishmen gravitated towards it in order to manage it, immediately they were made aware of it. The homes and families surviving in the Screen-Castlebridge area in which United Irishmen were alerted and responded promptly include Learys of Garrylough, Roches of Garrylough, Raths of Newfort, Mythens of Ballyruane, O'Connors of Garryhubbock, Kavanaghs of Boolabawn. Oral testimony of Mrs Maure Roche, Ballyhoobeg, Screen.
8. Luke Cullen Mss., cited in Dickson, *op. cit.,* pp 57-9; Sinnott, (1962) *loc. cit.,* p. 150; Musgrave, *op. cit.,* ii, p. 333; See note in Leslie, *op. cit.,* p. 120.
9. Hay, *op. cit.,* p. 301.
10. Lett Family Diary; Wheeler and Broadley, *op. cit.,* p. 86; See John Murphy's retort to Richards in Dickson, *op. cit.,* app. iii.
11. Wheeler and Broadley, *op. cit.,* p. 86; Sinnott, (1962), *loc. cit.,* pp 153-5.
12. Musgrave, *op. cit.,* i, p. 406 with footnote; Handcock, *op. cit.,* p. 23.
13. There are notices of the Roche family in Hore, *Wexford,* v.; R. Roche, 'The Roches of Wexford' in *Jn. Old Wex. Soc.,* ii (1969), p. 39, *et. seq.;* A. Gwynn and R. Handcock, *Medieval Religious Houses in Ireland* (London, 1970), pp 197-8.
14. Luke Cullen Mss., cited in Dickson, *op. cit.,* p. 60.
15. Sinnott (1962), *loc. cit.,* p. 150. The names of individual United Irishmen who accompanied George Sparks to the meeting point at Castle Ellis are still recalled. They were Mick Rossiter of The Mullawn (near Courtclough); Fortune from The Seabank, Ballyconniger; Cullen from Ballynaglogh; Kehoe from Ballynamona; Whelan from Askasilla and Kelly from Castle Ellis. Oral testimony of Phil Tobin, Kilmacow, Screen, who was given it by his father who was given the information by the two Miss Keatings of Ballinaclash who had vivid recollections of the Rebellion. Cullen, 'The 1798 Rebellion in Wexford,' pp 282, 290-4; Whelan 'Catholic Priest', p. 302.
16. Luke Cullen Mss., cited in Dickson, *op. cit.,* p. 60; Cullen, 'The 1798 Rebellion in Wexford', pp 290-1.
17. Hay, *op. cit.,* app. xxii, p. xxxiii. In this testimony of 27 July 1799, Hay's first cousin and friend, Edward FitzGerald of Newpark, is apparently given his title 'General' FitzGerald. Cullen, 'The 1798 Rebellion in Wexford', pp 290-1.
18. Luke Cullen Mss., cited in Dickson, *op. cit.,* p. 60.
19. Hay, *op. cit.,* i, p. 82.
20. Byrne, *op. cit.,* i, p. 49.
21. Luke Cullen Mss., cited in Dickson, *op. cit.,* p. 60; Sinnott (1962), *loc. cit.,* p. 51. Note Sinnott's interpretation of Cullen. A simple monument marks the spot where Fr. John Murphy stood and issued his orders before the action commenced.
22. Letter, 'Oulart Hill', *People,* 9 Apr. 1898.
23. Sinnott (1962), *loc. cit.,* p. 151; oral testimony of Phil Tobin, Kilmacow, Screen. Mr. Tobin's great grandfather fought in the Rebellion, was wounded but survived. Kavanagh, *op. cit.,* p. 106.
24. Kavanagh, *op. cit.,* pp 295-6; Musgrave, *op. cit.,* i, p. 421.
25. Kavanagh, *op. cit.,* app., pp 296-5. Oral testimony, J.J. Devereux, Drinagh. See McAnally, *op. cit.,* p. 48. It has been argued that these had become Protestant and 'loyal' in response to Lord Kingsborough's offer of land at low rent and long leases.
26. Dickson, *op. cit.,* pp 20, 65; Sinnott, (1962), *loc. cit.,* p. 152.
27. Luke Cullen Mss., cited in Dickson, *op. cit.,* p. 64. A monument was erected over their grave in 1988.

28. Letter, 'Oulart Hill', *People,* 9 Apr. 1898; Sinnott (1962), footnote, p. 152, 'Tom Donovan impulsively jumped the fence on discharging his gun and fell by the discharge of a reloaded musket'.
29. Musgrave, *op. cit.,* pp 419-22; Dickson, *op. cit.,* app. ii, p. 227.

Chapter Seven

1. Dickson, *op. cit.,* p. 66.
2. Sinnott (1938), *loc. cit.,* p. 26.
3. Dickson, *op. cit.,* p. 67.
4. Musgrave, *op. cit.,* i, pp 424-5.
5. The surplus from the great 1797 crop still lay in lofts and barns. See O'Brien, *op. cit.,* p. 124.
6. I.F.C. Schools Ms. 890, p. 88.
7. Hay, *op. cit.,* pp 161-3; Dickson, *op. cit.,* p. 197.
8. Dickson, *op. cit.,* p. 68; oral testimony, T.D. Sinnott.
9. Hay, *op. cit.,* p. 91; Lecky, *op. cit.,* iv, pp 19-20.
10. Hay, *op. cit.,* pp 266-9; Byrne, *op. cit.,* ii, pp 12-3; Dickson *op. cit.,* p. 17. The execution of the unfortunate Fr. John Redmond confused Bishop Caulfield. See letter to Troy, 2 Sept. 1798, Whelan, 'Catholic Priest', p. 315.
11. Musgrave, *op. cit.,* i, pp 412-3; Handcock Ms., cited in Pakenham, *op. cit.,* pp 177-8.
12. *Idem.*
13. Byrne, *op. cit.,* i, p. 58.
14. Musgrave, *op. cit.,* i, pp 401, 428; Sinnott (1948), *loc. cit.;* Whelan, 'Catholic Priest', p. 308.
15. Byrne, *op. cit.,* pp 53, 58, 59.
16. *Ibid.,* p. 53.
17. Whelan, 'Catholic Priest', pp 307-8.
18. Byrne, *op. cit.,* i, p. 58; Musgrave, i, p. 433; Dickson, *op. cit.,* pp 70-4.
19. Byrne, *op. cit.,* i, p. 59.
20. Sinnott (1962), *loc. cit.,* p. 143. The father of T.D. Sinnott's informant, Nicholas Keating, was one of those detailed by Edward Roche to set fire to Guttle Street (now John Street).
21. Handcock, *op. cit.,* pp 23, 40-2.
22. Cloney, *op. cit.,* p. 13; Hay, *op. cit.,* p. 92; T. Acres Ogle, *The Irish Militia Officer* (Dublin, 1873), p. 85; Dickson, *op. cit.,* p. 72.
23. Handcock, *op. cit.,* pp 43-6; Hay, *op. cit.,* p. 96.
24. Dickson, *op. cit.,* pp 73, 267; Whelan, 'Catholic Priest' p. 311, and source note 71, p. 538.
25. Letter, Trenbath to Bishop of Dromore, 22 Apr. 1797, Musgrave papers, N.L.I. Ms. 4,156.
26. Cloney, *op. cit.,* p. 15. This was repeated to the east, west and north of Enniscorthy.

Chapter Eight

1. Wheeler and Broadley, *op. cit.,* p. 87.
2. Dickson, *op. cit.,* pp 44-7.
3. Wheeler and Broadley, *op.cit.,* p. 87.
4. Byrne, *op. cit.,* i, p. 72; Cloney, *op. cit.,* p. 17; Lecky, *op. cit.,* iv, p. 362.
5. Byrne, *op. cit.,* i, pp 6, 14, 15, 24, 243, 279; iii, pp 82-3.

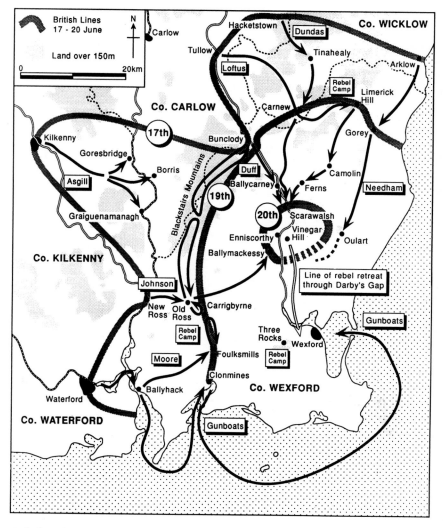

Rebel and enemy positions and movements before the Battle of Vinegar Hill
(Design: Kevin Whelan, Map: Mathew Stout).

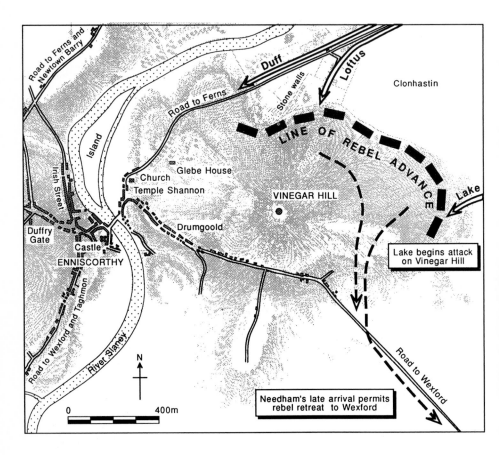

The Battle of Vinegar Hill. *(Map: Mathew Stout, redrawn from Musgrave's **Memoirs**).*

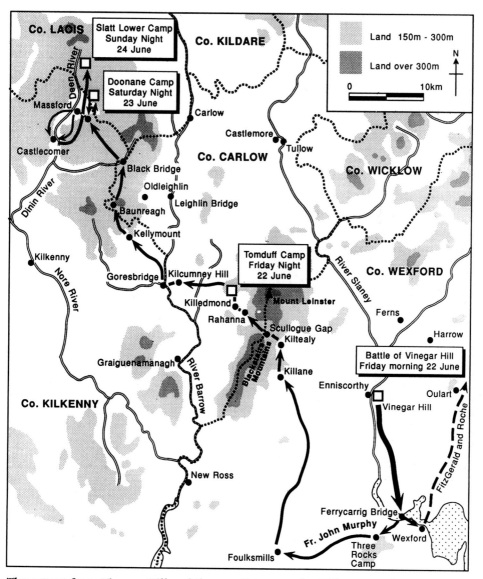

The retreat from Vinegar Hill and the march to counties Kilkenny and Laois.
(Mathew Stout).

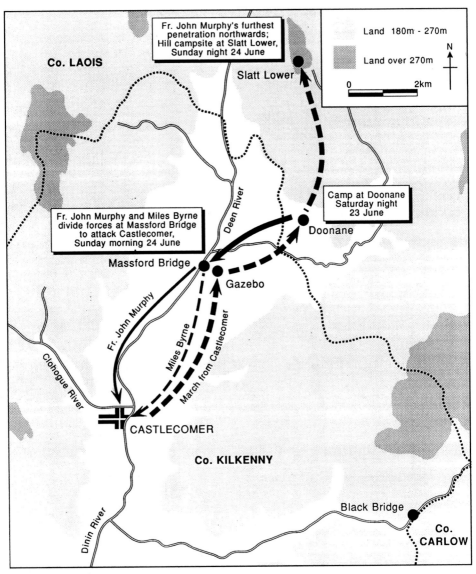

Co. LAOIS

Fr. John Murphy's furthest
penetration northwards;
Hill campsite at Slatt Lower,
Sunday night 24 June

Slatt Lower

Land 180m - 270m

Land over 270m

N

0   2km

Deen River

Camp at Doonane
Saturday night
23 June

Fr. John Murphy and Miles Byrne
divide forces at Massford Bridge
to attack Castlecomer,
Sunday morning 24 June

Doonane

Massford Bridge

Gazebo

Fr. John Murphy

Miles Byrne

March from Castlecomer

Clohogue River

CASTLECOMER

Co. KILKENNY

Dinin River

Black Bridge

**Co.
CARLOW**

The engagement at Castlecomer, 24 June, 1798. *(Mathew Stout).*

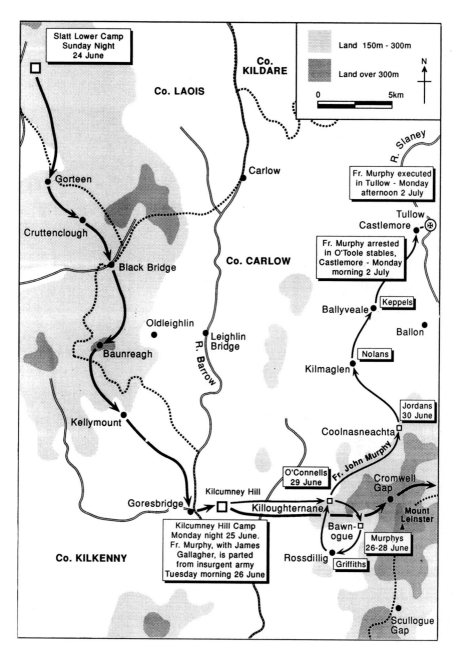

John Murphy's last journey, 24 June to 2 July, 1798. *(Mathew Stout).*

James Delany, bishop of Kildare and Leighlin, resident at Tullow in 1798.

Father Murphy's Monument, Market Square, Tullow.

Father Murphy monument, Market Square, Tullow.

The Mullawn graveyard overlooking the Slaney, on the outskirts of Tullow, where the remains of Fr. John Murphy lie. The exact location of his grave is unknown. *(J. B. Curtis).*

Oliver Sheppard's bronze memorial, depicting John Murphy and a croppy boy, in the Market Square, Enniscorthy.

The 1948 celebrations at the Three Rocks. Representing Edward Roche of Garrylough and Edward Fitzgerald of Newpark are Eamonn Foley of Crossabeg and Patrick O'Connor of Garryhubbock. Patrick O'Connor's great-great-grandfather was one of the Shelmalier United Irishmen who answered the sudden call to arms on Whit Sunday morning and who fought at Oulart Hill (*Irish Press*).

Miles Byrne of Monaseed in old age in Paris. This is a modern copy by the Guinness Museum of the original by E. Yatel (Paris), 1859, now in the President's collection of historical portraits in Áras an Uachtaráin. (*Courtesy of Her Excellency, the President and Peter Walsh, Guinness Museum*).

6. Whelan, 'Catholic Priest', pp. 304, 315; Cullen, 'The 1798 Rebellion in Wexford', p. 285; Flood, *op. cit.,* p. 62; Sinnott (1948), *loc. cit.,* p. 285.
7. Byrne, *op. cit.,* i, p. 66; Dickson, *op. cit.,* p. 206.
8. Cullen, 'The 1798 Rebellion in Wexford', pp 270, 277, 281; Whelan, 'Catholic Priest', p. 307; I.F.C. Schools Ms. 901, No. 16; Dickson, *op. cit.,* p. 210.
9. Cloney, *op. cit.,* p. 17.
10. Hay, *op. cit.,* p. 100; Byrne, *op. cit.,* i, p. 74; Dickson, *op. cit.,* p. 210.
11. Cloney, *op. cit.,* p. 18; Byrne, *op. cit.,* pp 71-2.
12. Byrne, *op. cit.,* pp 66-7; Dickson, *op. cit.,* p. 206.
13. Cloney, *op. cit.,* p. 18; Hay, *op. cit.,* pp 101-2.
14. Cullen, 'The 1798 Rebellion in Wexford', pp 291-3; Byrne, *op. cit.,* i, p. 73; Dickson, *op. cit.,* pp 79, 194, 196. There was no doubt in T. D. Sinnott's mind that Edward FitzGerald was to have been the overall commander. Sinnott was Grand Marshal of the great parade which marked the climax of the 140th anniversary celebrations in Enniscorthy in 1938. He placed the horseman who took the role of Edward FitzGerald in the leading position, alone at the head of that vast parade. The other leaders he represented on horseback at the head of their respective barony contingents. Information and programme from Sean Óg Ó'Dúbhaill, Honorary Treasurer, Comóradh '98, Enniscorthy.
15. Byrne, *op. cit.,* p. 73: Hay, *op. cit.,* pp 98-9.
16. Cloney, *op. cit.,* p. 198; Dickson, *op. cit.,* p. 79 and footnote 1, p. 93.
17. Dickson, *op. cit.,* pp 78, 206; Cullen, 'The 1798 Rebellion in Wexford', p. 262; Musgrave, *op. cit.,* i, p. 457.
18. Musgrave, *op. cit.,* ii, app. xix,; Dickson, *op. cit.,* pp 77-8.
19. Dickson, *op. cit.,* p. 77.
20. *Idem.*

Chapter Nine
1. Byrne, *op. cit.,* i, p. 75; Cloney, *op. cit.,* p. 20.
2. Byrne, *op. cit.,* i, p. 75; Cloney, *op. cit.,* p. 20.
3. *Idem.*
4. Cloney, *op. cit.,* p. 22.
5. Dickson, *op. cit.,* p. 82.
6. Musgrave, *op. cit.,* i, p. 476; Hay, *op. cit.,* pp 99-100.
7. Hay, *op.cit.,* p. 97; Musgrave, *op. cit.,* i, p. 420; Ogle, *op. cit.,* p. 87.
8. Musgrave, *op. cit.,* i, p. 476; Hay, *op. cit.,* p. 96.
9. Hay, *op. cit.,* p. 106; Ogle, *op. cit.,* p. 88; Cloney, *op. cit.,* p. 22. Cloney, who took part in the engagements at The Three Rocks, claims that the Wexford garrison attacking force numbered over one thousand men. Musgrave (i, p. 475) claims that the attacking force consisted of 200 Donegal Militia and 150 Yeoman Cavalry in support, hoping to link up with the expected reinforcements, the Thirteenth Regiment.
10. Hay, *op. cit.,* p. 118; Dickson, *op. cit.,* p. 88.
11. Cloney, *op. cit.,* pp 22-3.
12. Hay, *op. cit.,* p. 106; Byrne, *op. cit.,* i, p. 77.
13. Hay, *op. cit.,* p. 106, Ogle, *op. cit.,* p. 88; Musgrave, *op.cit.,* i, p. 478.
14. Wheeler and Broadley, *op. cit.,* p. 168.
15. Dickson, *op. cit.,* p. 83 and app. iii; Hay, *op. cit.,* pp 108-9; Cloney, *op. cit.,* p. 23.
16. Byrne, *op cit.,* i, p. 78; Taylor, *op. cit.,* p. 58.
17. Byrne, *op. cit.,* i, p. 80; Gordon, *History,* p. 259.

18. Hay, *op. cit.*, p. 112, *et seq.*; Cloney, *op. cit.*, pp 623-4; Musgrave, *op. cit.*, i, pp 480-1.
19. Handcock, *op. cit.*, p. 57.
20. Hay, *op. cit.*, p. 125.
21. Wheeler and Broadley, *op. cit.*, p. 187.
22. Byrne, i, *op. cit.*, p. 80; Hay, *op. cit.*, pp 110-13. This was a taunt used for many years against their families and descendants.
23. Hay, *op. cit.*, p. 114; Taylor, *op. cit.*, p. 60.
24. Dickson, *op. cit.*, app. xii.
25. Hay, *op. cit.*, p. 121; Cloney, *op. cit.*, p. 206; Byrne, *op. cit.*, i, p. 79.
26. Hay, *op. cit.*, p. 117; Dickson, *op. cit.*, p. 88.
27. Handcock, *op. cit.*, p. 421; Musgrave, *op. cit.*, i, p. 549; Hay, *op. cit.*, p. 163, includes a sinister reason for Handcock's urgency. Cloney, *op. cit.*, p. 220.
28. Hay, *op. cit.*, pp 112-3.
29. Wheeler and Broadley, *op. cit.*, p. 178.
30. Caulfield to Troy, letter of 2 Sept. 1798, cited in Whelan, 'Catholic Priest', p. 315; Caulfield to Troy, 2 May 1799, D.D.A.; Dickson, *op. cit.*, pp 54-5; Byrne, *op. cit.*, p. 86.
31. Cloney, *op. cit.*, p. 257; Wheeler and Broadley, *op. cit.*, p. 176.
32. Musgrave, *op. cit.*, ii, p. 392.
33. Luke Cullen Mss., cited in Dickson, *op. cit.*, p. 52; Caulfield, *op. cit.*, p. 3.
34. Hay, *op. cit.*, p. 152; Cloney, *op. cit.*, p. 105; Byrne, *op. cit.*, pp 83-4. The present writer's great, great, great grandfather, Nicholas Furlong of Rathaspeck, was involved in this phase. He was a tenant farmer living in the house later incorporated into the Conboy home. The consistent account, handed down through the female line, is that he went with other neighbours to Cornelius Grogan of Johnstown Castle to protest at burnings and shootings by the retreating Wexford garrison and that they persuaded Grogan to inspect the destruction. On doing so, Grogan 'brought the men of the district with him into Bagenal Harvey at Wexford'. They later fought at the battle of Ross where Nicholas Furlong was mortally wounded. He died of his wounds and was buried by his comrades somewhere near Carrigbyrne. The family account has always held that his ghost was seen by his teenage children in the lane at the rear of their home at the estimated time of his death. (This matter of fact account was never regarded as extraordinary). What was NOT handed down and what remained a close secret until Elizabeth Richard's diary was made public was that there was an active United Irishman cell in the parish with a local command structure. Patrick O'Brien and William Codd were captains of this unit. Patrick O'Brien was a schoolteacher, a nephew of Fr. John Corrin, parish priest of Wexford, and grandnephew of Bishop Nicholas Sweetman. None of this was passed on in my family's account.
35. Hay, *op. cit.*, p. 120; Cloney, *op. cit.*, p. 206.
36. Cloney, *op. cit.*, pp 29-30; Byrne, *op. cit.*, i, p. 81; Hay, *op. cit.*, p. 121. See note 63, Cullen, 'The 1798 Rebellion in its eighteenth century context', p. 113.
37. Sinnott (1948), *loc. cit.*
38. Byrne, *op. cit.*, i, pp 53-4; Sinnott (1948), *loc. cit.*, writes: 'Fr. John Murphy was the only leader gifted with the strength of character, the instinctive military genius and the power of evoking blind loyalty necessary for the control and direction of the peasant army, and a mistaken policy condemned him to a subordinate position'. Sinnott states (1962), *loc cit.*, p. 155: 'Fr. John was the only leader, with the possible exception of John Kelly, who realised the necessity for speed of movement'. Hay's depiction of Harvey is not flattering and suggests an understandable reaction to the

failure of his friend and first cousin, Edward Fitzgerald, to become, as was anticipated, overall military commander at the Windmill Hill conference. Hay, *op. cit.*, p. 107.

39. P. Sinnott, 'Duncannon Fort' in *Jn. Old. Wex. Soc.*, iii (1970), p. 79.
40. Byrne, *op. cit.*, i, p. 82; Cloney, *op. cit.*, p. 41.
41. Byrne, *op. cit.*, i, pp 85-6; Musgrave, *op. cit*, i, p. 485; Dickson, *op. cit.*, p. 90.
42. Byrne, *op. cit.*, i, p. 86; Dickson, *op. cit.*, p. 90.
43. Musgrave, *op. cit.*, i, p. 548; Byrne, *op. cit.*, i, p. 84; Dickson, *op. cit.*, pp 89, 213.
44. Hay, *op. cit.*, p. 129; Byrne, *op. cit.*, i, p. 82.
45. Hay, *op. cit.*, p. 131.
46. *People,* Supplement, 11 Nov. 1977; Byrne, *op. cit.*, i, p. 82; Musgrave, *op. cit.*, i, p. 577.
47. Musgrave, *op. cit.*, i, p. 551; Cloney, *op. cit,* pp 196, 212; Diary of Elizabeth Richards; Ogle, *op. cit.*, p. 109; Wheeler and Broadley, *op. cit.*, p. 174; Dickson, *op. cit.*, p. 89.
48. Hay, *op. cit.*, pp 125-6.
49. Caulfield to Troy, 21 May 1799, D.D.A.; [Veritas] *A vindication,* p. 47. I am grateful to Dr. Thomas Sherwood, St. Peter's College Wexford, for clarification of points of Canon Law.
50. Caulfield to Troy, 23 Sept. 1799, D.D.A.; Edward O'Cullen, to Fr. P. J. Roche, O.F.M., Franciscan Friary, Wexford. I am grateful to Fr. Laurence Murphy, Guardian, for access to this document.
51. Oral testimony, Fr. P. Murphy, Glynn and Fr. M. Berney, Monaseed.
52. Hay, *op. cit.*, p. 142; Dickson, *op. cit.*, pp 208-9; Wheeler and Broadley, *op. cit,* p. 178, citing Mrs Brownrigg's journal, claims a figure of 300 men for the John Street Corps. Whelan, 'Religious Factor', p. 76.
53. Dickson, *op. cit.*, p. 197.
54. Dickson, *op. cit.*, pp 97-8; Hay, *op. cit.*, p. 122; Byrne, *op. cit.*, i, p. 85.

Chapter Ten

1. Byrne, *op. cit.*, i, pp 85-6.
2. *Ibid.,* pp 96, 104. Perry is first mentioned by name on p. 104. Gordon, *History of Ireland,* p. 453.
3. Byrne, *op. cit.*, i, pp 104, 127.
4. Taylor, *op. cit.*, p. 67; Wheeler and Broadley, *op. cit.*, p. 105; Dickson, *op. cit.*, p. 98.
5. Byrne, *op. cit.*, i, p. 92.
6. Taylor, *op. cit.*, p. 67, *et. seq.;* Wheeler and Broadley, *op. cit.*, p. 105; Dickson, *op. cit.*, pp 99-100.
7. Byrne, *op. cit.*, i, p. 91; Dickson, *op. cit.*, p. 95.
8. Byrne, *op. cit.*, i, p. 91; Musgrave, *op. cit.*, i, pp 492-3.
9. Byrne, *op. cit.*, i, p. 98.
10. *Idem.,* p. 99.
11. Wheeler and Broadley, *op. cit.*, p. 109.
12. This description of John Murphy in battle was written by Byrne (*op. cit.*, i, p. 136) in relation to the battle of Arklow. John Murphy did not take part in the battle of Arklow. In my opinion Byrne was confusing Arklow with Tubberneering. See letter in *People,* 9 July 1898.
13. Dickson, *op. cit.*, p. 194.
14. *Idem.,* p. 103.
15. Maxwell, *History,* footnote, p. 111.
16. Dickson, *op. cit.*, p. 104.

17. *Ibid.*, app. iv; Byrne, *op. cit.*, i, p. 103; Wheeler and Broadley, *op. cit.*, pp 109, 110; Maxwell, *op. cit.*, p. 109.
18. Musgrave, *op. cit.*, i, p. 499; Dickson, *op. cit.*, p. 104.
19. Byrne, *op. cit.*, i, p. 101.
20. *Ibid.*, pp 102-3; Dickson, *op. cit.*, p. 200; Cullen, 'The 1798 Rebellion in Wexford', pp 269, 280-2.
21. Dickson, *op. cit.*, p. 240; Musgrave, *op. cit.*, i, p. 537.
22. Letter, Castlereagh to Pelham, 8 June 1798. Add. Mss., 22, 105 (398).

Chapter Eleven
1. Byrne, *op.cit.*, i, p. 114; Dickson, *op. cit.*, p. 106.
2. Byrne, *op. cit.*, p. 113.
3. *Ibid.*, p. 125; Hay, *op. cit.*, pp 161, 180; Kavanagh, *op. cit.*, p. 179.
4. Byrne, *op. cit.*, i, p. 125.
5. Sinnott (1948), *loc. cit.*; Kavanagh, *op. cit.*, p. 134; Kavanagh, *op. cit.*, p. 134.
6. *Idem.*
7. Dickson, *op. cit.*, p. 108.
8. Byrne, *op. cit.*, p. 116.
9. *Ibid.*, p. 118.
10. *Ibid.*, p. 124.
11. *Ibid.*, p. 125; Barrington, *Rise and Fall*, p. 447.
12. Sinnott (1948), *loc. cit.*; Taylor, *op. cit.*, p. 137. The dispute between Fr. John and Fr. Michael Murphy was bitter and divisive, according to T. D. Sinnott.
13. Byrne, *op. cit.*, i, p. 33.
14. Musgrave, *op. cit.*, ii, app. xxii and xxiii.
15. Byrne, *op. cit.*, i, p. 45, for notice of Wheatley.
16. Hay, *op. cit.*, pp 160-1; Musgrave, *op. cit.*, ii, p. 399; Taylor *op. cit.*, pp 101-3.
17. Byrne, *op. cit.*, i, p. 33; Musgrave, *op. cit.*, i, p. 579, ii, app. xxii; Taylor, *op. cit.*, pp 125, 176-80; Kavanagh, *op. cit.*, p. 191.
18. Byrne, *op. cit.*, i, p. 176, *et. seq.*;
19. Dickson, *op. cit.*, p. 129.
20. Byrne, *op. cit.*, i, pp 131-2.
21. *Idem.*, p. 150; Musgrave, *op. cit,* ii, app. xxii and xxiii; Taylor, *op. cit.*, pp 176, 180; Maxwell, *op. cit.*, p. 139; Gordon (1801), *op. cit.*, p. 164.
22. George III to Pitt, 3 June 1798, cited in Pakenham, *op. cit.*, p. 276.
23. *Ibid.*, p. 278.
24. *Ibid.*, pp 267-8.
25. Byrne, *op. cit.*, i, p. 133; Letter, 'Oulart Hill' *New Ross Standard,* 28 May 1898; Letter, *People,* 19 June, 1948; Dickson, *op. cit.*, pp 129-30.
26. Letter, 'Oulart Hill', *New Ross Standard,* 28 May 1898.
27. Taylor, *op. cit.*, pp 97, 137; Kavanagh, *op. cit.*, footnote, p. 186; Sinnott (1948), *loc. cit.*; Letter, *People,* 19 June, 1948.
28. Dickson, *op. cit.*, app. v, viii, ix.
29. Byrne, *op. cit.*, i, pp 138-42.
30. *Ibid.*, p. 21; Hay, *op. cit.*, p. 189. Both were nonetheless regarded with suspicion, arrested and jailed in Dublin without charge on 12 June 1798. Dr. John Esmonde, brother of Sir Thomas was hanged in Dublin for his participation in the Kildare rising.
31. Byrne, *op. cit.*, i, p. 53.
32. Dickson, *op. cit.*, app. v, ix.

33. *Ibid.,* app. viii; Wheeler and Broadley, *op. cit.,* p. 125.
34. Sinnott (1948), *loc. cit.;* Gordon (1801), *op. cit.,* p. 157.
35. Dickson, *op. cit.,* app. xii.
36. Byrne, *op. cit.,* pp 143-4.
37. Dickson, *op. cit.,* app. v, p. 245.
38. Needham to Lake, 10 June 1798, cited in Pakenham, *op. cit.,* p. 281.
39. Camden to Portland, 10 and 11 June 1798, cited in Pakenham, *op. cit.,* p. 282.
40. Castlereagh to Pelham, 13 June, 1798, cited in Pakenham, *op. cit.,* p. 282.
41. Pakenham, *op. cit.,* pp. 266-76.
42. Dickson, *Revolt in the North,* chapters 18 to 22.

Chapter Twelve
1. Sinnott (1948), *loc. cit.*
2. Taylor, *op. cit.,* p. 136; Byrne, *op. cit.,* i, p. 143; Hay, *op. cit.,* p. 182.
3. Cloney, *op. cit.,* p. 224; Gordon (1801), *op. cit.,* pp 258-9.
4. Byrne, *op. cit.,* i, p. 148; Gordon (1801), *op. cit.,* pp 258-9.
5. *Idem.*
6. Cloney, *op. cit.,* p. 199.
7. Byrne, *op. cit.,* i, 149.
8. Musgrave, *op. cit.,* i, p. 579, ii, p. 359, app. xxii; Caulfield, *op. cit.,* p. 52. Owen survived the Rebellion. For some details see Ogle, *op. cit.,* p. 98; Leslie, *op. cit.,* pp 96, 167, 208; J. Adams in T. Croker (ed.), *Researches in the South of Ireland* (London, 1824) app.; N. Furlong, 'History of Land Reclamation in Wexford Harbour' in *Jn. Old Wex. Soc.,* ii (1969), p. 53.
9. Byrne, *op. cit.,* i, pp. 148, 165.
10. Wheeler and Broadley, *op. cit.,* p. 138.
11. Byrne, *op. cit.,* p. 256.
12. Dickson, *Revolt in the North,* p. 163, app. xix.
13. Pakenham, *op. cit.,* p. 256.
14. Byrne, *op. cit.,* i, p. 153.
15. Dickson, *Wexford Rising,* pp 136-60.
16. *Idem.*
17. Byrne, *op. cit.,* i, p. 153.
18. *Idem.*
19. Wheeler and Broadley, *op. cit.,* p. 143; Dickson, *op. cit.,* p. 160.
20. Musgrave, *op. cit.,* i, pp 4-5; Dickson, *op. cit.,* p. 138.
21. Dickson, *Wexford Rising,* p. 136.
22. Byrne, *op. cit.,* i, p. 160.
23. *Ibid.,* p. 161; Gordon (1801), *op. cit.,* p. 193.
24. Musgrave, *op. cit.,* ii, p. 4; Maxwell, *op. cit.,* p. 138; Dickson, *Wexford Rising,* p. 138.
25. Jones, 'An Impartial Narrative ... from Authentic Letters', cited in Dickson, *op. cit.,* p. 138.
26. Byrne, *op. cit.,* ii, p. 163.
27. Dickson, *Wexford Rising,* p. 138.
28. Byrne, *op. cit.,* ii, pp 163-8. Loftus to Lake (Dickson, *op. cit.,* app. iv) indicates that Vinegar Hill was a reasonable option: 'I beg to impress on you that in an enclosed country like this, where the cavalry cannot act, the enemy is very formidable and can only be met by a sufficient force and a well regulated artillery, for every hill and ditch is a post for them'.
29. Byrne, *op. cit.,* i, p. 164.

Chapter Thirteen

1. Musgrave, *op. cit.*, ii, p.1, *et. seq.*
2. Maxwell, *op. cit.*, p. 134; Pakenham, *op. cit.*, p. 293.
3. Byrne, *op. cit.*, i, p. 171.
4. Dickson, *Wexford Rising*, p. 197.
5. Byrne, *op. cit.*, i, p. 168; Hay, *op. cit.*, p. 203.
6. Byrne, *op. cit.*, i, p. 166.
7. *Ibid.*, p. 167.
8. *Ibid.*, p. 168; Hay, *op. cit.*, p. 255.
9. Cloney, *op. cit.*, p. 71; Hay, *op. cit.*, p. 203.
10. Dickson, *op. cit.*, app. v.
11. Byrne, *op. cit.*, i, p. 170.
12. *Ibid.*, p. 167; Dickson, *Wexford Rising*, p. 162.
13. Musgrave, *op. cit.*, ii, p. 6.
14. Maxwell, *op. cit.*, p. 145.
15. MacSuibhne, *'98 in Carlow*, p. 12. Kavanagh; *op. cit.*, p. 304; Letter from Patrick Murphy, *Wexford Free Press*, 2 Mar. 1898.
16. Byrne, *op. cit.*, i, p. 172.
17. Barrington, cited in Kavanagh, *op. cit.*, pp 208-9.
18. Byrne, *op. cit.*, i, p. 174; Kavanagh, *op. cit.*, p. 209; Dickson, *Wexford Rising*, p. 162, *et seq.*
19. Byrne, *op. cit.*, p. 173.
20. Dickson, *Wexford Rising*, app. v.
21. *Ibid.*, p. 164; Wheeler and Broadley, *op. cit.*, pp 157-8.
22. Dickson, *Wexford Rising*, app. x; Hay, *op. cit.*, p. 229.
23. Byrne, *op. cit.*, pp 68-9; Byrne, *op. cit.*, p. 211; Maxwell, *op. cit.*, p. 146.
24. Cloney, *op. cit.*, pp 68-9; Byrne, *op. cit.*, i, p. 179; Dickson, *Wexford Rising*, pp 163-5.
25. Barrington, *Personal Sketches*, p. 146; Cloney, *op. cit.*, p. 218. (Cloney gives the number as 76); Hay, *op. cit.*, p. 235. General Lake repeated this chastisement at the capture of Wexford. He burned down the Infirmary in Hill Street with fifty seven wounded and sick insurgents inside. Cloney, *op. cit.*, p. 218.

Chapter Fourteen

1. Cloney, *op. cit.*, pp 68-9.
2. Letter, *Wexford Free Press* Patrick Murphy, Strahart, 2 Mar. 1898. In order to get through the lines, Moses Murphy's wife disguised her relationship by using her loyalist sounding maiden name of Proctor. Despite the closest search, Patrick's body was never found.
3. Cloney, *op. cit.*, pp 66-7; Hay, *op. cit.*, p. 236.
4. Dickson, *Wexford Rising*, p. 166; Sinnott (1962) *loc. cit.*, p. 158; *Ibid* (1938), p. 27.
5. Sinnott (1938), *loc. cit.*, p. 27.
6. Hay, *op. cit.*, pp 237-8; Caulfield, *op. cit.*, p.16.
7. Byrne, *op. cit.*, i, p. 189.
8. For a succinct account of Philip Roche's experiences and the events at Scullabogue and Wexford Bridge, see Dickson, *Wexford Rising*, pp 119-24, 148-54 and footnote, p. 193; Kavanagh, *op. cit.*, pp 156-9.
9. Dickson, *op. cit.*, p. 209.
10. *Ibid.*, pp 166-74; Byrne, *op. cit.*, i, pp 191-2.
11. Byrne, *op. cit.*, i, p. 193; Oral testimony, T. D. Sinnott.

12. Byrne, *op. cit.*, i, p. 225; T. Lyng, *Castlecomer Connections* (Castlecomer, 1984), p. 267.
13. Lyng, *op. cit.*, p. 215; Oral testimony, T. Lyng.
14. Musgrave, *op. cit.*, ii, pp 76-7; Oral testimony, T. Lyng.
15. Byrne, *op. cit.*, i, pp 202-3.
16. Cloney, *op. cit.*, p. 81.
17. Byrne, *op. cit.*, 1, pp 204-5.
18. *Idem.*
19. Gordon (1805), *op. cit.*, p. 399; Lecky, *op. cit.*, iv, p. 428; Ogle, *op. cit.*, p. 107. The execution was carried out by sailors of the Royal Navy.
20. Byrne, *op.cit.*, i, p. 206.
21. MacSuibhne, *'98 in Carlow,* pp 69-70.
22. Byrne, *op. cit.* i, p. 208; Musgrave, *op. cit.*, ii, p. 73.
23. MacSuibhne, *'98 in Carlow,* p. 36.
24. Byrne, *op. cit.;* p. 208; Musgrave, *op. cit.*, ii, p. 73.
25. MacSuibhne, *'98 in Carlow,* p. 58 (notes).
26. Byrne, *op. cit.*, i, p. 208.
27 Musgrave, *op. cit.*, ii, p. 73; MacSuibhne, *'98 in Carlow,* p. 37.
28. Byrne, *op. cit.*, i, p. 209.
29. *Ibid.*, p. 212.
30. Cloney, *op. cit.*, p. 82; Dickson, *Wexford Rising,* p. 171.
31. *Ibid.;* Byrne, *op. cit.*, i, p. 210; MacSuibhne, *'98 in Carlow,* p. 39.
32. Byrne, *op. cit.* i, pp 211-3.
33. *Ibid.*, p. 212.
34. *Idem.*
35. MacSuibhne, *'98 in Carlow,* pp 77-8.
36. Byrne, *op. cit.*, i, p. 212; Musgrave, *op. cit.*, ii, pp 74-5; Dickson, *Wexford Rising,* pp 170-1.
37. MacSuibhne, *'98 in Carlow,* p. 43.
38. *Ibid.* p. 42.
39. *Idem.*
40. Byrne, *op. cit.*, i, p. 213; Lyng, *op. cit.*, p. 272.
41. Byrne, *op. cit.*, i, 213.

Chapter Fifteen

1. Lyng, *op. cit.*, p. 267.
2. *Ibid.*, pp 282-9.
3. MacSuibhne, *'98 in Carlow,* p. 42; Oral testimony, T. Lyng.
4. Dickson, *Wexford Rising,* p. 171.
5. Musgrave, *op. cit.*, ii, pp 80-1; Teeling, *Sequel,* p. 266.
6. Oral testimony, T. Lyng.
7. Lyng, *op. cit.*, p. 272; Teeling, *op. cit.*, p. 268.
8. Byrne, *op. cit.*, i, pp 115-20.
9. Teeling, *op. cit.*, p. 266.
10. Lyng, *op. cit.*, p. 273, Oral testimony, T. Lyng.
11. *An Intercepted letter from J-T-, Esq., written at Canton to His Friend in Dublin, Ireland* (Dublin, 1804), p. 49; MacSuibhne, *'98 in Carlow,* p. 45.
12. Byrne, *op. cit.*, pp 221-3.
13. Asgill to Castlereagh, cited in MacSuibhne, *'98 in Carlow,* p. 44.
14. Lyng, *op. cit.*, p. 267.

15. Oral testimony, T. Lyng.
16. Lyng, *op.cit.*, p. 268.
17. Byrne, *op. cit.*, pp 223-4; MacSuibhne, *'98 in Carlow*, pp 45-8.
18. Oral testimony, Michael Daly, Slatt Lower, county Laois.
19. Byrne, *op. cit.*, p. 227; MacSuibhne, *'98 in Carlow*, p. 46, notes, pp 58, 59. Thomas Lyng supports the cultural difference theory made clear by Miles Byrne. Lyng believes that a gulf between colliers and insurgents of farming background opened after the attack on Castlecomer.
20. Account of the Action at Slatt, Castlecomer and Kilcumney, by W. Pole, in N.L.I., Pery papers (uncatalogued); MacSuibhne, *'98 in Carlow*, pp 46-58.
21. Lyng, *op. cit.*, p. 275; Byrne, *op. cit.*, i, pp 224-5.

Chapter Sixteen
1. Byrne, *op. cit.*, i, p. 225; MacSuibhne, *'98 in Carlow*, p. 47.
2. *Ibid.*, p. 54.
3. T. Lyng, *Deenside*, Christmas issue (Castlecomer, 1980), ballad, p. 16. Oral testimony of John Barker, Wexford, a kinsman of William Barker. This is the persistent county Wexford tradition invoked to this day against Kilkenny supporters during inter county hurling matches. Lyng has pointed out that Doonane is in county Laois.
4. Byrne, *op. cit.*, i, p. 226; Kavanagh, *op. cit.*, p. 235.
5. Byrne, *op. cit.*, p. 227; MacSuibhne, *'98 in Carlow*, pp 66-8; Action at Slatt, Castlecomer and Kilcumney, by W. Pole, N.L.I., Pery papers.
6. Byrne, *op. cit.*, i, p. 227.
7. Cloney, *op. cit.*, p. 87; MacSuibhne, *'98 in Carlow*, pp 66, 77.
8. Petition of J. McNabb to Philip, Earl of Hardwick, Lord Lieutenant, S.P.O.R.P., 620/60/31.
9. MacSuibhne, *'98 in Carlow*, pp 52, 67-8; W. Nolan, 'Fr. John's Last Journey, 1798' in *Carloviana*, i, No. 18 (1969), p. 23.
10. MacSuibhne, *'98 in Carlow*, p. 72.
11. *Ibid.*, pp 66-7.
12. *Ibid.*
13. Asgill to Castlereagh, 26 June 1798 in MacSuibhne, *'98 in Carlow*, pp 48-9; *Finn's Leinster Journal*, Kilkenny, 25-7 June 1798. These reports created later confusion. Musgrave, amongst others, accepted both reports. After it was established that it was Fr. John Murphy of Boolavogue who was executed in Tullow on 2 July, he concluded that there had been two Fr. John Murphys at Kilcumney, one the Boolavogue priest's 'aide-de-camp'. See Musgrave, *op. cit.*, ii, p. 89.
14. MacSuibhne, *'98 in Carlow*, p. 71.
15. *Ibid.*, p. 73. The Jordans preserved the two small bronze candlesticks which he used at Mass as a memento. They were suited to the old tallow candles.
16. *Ibid.*, p. 87.
17. *Ibid.*, pp 52-74; Nolan, *loc. cit.*, p. 23.
18. MacSuibhne, *'98 in Carlow*, pp 16-19.
19. M. Gibbons, *Glimpses of Catholic Ireland in the Eighteenth Century* (Dublin, 1932), p. 189; Nolan, *loc. cit.*, p. 18; Sinnott (1962), *loc. cit.*, p. 159.
20. MacSuibhne, *'98 in Carlow*, pp 53-9, 77-8.
21. S.P.O.R.P., 620/60/31.
22. MacSuibhne, *'98 in Carlow*, p. 59.

23. *Ibid.*, p. 53; Musgrave, *op. cit.*, ii, p. 89.
24. Nolan, *loc. cit.*, p. 24.
25. Musgrave, *op. cit.*, ii, p. 90; MacSuibhne, *'98 in Carlow*, p. 53; Sinnott (1962), *loc. cit.*, p. 159.
26. Musgrave, *op. cit.*, ii, pp 89-90; Plowden, *op. cit.*, ii, p. 478; *Irish Magazine and Monthly Asylum for Neglected Biography* (June, 1811).
27. Plowden, *op. cit.*, p. 478.
28. Sinnott (1962), *loc. cit.*, p. 160.
29. MacSuibhne, *'98 in Carlow*, pp. 21-3; Gibbons, *op. cit.*, p. 189; Comerford, *Collections*, iii, p. 392.
30. *Idem.*
31. Caulfield to Troy, cited in Whelan, 'Catholic Priest', p. 315.
32. Letter, Patrick Murphy, Strahart in *Wexford Free Press*, 2 Mar. 1898.
33. *Irish Magazine,* June, 1811.
34. Comerford, *op. cit.*, iii, p. 392.
35. MacSuibhne, *'98 in Carlow*, p. 54. See also p. 87.
36. *Ibid.*, pp 82-3.
37. Byrne, *op. cit.*, i, p. 230; *An Intercepted Letter from J-T-, Esq.*, 30 Aug. 1798, pp 51-2, repeats the report that amongst the dead at Kilcumney was 'the invulnerable commander Murphy'; Sinnott (1962), *loc. cit.*, p. 160; Nolan, 'Fr. John's last Journey', *loc cit.*

EPILOGUE
1. Byrne, *Memoirs,* i, p. 231.
2. *Ibid.*, p. 242.
3. *Ibid.*, p. 298.
4. Pakenham, *op. cit.*, p. 317.
5. *Ibid.*, p. 341.
6. R. Fraser, *A statistical survey of county Wexford* (Dublin, 1807), p. 56; Dickson, *op. cit.*, p. 177.
7. T.D. Sinnott, U.C.D. extra-mural lectures, Wexford, 1951. Deportations continued 'by the cartload at frequent intervals for upwards of two years after the fighting ceased'.
8. List of arms captured, 19 August, 1798, cited in Pakenham, *op. cit.*, p. 334.
9. Dickson, *Wexford Rising*, pp 196-8.
10. *Ibid.*, pp 194, 203.
11. *Ibid.*, p. 196.
12. *Ibid.*, pp 196-7.
13. *Ibid.*, p. 192.
14. *Ibid.*, p. 213; Ogle, *Irish Militia*, pp 107-8.
15. Dickson, *Wexford Rising*, p. 201.
16. *Ibid.*, p. 202.
17. *Ibid.*, p. 214.
18. *Ibid.*, p. 211.
19. Cloney, *op. cit., passim;* J. Joyce, *General Thomas Cloney* (Dublin 1988); Cullen, '1798 Rebellion in Wexford'; S. Cloney, 'The Cloney families of county Wexford' in Whelan, *Wexford,* pp 316-41.
20. W. Sweetman, 'Edward Hay' in *The Past,* xv (1984), pp 55-68.
21. Byrne, *op. cit.*, p. 230.
22. Dickson, *op. cit.*, pp 206-8.

23. Caulfield to Troy, 3 Nov., 1798, D.D.A.
24. Caulfield to Troy, 2 June, 9 July, 23 Aug., 1799, D.D.A.
25. Pastoral letter of James Caulfield, 13 Sept., 1798, in Moran, *Spicilegium Ossoriense*, pp 572-7.
26. Grattan Flood, *op. cit.*, p. xx; Hay, *op. cit.*, p. 294.
27. Musgrave, *op. cit.*
28. Leslie, *op. cit.*, p. 168.
29. Jane Barber, Memoir, typescript, Wexford County Library.
30. Dickson, *Wexford Rising*, p. 178.
31. Cited in Whelan, 'Catholic priest', p. 315.
32. Oral testimony, Art Sinnott, Boolavogue.

INDEX OF PEOPLE

Hatton, William:
15, 41, 88.
Hay, Captain Philip:
84, 94, 104, 105, 115.
Hay, Edward:
84, 86, 88, 91, 103, 104, 166.
Hay, John:
16, 41, 71, 76, 81, 84, 86, 88, 89, 91, 94, 97, 103, 104, 166.
Hay, Philip:
113.
Hayden, Rev. Samuel:
69.
Hays of Ballinkeele:
14.
Hoche, General Lazare:
22.
Honam, Thomas:
See Tom the Devil.
Howlett, Thomas:
24.
Hughes, Henry:
16, 88, 89.
Hunt, Lieutenant:
69.
Hunte, Le, Captain:
54, 56, 58, 60.
Hunter, General:
165.

Jacob, Archibald Hamilton:
48, 76, 78, 85, 119, 168.
Jacob, Ebenezer:
84, 90.
James II, King:
71.
Johnson, General:
127, 128, 129, 132, 133.
Jordans of Coolnasneachta:
158.

Kane, Castlecomer:
150.
Kavanagh, Fr. Francis:
120.
Kavanagh, Jeremiah:
57.
Keane, Fr. John:
28.

Kearney, William:
90.
Kearns, Fr. Mogue:
24, 25, 66, 70, 88, 90, 91, 96, 130, 134, 135, 139, 141, 157.
Kearns, Padraig Ruadh:
25.
Kehoe [Tenant farmer]:
154.
Kelly, John:
71, 76, 85, 86, 88, 89, 110, 141, 165, 170.
Kennedy, Hugh:
95.
Keogh [Ensign]:
60.
Keogh, Michael:
62.
Keppel, Anne:
158.
Keppel, George:
158, 159.
Keugh, Matthew:
16, 41, 86, 88, 90, 136, 140, 165, 170.
King, Jonah:
85.
Kingsborough, Earl of:
38, 110, 137.
Kingsmill, Admiral:
83.
Kirwan, Daniel:
123, 132, 135.
Kyan, Esmond:
16, 101, 103, 105, 114, 115, 119, 138, 165, 170.

Lake, General:
123, 124, 125, 126, 127, 132, 133, 134, 135, 136, 140, 142, 165, 167.
Lett, Mrs.:
86.
Little, Mary:
142.
Loftus, Major General:
97, 99, 100, 101, 103, 104, 105, 106, 121, 124, 127, 128, 129.

Lombard, Major:
60.
Louis XVI, King of France:
13.
Lyng, Mrs.:
145.

Maguire, Hugh:
23.
Manzors:
162.
Marie Antoinette, Queen:
13.
Matthews, Major:
155.
Maxwell, Colonel:
78, 96.
McClintock, Captain:
160.
McLaren, Sergeant Archibald:
102, 115, 116.
McNabb, John:
156, 160.
Meagher, Mrs.:
123.
Mernagh, Matt:
66.
Monaghan, Richard:
See Dick Monk.
Monk, Dick:
88, 92, 101, 111, 114, 115, 120, 130, 131, 135, 138, 140, 144, 156, 165, 170.
Moore, General John:
18, 127, 128, 129, 131, 137, 139, 165, 168.
Mountnorris, Lord:
9, 14, 20, 24, 25, 30, 31, 32, 34, 36, 37, 40, 46, 52, 53, 63, 64, 118.
Murphy, Fr. Bryan:
28.
Murphy, Fr. Michael:
27, 64, 65, 70, 71, 89, 91, 94, 95, 99, 103, 105, 106, 110, 114, 115, 118, 121, 170.
Murphy, James:
1, 3, 9.

INDEX OF PLACES

Associate Sponsors

Bernard and Mary Browne, Seattle, U.S.A.

Denis Cloney, Curracloe.

Most Rev. Brendan Comiskey, Bishop of Ferns.

Drinagh Antiques, Wexford.

James Hall, Boolavogue.

Edmund Hassett Ltd., North Main St., Wexford.

Patrick and Ina Jordan, Vancouver, Canada.

Kehoe and Haythornthwaite, Wexford.

Kelly's Strand Hotel, Rosslare.

Peter McDonald Engineering, New Ross.

James J. O'Connor, Ardara.

Most Rev. Laurence Ryan, Bishop of Kildare and Leighlin.

St. Peter's College Seminary, Wexford.

South East Tourism.

Steel Co. Ltd., New Ross.

Denis and Blaihín Taylor,Vancouver, Canada

Wallace-Howlin Holdings, Wellingtonbridge.

Wexford Creamery.

Tom and Marie Williams, Park House, Wexford.

Culleton Insurances, Wexford.

Patrick Jordan, Jr., Coquitlam, Vancouver, Canada.

Trudy Jordan, Vancouver, Canada.

Rt. Rev. Monsignor Mícheál Ledwith, President, St. Patrick's College, Maynooth.

SUBSCRIBERS

Bank of Ireland.
John Bolger and Co. Ltd., Ferns.
John Bolger, Nottingham, England.
Bernard and Mary Browne, Seattle,
  Washington, U.S.A.
F.X. Butler, Coolcotts, Wexford.
Seamus Codd, A.C.C., Wexford.
Most Rev. Brendan Comiskey, Bishop
  of Ferns.
Professor Patrick J. Corish, St. Patrick's
  College, Maynooth.
Dr. Barty Curtis, St. Aidan's, Wexford.
Rev. Patrick Cushen, R.C.A., Wexford.
Very Rev. James B. Curtis, P.P., V.F.,
  Ferns, Co. Wexford.
Very Rev. Seamas S. de Vál, S.P., An
  tAbhallort, Co. Loch Garman.
J. J. Devereux, Broom Cottage, Drinagh
  Wexford.
Jim Doyle, New Ross.
Rita Doyle, 81 North Main St., Wexford.
Jarlath Glynn, Chairman, Wexford
  Historical Society.
Sir David Goodall, British High
  Commissioner to India.
Jim Hall, Boolavogue.
Edmond Hassett Ltd., Wexford.
Adrian Haythornthwaite, Wexford.
Professor Frank Horlbeck, University of
  Wisconsin, U.S.A.
Irish National Insurance Co.
Robbie Jacob, F.B.D., Enniscorthy.
Patrick and Ina Jordan, Vancouver,
  Canada.
Trudy Jordan, Vancouver, Canada.
John and Mrs. Joyce, Graiguenamanagh,
  Co. Kilkenny.
Brian and Martina Kealy, Castleknock.
John Keane, Custom House Quay,
  Wexford.
Eva Kelly, New Ross.
Kelly's Strand Hotel, Rosslare.
Muriel McCarthy, Marsh's Library, Dublin.
Peter McDonald Engineering, New Ross.
Martin McCullough, Belgrave Sq., Dublin.
Dr. Patrick McKiernan, Wexford.
Rory Murphy, M.C.C., Bunclody
  Historical Society.
New Ireland Assurance Co.

Rev. Hugh O'Byrne, Adm., Wexford.
Tomás Ó Ceallaigh, Inis Corthaidh.
Russel and Paula Panczenko,
  University of Wisconsin, U.S.A.
Helen Doyle Roche, Wexford.
Michael Murphy, Golden Pages, Dublin.
Eoin Ryan, Dublin.
Most Rev. Laurence Ryan, Bishop of
  Kildare and Leighlin.
Sean Scallan, St. Magdalen's, Wexford.
St. Peter's College Seminary, Wexford.
Jim Sutton, New Ross.
Denis and Blaihín Taylor, Vancouver,
  Canada.
Dermot Traynor, Clonard, Wexford.
Ui Cinsealaigh Historical Society.
Wexford Creamery.
Tom and Marie Williams, Park House,
  Wexford.
Right Rev. Noel V. Willoughby, Bishop of
  Cashel, Ferns and Ossory.
B. Wright, Tullow Phelim Historical
  Society.
Lily Wright, Waterford.